Judicial Decision Making
Is Psychology Relevant?

Perspectives in
Law & Psychology

Sponsored by the American Psychology-Law Society/Division 41 of the American Psychological Association

Series Editor: RONALD ROESCH, *Simon Fraser University*
Burnaby, British Columbia, Canada

Editorial Board: MARY DURHAM, JANE GOODMAN-DELAHUNT, THOMAS GRISSO, STEPHEN D. HART, MARSHA LISS, EDWARD P. MULVEY, JAMES R. P. OGLOFF, NORMAN G. POYTHRESS, JR., DON READ, and REGINA SCHULLER

A Continuation Order Plan is available for this series. A continuation order will bring delivery of each new volume immediately upon publication. Volumes are billed only upon actual shipment. For further information please contact the publisher.

Judicial Decision Making

Is Psychology Relevant?

Lawrence S. Wrightsman

University of Kansas
Lawrence, Kansas

KLUWER ACADEMIC / PLENUM PUBLISHERS
NEW YORK, BOSTON, DORDRECHT, LONDON, MOSCOW

ISBN 0-306-46154-4

©1999 Kluwer Academic / Plenum Publishers, New York
233 Spring Street, New York, N.Y. 10013

10 9 8 7 6 5 4 3 2 1

A C.I.P. record for this book is available from the Library of Congress

Printed in the United States of America

To the memory of Jeffrey Z. Rubin
—LSW

Preface

In the mid-1970s, as a social psychologist dedicated to the application of knowledge, I welcomed our field's emerging interest in the legal system. I have always been fascinated by jury trials—something about the idea that two conceptions of the truth were in irrevocable conflict and jurors could choose only one of them. More important, the criminal justice system is a major social force that has been ignored by social psychologists for most of the twentieth century. As I systematically began to explore the applications of social psychological concepts to the law 20 years ago, I experienced the delight of discovery similar to that of a child under a Christmas tree. It has been satisfying to be among the cohort of researchers who have studied the legal system, especially trial juries, from a psychological perspective. I believe we have learned much that would be useful if the system were to be revised.

"If the system were to be revised". . . there's the rub. As I have stated, my original motivation was the application of knowledge. Like other social scientists, I believed—perhaps arrogantly—that the results of our research efforts could be used to make trial juries operate with more efficiency, accuracy, and satisfaction. Over the last two decades, much knowledge has accumulated. How can we put this knowledge to work?

Judges are the gatekeepers of the legal system. My interest began to shift from a curiosity about the impact of the system on jury behavior to the impact of our research findings on judges' actions in the courtroom. How do we disseminate our findings to judges? Most judges do not read psychology journals or scholarly books; some do not even read law reviews.

I explored one possible avenue of influence: speaking at conferences attended by judges. I found judges' reactions to my proposals for change to be variable. Once, when I was on my soapbox about the need for judges to admonish the jury to give time and thought to whom it selects as foreperson (the typical jury spends about 0.35 of a minute on this task), a judge disdained my efforts, saying, "The foreman (sic) is only an errand boy for the judge." On another occasion, a trial judge seemed genuinely impressed with the Kassin and Wrightsman finding that if jurors are given the instruction about reasonable doubt *before* hearing the evidence, they retain more of the evidence during deliberations. He promised to implement this finding in his courtroom.

These experiences led me to explore more systematically the question of how (and even whether) psychology can influence judicial behavior. I learned that the American Psychological Association had submitted more than 90 *amicus curiae* briefs to the U.S. Supreme Court and other appellate courts in an effort to influence judicial decisions. I examined a selection of these briefs and compared them with the Court's eventual decision in an effort to determine what was effective and what was not. The second half of this book reflects this effort.

Through this work, I began to get a better understanding of the applicability of psychology to judicial decision making. I realized, however, that the question of psychology's relevance was legitimately a broader one. How *do* judges make decisions? When a trial judge is asked to determine the facts in a case, when an appellate judge must decide the applicability of previous rulings, does the judge act in ways that are different from those of other experts when they make job-related decisions? This book offers answers to these questions.

Though the field of psychology has extensively studied the process of judgment and the act of decision making, it has for the most part, ignored the applications of this knowledge to the field of jurisprudence. The first half of this book seeks to redress this imbalance. For the decision making of appellate judges—who act in panels—the field of social psychology is especially appropriate. In addition to its emphasis on attitudes, persuasion, conformity, and group dynamics, social psychology (in contrast to other subfields of psychology or to sociology) uses both the individual and the group as its units of behavior. The study of decision making by the Supreme Court, for example, cannot ignore the fact that individual justices form early opinions without input from their colleagues; neither can it ignore the fact that the final result—even granted that it is an opinion written by one justice—reflects a *group* process of information exchange, negotiation, revision, and compromise.

The teaser in the title of this book—*Is Psychology Relevant?*—consequently seeks to answer two questions. First, can a psychological analysis provide us with useful information about how judges make their professional decisions? Second, has the field of psychology been effective in influencing the Court? Although my conclusions in response to these questions are not always reassuring, I hope they will provide illumination for those who, like me, seek to improve the legal system.

Acknowledgments

I am grateful to many people for their help.

First, chronologically, is Dyane Swanson, who as an undergraduate 4 years ago, worked with me in developing a system to analyze a number of *amicus* briefs prepared by the American Psychological Association.

Second, I gained much from the opportunity to share a draft of this book with the doctoral and law students who participated in my seminars on judicial decision making during the 1996–97 and 1997–98 school years. These students responded to the chapters, raised issues I had overlooked, and often went out of their way to provide materials that I incorporated in the final version. I appreciate the contributions of Aaron Hull, Lisa Kreiner, Paul Silvia, Lisa Thompson, Catherine Hess, Kathleen Feagen, Amy Eshleman, Jo-Ann Tsang, Greg Nichols, Jennifer Gottschalk, Rachel Lee, Melisa Rempfer, Catherine Theisen, Noel Jacobs, Natasha Brown, Camille Randall, and Kirsten Kakolewski.

My three undergraduate research assistants, Adrienne LeFevre, Alexis McKinley, and John Mendenhall, tracked down elusive references in the law library and summarized materials for me. John Mendenhall was especially indispensable; he has continued to serve as my helper during the final stages of polishing the manuscript.

I benefited greatly from the perspective and contributions of two of my colleagues from the Department of Political Science at the University of Kansas. One, C. K. ("Pete") Rowland, team-taught the judicial decision-making course with me during the Fall 1997 semester; the other, Ryan Beasley, sat in on the course and made a number of insightful comments that I have tried to incorporate into the manuscript.

My colleague in the Department of Psychology, Allen Omoto, read and responded to portions of the book and provided me with materials that were useful for Chapter 1. Alan Reifman and Dan Simon have provided support and made helpful suggestions via e-mail.

Ronald Roesch, editor of the *Perspectives in Law and Psychology* series, has served as a thoughtful yet meticulous reviewer, and I am indebted to him for his support and patience.

Last, but by no means least, is my gratitude to Bea Gray, who checked every line of the text for typing errors and produced the completed manuscript. Even more important, she was endlessly encouraging and patient as I obsessed over the completion of this task.

Contents

1

How Do Judges Decide?

It all began in December 1990, but few Americans were aware of it until the spring of 1996, when the issue leapt into our national consciousness and initiated an intense debate. At issue: the legality of same-sex marriages. In Hawaii three same-sex couples (a pair of men and two pairs of women) had applied for marriage licenses, based on their reading of that state's Equal Rights Amendment. Their requests were quickly rejected by a judge. (The denial of the application was not a surprise, as detailed below). When the couples appealed the decision, the supreme court of the state of Hawaii ruled in May of 1993 (in the case of *Baehr v. Lewin*, later retitled *Baehr v. Miike*) that the denial of marriage licenses to these couples conflicted with provisions against sex discrimination in Hawaii's state constitution. But rather than summarily proclaiming that the state must honor same-sex marriages, the court remanded the case to the trial judge "to undertake a strict-scrutiny review to determine whether a compelling state interest justifies the discriminatory effects of not recognizing same-sex marriages" (Greenberg & Gasman, 1996, p. B8). Unless such a "compelling" interest could be demonstrated, such requests would henceforth be honored by the courts.

The background of this case is as follows.

When Ninia Baehr and Genora Dancel applied to the Hawaii Department of Health for a marriage license on December 17, 1990, they had a hunch they would be turned down. Baehr and Dancel had known each other since

June, when Baehr's mother had introduced them. After several conversations, they began to date. In September, following a trip to San Diego, Dancel purchased an engagement ring and popped the question. Baehr enthusiastically said yes (Eskridge, 1996b).

They knew that gay and lesbian couples were not allowed to marry anywhere in the United States. Still, they were surprised when, after requesting a change in their life insurance policies to name each other as beneficiaries, the insurance companies refused, saying that only legal spouses could be beneficiaries (Eskridge, 1996b). When they sought legal advice on this matter, Bill Woods, an attorney and gay activist in Honolulu, mentioned that Hawaii's prohibition against same-sex marriages might be susceptible to a constitutional challenge. Were they willing to make that challenge?

After much thought, they agreed to do so, as did two other couples, Tammy Rodrigues and Antoinette Pregil, and Pat Lagon and Joseph Melillo. All three couples qualified for marriage licenses except for the requirement that the applicants be of different sexes. The director of the state's health department, John C. Lewin, requested an opinion from the state attorney general's office as to the legality of same-sex marriages; the attorney general ruled that the right to marry was not available to same-sex couples. In his view constitutional rights were limited to decisions "to marry and raise [a] child in a traditional family setting" (quoted by Eskridge, 1996b, p. 4). He drew upon an opinion of a Kentucky appeals court from 1973 (*Jones v. Hallahan*) that stated that marriage has "always" been the union between a man and a woman.

William Eskridge's book describes the next steps:

On April 12, 1991, the Hawaii Department of Health wrote Baehr and Dancel, rejecting their application "since you are both of the same sex and for this reason are not capable of forming a valid marriage contract within the meaning of [the marriage statute]. Even if we did issue a marriage license to you, it would not be a valid marriage under Hawaii law" (quoted by Eskridge, 1996b, p. 4).

On May 1, 1991, Baehr and Dancel, along with the two other couples, filed a complaint that the exclusion of same-sex couples was invalid under either the U.S. Constitution or the Hawaii Constitution. The same day, the two women moved in together. The trial judge upheld the exclusion, so the couples appealed to the supreme court of Hawaii. During oral arguments of September 13, 1992, the state defended the exclusion as "permissible" discrimination (Eskridge, 1996b, p. 5).

On May 5, 1993, the Hawaii Supreme Court found the exclusion discriminatory under Hawaii's state constitution; it remanded the case to a trial judge to determine whether the discrimination was, in fact, "permissible" because of a "compelling" state interest.

The plaintiffs anticipated that at the September 10, 1996 hearing the state of Hawaii would give three arguments why it had a "compelling interest" in preserving the legalization of marriage for only different-sex couples. Drawing on the state's earlier brief, Eskridge (1996b, p. 138) described these as follows:

1. Same-sex marriage interferes with the state's "compelling interest in fostering procreation" because same-sex couples cannot, as couples, conceive children. The earlier brief went on to conclude that "a child is best parented by its biological parents living in a single household."
2. "Same-sex couples will have disproportionate incentives to move to and/or remain in Hawaii" and that would "distort the job and housing markets" and "alter the State of Hawaii's desirability as a visitor destination."
3. "Allowing same-sex couples to marry conveys in socially, psychologically, and otherwise important ways approval of nonheterosexual orientations and behaviors" (quoted by Eskridge, 1996b, p. 138).

The first of these was apparently the one emphasized by the state when the judge heard the case in September 1996. Meanwhile, Baehr and Dancel had moved to Baltimore, to avoid publicity resulting from the case.

THE STATUS OF SAME-SEX MARRIAGES

Hawaii has yet to approve any applications for same-sex couples. At the September hearing, the state argued its position before a local judge, a different judge from the one who made the original ruling: The state's main claim was that the ban was aimed at giving Hawaii's children the best possible upbringing. Judge Kevin Chang did not agree; he ruled that the state may not forbid same-sex marriages, but he put off implementing the decision so as to permit an appellate review. The next day the state announced that it would, in fact, again appeal the ruling to the supreme court of Hawaii. A final state court resolution has not yet been announced. Meanwhile the state legislature, in an effort to disempower any court sanction, decided to put before the state's voters an amendment to Hawaii's constitution that would ban gay marriages. The legislature was confident that the state's voters would endorse it.

In light of the fact that one of this book's purposes is to examine psychology's impact on judicial decision making, it is of interest to ask what role, if any, specific psychologists played in the Hawaii lawsuit. The short answer is that psychologists participated on both sides. In response to the state's assertion that children profit most when they are part of families with two biological parents, eight psychologists and a psychiatrist filed an *amicus curiae* ("friend of the court") brief in support of the plaintiffs. The brief cited research in concluding:

- Gay men and lesbians are as effective at parenting as heterosexual persons are.
- Homosexual relationships are just like heterosexual relationships in all ways that have an impact on parental fitness.
- Children raised by lesbian and gay parents are as well adjusted and socially mature as children raised by heterosexual parents (Clay, 1997).

The brief also argued that preventing the marriage of same-sex couples denied children the benefits that a second legal parent can provide. Psychologist Charlotte J. Patterson of the University of Virginia provided expert testimony for the plaintiffs; her research on the adjustment level of children of gay and lesbian parents was consistent with the *amicus* brief.

In opposition the state called on Richard N. Williams, a psychology professor at Brigham Young University, to assess the quality of the research described in the plaintiff's brief and in the testimony of Dr. Patterson. He labeled the studies methodologically flawed, claiming they had too-small sample sizes and infrequent control groups. "This is not a very good body of research," he said (Clay, 1997, p. 40).

Observers anticipate that the Hawaii Supreme Court will approve of such marriages, even though the Hawaii state legislature passed a bill in 1994 affirming that marriage was intended only for what it called "man–woman units" capable of procreating (Dunlap, 1996a). If same-sex marriage becomes legal in Hawaii, it is assumed that many gay and lesbian couples from other states will travel there to get legally married. When they return to their homes in, say, Maine or Missouri with official marriage licenses, they will expect the benefits that other married persons have, from family rates at the neighborhood health club to family-based medical coverage, inheritance rights, and joint parental custody of children. Laurie McBride, executive director of the Lobby for Individual Freedom and Equality, a gay and lesbian group, said, "California is going to have literally thousands of couples who are going to come back from Hawaii expecting their marriage to be treated with the respect and dignity given every other marriage." When asked if she and her partner of 11 years, Donna Yutzy, would be among them, Ms. McBride answered, "In a heartbeat" (quoted by Dunlap, 1996a, p. A7).

In addition to dignity and respect, gay and lesbian couples seek the economic benefits of marriage. Fran De Benedictis and Emma Llaurado, police officers in New York City who have been together for 11 years, deplore how much more it cost in legal fees to jointly adopt their child without the benefit of marriage; furthermore, as "unmarrieds," neither can collect the other's size-

able line-of-duty death benefits (Rich, 1996a). Likewise, gay couples are denied health care benefits in most programs, although in the last few years,
IBM, Microsoft, American Express, and numerous other companies have extended family coverage to gay couples who live together and are "financially
interdependent" (Dunlap, 1996b). The policy received national publicity in
June 1997, when the Southern Baptist Convention voted to boycott Disney-
owned operations because Disney is among the 300 companies that offer health
care coverage to the gay partners of their employees.

RESPONSE OF THE FEDERAL GOVERNMENT AND OF OTHER STATES

Responding to developments in Hawaii, some states began passing laws in
early 1996 restricting eligibility for marriage. As of late 1998, 18 states had
passed such legislation. Typically, these bills did not just prohibit same-sex
marriages; most included a provision barring the state from recognizing same-
sex marriages solemnized in other states. (Such legislative measures failed or
stalled in 20 other states, however, and in Colorado the governor vetoed such
a bill.) Congress introduced an equivalent federal law, "Defense of Marriage
Act," which was proposed by thrice-married Robert Barr of Georgia. The bill
defined marriage as a "legal union between one man and one woman" for
federal purposes. Though it did not block any state from conferring its own
legal status to same-sex unions, it relieved the other states of any obligation to
respect Hawaii's marriages. The bill was explicit on the point that same-sex
couples would remain ineligible for a wide range of federal benefits, including
Social Security payments and veterans' pensions; it passed the House in July
1996 by a vote of 342 to 67, and the Senate overwhelmingly adopted it after
the summer recess (only 14 senators voted against it). President Clinton, though
criticizing the bill as divisive and unnecessary, signed it.

DETERMINING THE LEGALITY OF SAME-SEX MARRIAGES

Are same-sex marriages legal? We can expect that this question will eventually find its way to the U.S. Supreme Court for resolution. How will the Court
decide? Already we have seen, in the decisions of two trial judges and of the
Hawaii Supreme Court, an inconsistent response. One purpose of this book is
to examine, from a psychological perspective, how appellate court decisions
are made. Conventional wisdom assumes that judges use legal principles to
guide their decisions and that they use a rather intellectualized process, but
for the last 50 years political scientists have said that these decisions reflect
more the attitudes and values of the decision makers—that judges, like the rest
of us, are not emotion-free even when making the momentous choices that
are central to their job.

Identifying the determinants of judicial decisions is by no means easy. In the matter of the constitutionality of same-sex marriages, the task is even harder. For example, what specific question will be posed? The right of states to disregard the laws of another state? The right of states to establish their own marriage requirements? The power of the federal government to pass laws that abridge the implicit authority of individual states? Let us assume that the supreme court of Hawaii allows same-sex marriages. The actual case that might come before the U.S. Supreme Court could, for example, be the state of Hawaii versus the United States. Individual states have long been given the autonomy to make their own regulations in such matters; each state, for example, determines its own speed limits. But at the same time, federal regulations are assumed to outweigh contradictory state rules. In the words of Segal and Spaeth (1993), "if a state were free to determine the compatibility of its own actions with those of the federal government, any given provision of the Constitution, act of Congress, or U.S. treaty would likely mean something different in each state" (p. 77). Of relevance to this argument is the fact that in 1967, the U.S. Supreme Court, in *Loving v. Virginia*, outlawed the antimiscegenation laws, which at that time were on the books of many states. With such contradictory precedents operating, decision making by judges becomes more complex.

THE "FULL FAITH AND CREDIT" CLAUSE OF THE UNITED STATES CONSTITUTION

The actual case coming before the Supreme Court is likely to take a different form, however. Let us say that a same-sex couple from Utah goes to Hawaii for a week, gets married, and returns to Utah. Attempting to receive health insurance benefits as a couple, they are told that same-sex marriages are illegal in Utah. They appeal, citing the "full faith and credit" clause of the U.S. Constitution. Article 4, Section 1, of the Constitution begins by providing that "full faith and credit shall be given in each state to the public acts, records, and judicial proceedings of every other state. Some experts conclude that a marriage ceremony fits all three of these categories, that is, it is a "public act," a "record," and often a "judicial proceeding" (Greenberg & Gasman, 1996). The same-sex couple might also cite *Shapiro v. Thompson* (1969), in which the Supreme Court recognized that states may not "unduly interfere with the right to migrate, resettle, find a new job and start a new life" (p. 629) and that "the nature of our Federal union and our constitutional concepts of personal liberty unite to require that all citizens be free to travel throughout the length and breadth of our land uninhibited by statutes, rules or regulations which unreasonably burden or restrict this movement" (p. 629). If a Hawaii driver's license is legal in Utah, why isn't a Hawaii marriage license?

Another way the issue could come before the Court is through a conflict between the legislative and the judicial branches. The sentence that follows the above-quoted one on "full faith and credit" states: "And the Congress may by general laws prescribe the manner in which such acts, records and proceedings shall be proved, and the effect thereof. Does that mean that the authority of Congress to "prescribe the effect" of state marriages gives Congress the power to take away constitutional rights? What was the intent of its framers when they composed those two sentences? For some experts (see Eskridge, 1996a), the intent was for states to recognize each other's records and judgments as fundamental rights, not merely as matters of discretion. William Eskridge, a law professor at Georgetown University, concluded that "never in the nation's history has Congress invoked the 'prescribe the effect' sentence to undermine the guarantees of the 'full faith and credit' clause as interpreted by the courts" (p. 11). But sponsors of the Defense of Marriage Act point to this very sentence to support their claim that Congress can take away a state's constitutional rights. For Eskridge, the Defense of Marriage Act "raises grave constitutional concerns" (p. 11).

Does a procedure adopted by one state carry over to other states automatically, as indicated above? Another interpretation of the relevance of the "full faith and credit" clause is offered by law professor Linda Silberman. Silberman (1996) makes a distinction between state laws and state *judicial proceedings* with respect to the applicability of the "full faith and credit" clause. In response to a *New York Times* editorial, Silberman wrote:

> You imply that should Hawaii authorize same-sex marriages, other states would be required under the 'full faith and credit' requirement in the Constitution to recognize such marriages. The mistake is to equate the 'full faith and credit' requirement as it applies to judicial proceedings with the quite different 'full faith and credit' principle relevant to laws. Supreme Court precedents have made clear that the role for accommodating competing state interests is different depending on whether 'full faith and credit' is owed to a judgment of a sister state or only to its laws. Because a judgment concludes a judicial proceeding, interests of finality and stability are thought to preclude a sister state from reexamining the issues in light of its own interests. However, when a state enacts a law—until it has been applied in a judicial proceeding—a sister state is free to decide whether to apply that law or its own. (1996, p. A14)

Professor Silberman concluded that a marriage ceremony is not a "judicial proceeding" and therefore another state can consider its own interests in deciding what law to apply. She noted that there has always been a public policy exception when a state finds a law to be inconsistent with its own policies. She wrote, "A state that regards a marriage between an uncle and a niece as prohibited incest is not required by any full-faith-and-credit principle to honor an uncle-niece marriage valid in a sister state, even if the couple moves to the state of prohibition 10 years after the marriage" (1996, p. A14).

Professor Eskridge also considers the "full faith and credit" clause's applicability, and he even uses an example similar to Professor Silberman's, but his take is a little different. Noting that some states recognize "incestuous" first cousin marriages if they are legal in the state where the couple married (and in 11 states and the District of Columbia, they are), he believes that this courtesy is offered "at least in part out of constitutional obligation" (1996a, p. 11). Like Professor Silberman, he notes that other states refuse to recognize such marriages and that they base their refusal on the above-mentioned public-policy exception to the full faith and credit obligations. He believes that the Supreme Court has not "definitively" ruled on the legality of a public-policy exception.

PREDICTING THE REACTIONS
OF SUPREME COURT JUSTICES

It is fascinating to speculate on how each justice on the U.S. Supreme Court would vote on the legality of same-sex marriages. Previous Court decisions regarding the rights of homosexual persons do not provide a consistent guide; in fact, the two most recent decisions are strikingly inconsistent. Some would say that the Supreme Court would make the decision on the basis of legal precedents and past judicial decisions. Although such considerations may be a factor, they are not the whole story, and precedents and past judicial decisions may conflict. Which specific precedents does a Supreme Court justice choose to emphasize?

The Court considered two cases dealing with the rights of homosexual persons in the decades of the 1980s and 1990s. The final rulings in these two cases—which, admittedly, had a 10-year interval between them—left some court observers questioning the consistency of the Court's decisions.

The first decision, *Bowers v. Hardwick* (1986), responded to a challenge of Georgia law that made sexual relations between homosexual persons illegal. In a close vote, the Supreme Court decided to uphold that law, concluding that the privacy rights implied in the Constitution did not extend to "acts of sodomy" by homosexual persons. The decision was justified on the grounds of long-standing censure of homosexuality in Western civilization.

The specific issue in the second case, *Romer v. Evans* (1996), was quite different. In November of 1992, Colorado voters approved a state constitutional amendment (Amendment 2) that stated the following:

> NO PROTECTED STATUS BASED ON HOMOSEXUAL, LESBIAN, OR BISEXUAL ORIENTATION. Neither the State of Colorado, through any of its branches or departments, nor any of its agencies, political subdivisions, municipalities or school districts, shall enact, adopt or enforce any statute, regulation, ordinance or policy whereby homosexual, lesbian or bisexual orientation, conduct, practices or relationships shall constitute or otherwise be the basis of, or entitle any person or class of persons to have or claim any minority status, quota preferences, protected

status or claim of discrimination· This Section of the Constitution shall be in all
respects self-executing. (From Cole. Rev. State Const., Art. II, # 30b [1994 Supp.]

This amendment, which was approved by a slight majority of Colorado
voters, clearly has complex and cumbersome wording. It is no surprise that
people differed in what they thought it meant. Did it mean that homosexual
persons were not entitled to special treatment or favoritism? The state concluded that it meant that ordinances in three Colorado cities that had protected homosexual persons from discrimination in employment, housing, and
public accommodations were repealed. Furthermore, for some observers, the
wording permitted the state or its political subdivisions (cities, counties) to
adopt policies that would discriminate against gay men, lesbians, and bisexual
persons.

The constitutionality of Amendment 2 was immediately challenged in
Colorado's state court. The district court granted the respondent's motion for
a temporary injunction against its enforcement, so it never took effect. In 1993
the Colorado Supreme Court upheld the injunction, ruling that the amendment "fenced out" an identifiable class of persons and infringed upon their
fundamental right to participate equally in the political process. The state of
Colorado appealed the local court decision to the U.S. Supreme Court.
Colorado's governor at the time was Roy Romer; hence the Supreme Court
case was called *Romer v. Evans*. Although Governor Romer opposed the amendment, as governor his name was on the petition representing the state. Later,
in 1996, Romer became the first governor to veto his state legislature's bill
outlawing same-sex marriages. Although personally opposed to same-sex
marriages, Romer felt that his state's law was a "mean-spirited and unnecessary [attempt] to single out and condemn the life style of gay and lesbian people"
(Rich, 1996b, p. A11).

In its defense, Colorado argued that the amendment did not reflect discrimination, but rather the removal of special protections extending civil rights
to homosexual persons through the ordinances adopted in Boulder, Aspen,
and Denver. So the question was: Are these "special rights" or "equal rights"?

On May 20, 1996, the Supreme Court ruled that Amendment 2 was unconstitutional. Writing for the 6-to-3 majority, Justice Anthony Kennedy said
that a state cannot so deem a class of persons a stranger to its laws" and that
Amendment 2 had placed homosexual persons in Colorado in a "solitary class,"
thus violating the Constitution's guarantee of equal protection. He rejected
Colorado's claim that the amendment only deprived homosexual persons of
"special" rights; "To the contrary," he wrote, "the amendment imposes a special disability on those persons alone" (p. 4357) by requiring a new constitutional amendment to restore local protections. Justice Kennedy concluded:

> We find nothing special in the protections Amendment 2 withholds. These are
> protections taken for granted by most people either because they already have

them or do not need them; these are protections against exclusion from an almost limitless number of transactions and endeavors that constitute ordinary civil life in a free society. (p. 4358)

He reasoned that such an act was inexplicable on any basis other than "an animus toward the class that it affects"—that is, prejudice against gay persons. The majority opinion stated that the amendment did not meet even the lowest level of scrutiny afforded any official action challenged as a violation of the constitutional guarantee of equal protection. Under such a test, "a law must bear a rational relationship to a legitimate governmental purpose, and Amendment 2 does not" (p. 4358).

In his majority opinion, Justice Kennedy used a line of argument advocated in a 13-page *amicus* brief filed by Harvard Law School professor Laurence Tribe with the assistance of several other constitutional scholars. The brief was short on precedent and long on logic. "Amendment 2 is a rare example of a *per se* violation of the Equal protection Clause" (quoted by Greenhouse, 1996a, p. C19). Tribe later told an interviewer, "I really started with the words of the Constitution—'equal protection of the laws.' The law protects people by giving them remedies when they've been wronged. What Amendment 2 did was say that some people can't get the same protections as others. The protection is not equal. It sounds like third-grade reasoning, but that's how I came to it" (quoted by Toobin, 1996, p. 44). Tribe continued:

> What you had with this law was a particular group of people declared ineligible under the laws of Colorado for any legal protection against discrimination. The law meant that gays could not claim discrimination if, say, the police intentionally refused to answer their 911 calls, or if hospitals refused to give them blood transfusions, or if they were assaulted because they were gay. This is a *per se* violation of equal protection of the laws under the Fourteenth Amendment— something that was unique in my experience with cases before the Court. Even if you disapprove of gay people—even if what gay people do is wrong—you can't deny them the protection of the law. And it has nothing to do with their being gay. You couldn't have a law like this one for gamblers, or even for bank robbers. My approach offered the Court a way to decide this case which didn't require it to give any special recognition to gay rights as such. (Toobin, 1996, pp. 44–45)

Justice Kennedy agreed with Professor Tribe's brief, stating that any law that makes it more difficult for one group of citizens than for others to seek relief from the government "is itself a denial of equal protection of the laws in the most literal sense." (In keeping with the general inconsistency of previous decisions on this issue, Professor Tribe had previously represented Michael Hardwick, arguing the losing side in *Bowers v. Hardwick*).

Justices Stevens, O'Connor, Souter, Ginsburg, and Breyer joined in the majority decision. Clearly they were an ideological mixture; four of the six had been appointed by Republican presidents. The opinion writer, a Reagan appointee, had—15 years earlier—authored a Circuit Court of Appeals decision that had labeled as "rational" a U.S. Navy policy that discharged any members of the navy known to be homosexual.

Justice Scalia filed a stinging dissent, calling the majority opinion "preposterous" and claiming that the majority had taken sides in "the culture wars (through] an act not of judicial judgment but of political will" (quoted by Greenhouse, 1996a, p. A1). He noted that the voters of Colorado had passed the amendment by 53% to 47%, and that such a vote by citizens was the "most democratic of procedures," especially "since the Constitution of the United States says nothing about this subject." He viewed the amendment differently from Justice Kennedy, seeing it as "a modest attempt by seemingly tolerant Coloradans to preserve traditional sexual mores against the efforts of a politically powerful minority to revise those mores through the use of the laws." In a further statement, he revealed his attitude toward the majority decision: "This Court has no business imposing upon all Americans the resolution favored by the elite class from which the members of this institution are selected, pronouncing that 'animosity' toward homosexuality . . . is evil."

Justices Rehnquist and Thomas also dissented, agreeing with Justice Scalia that the Colorado amendment was an "eminently reasonable [means of preventing the] piecemeal deterioration of the sexual morality favored by a majority of Coloradans" (quoted by Greenhouse, 1996a, pp. A1, C19)

The majority opinion did not refer to *Bowers v. Hardwick* (1986). Conservative columnist Mona Charen, only slight exaggerating, wrote that "if a law student had written a memo on the law regarding homosexuality and omitted that case, he or she would have flunked" (1996, p. 7B). Justice Scalia did not let his colleagues forget it; he wrote: "In holding that homosexuality cannot be singled out for disfavorable treatment, the Court contradicts a decision, unchallenged here, pronounced only ten years ago, see *Bowers v. Hardwick* (1986), and places the prestige of this institution behind the proposition that opposition to homosexuality is as reprehensible as racial or religious bias." Further, he wrote:

> The case most relevant to the issue before us today is not even mentioned in the Court's opinion: In *Bowers v. Hardwick* we held that the Constitution does not prohibit . . . making homosexual conduct a crime. . . . If it is constitutionally permissible for a state to make homosexual conduct criminal, surely it is constitutionally permissible for a state to enact other laws merely disfavoring homosexual conduct. [That is, if it was constitutionally permissible for a state to make homosexuality a crime, it was certainly permissible to adopt a provision] merely prohibiting all levels of state government from bestowing special protections upon homosexual conduct. (quoted by Greenhouse, 1996a, p. C19)

How can we reconcile the *Romer v. Evans* decision with that of *Bowers v. Hardwick*? The first decision upheld the criminalization of homosexual sexual behavior. A number of states have such laws on their books. The more recent decision concluded that identifiable groups could not be singled out for discriminatory treatment by the state. Justice Kennedy seemed to be saying that the fact that the allegedly disenfranchised group was the gay community was irrelevant, in that any such group so treated would have received the same reaction. Perhaps Kennedy saw no relationship between the two cases and that was the reason he did not mention the earlier decision.

Observers have asked: Is the *Bowers v. Hardwick* decision no longer operative? The experts generally think so (see, for example, Toobin, 1996, p. 46); the *Hardwick* decision may "simply become irrelevant" (Coyle, 1996a, p. A11). These experts also believe that the Court now has enough votes to overrule the earlier decision. It should be noted, however, that the *Romer* decision does not provide affirmative *rights* for gay persons; rather it states the unconstitutionality of placing burdens on them not placed upon other groups of people. We cannot assume from this that five votes exist to uphold the legality of same-sex marriages; that is another matter.

To what degree are Supreme Court justices bound by legal and constitutional considerations? Are they able to view issues free of personal biases? Each justice is only human, and being human means sometimes making decisions that are self-serving or in other ways biased. Thus psychology comes into play as a tool for understanding the process of judicial decision making.

The fact that even Supreme Court justices are susceptible to self-serving biases is revealed in a Court decision rendered shortly after a federal income tax was implemented in 1913. Incredibly, for the next 26 years the Supreme Court justices concluded that this tax did not apply to themselves, or to any federal judges. Why not? Because Article 3, Section 1, of the Constitution guarantees that federal judges' salaries cannot "be diminished during their continuance in office." The justices concluded that any taxation of their salaries would diminish them, and it was not until 1939 that the justices overruled their predecessors and allowed themselves to be taxed just like the rest of us (Segal & Spaeth, 1993, p. 3). (The issue of judges and taxes recently resurfaced; on the first day of the Supreme Court's 1996-97 term, the Court considered the appeal of 16 federal judges who claimed that Congress had violated the constitution by passing a 1984 law forcing federal judges—for the first time—to pay Social Security and Medicare taxes. In 1995 an appellate court had agreed—not surprisingly—that these intrusions represented an unconstitutional reduction in pay. Four justices—all of whom were federal judges in 1984—recused themselves, depriving the Supreme Court of a quorum, thus leaving operative the lower court's ruling [in *United States v. Hatter*], meaning that about 80 federal judges, including Supreme Court justices, would gain as much as $75,000 in back pay.)

So judges, like all humans, are susceptible to responding on the basis of their needs and values. But each judge is an *individual*, and each has a some what different set of values and attitudes that contribute to how he or she interprets and emphasizes past precedents and decisions. Smolla (1995) wrote:

> The personalities and jurisprudential leaning of the nine Justices . . . are always brightly in evidence. . . . That is partly because those who watch the Court regularly come to see it not as mystical and mythical, an oracular institution pronouncing the sacred truths of the republic from on marble high but rather as a collection of nine quite distinct individuals, men and women who often squabble and struggle as they wrestle each other for the votes necessary to resolve many of the deepest conflicts of our national identity. (p. 4)

And even then Chief Justice Warren Burger acknowledged that the Supreme Court justices comprise a "select company not because we are all-knowing, but because we were selected and we are here" (quoted by Menez, 1984, p. 1).

On what basis would each justice decide? For some justices, clear and consistent legal philosophies have emerged; Chief Justice William Rehnquist emphasizes states' rights over federal rights. Justice Antonin Scalia is explicit about the legitimacy of legislative procedures and constricted meanings for constitutional principles. Justice Clarence Thomas reflects a position that courts should not legislate and that the Constitution should be interpreted on the basis of its writers' "original intent." Based on the votes from the 1996–97 term, one could accurately predict Justice Thomas's vote from Justice Scalia's. Of 80 signed decisions, they voted the same way on 79; they disagreed only on the outcome of an obscure estate-tax case.

The attitudes and values of other justices are sometimes less discernible. On occasion, justices vote in ways that are inconsistent with what "experts" declare the justices' values to be. A Reagan appointee and survivor of his "litmus test" for conservative values, Justice Anthony Kennedy has rendered some surprising decisions, including decisions that have upheld abortion rights. Justice Ruth Bader Ginsburg, though characterized as a "liberal" and an "activist" by the media, has generally taken a middle-of-the-road track and has recently sided with the conservatives in several important votes (Biskupic, 1995). Justices John Paul Stevens and (to lesser extent) David Souter have an idiosyncratic bent. Justice Stevens was the lone dissenter in five 8-to-1 decisions during the 1996–97 term. The oldest member of the Court, he has frequently provided a concurring or dissenting opinion to the effect that another issue was really the central one. Law professor Susan Estrich admires his uniqueness, saying, "He is not an ideologue. He is not a politician. He did not come to the Court with an agenda" (1995, p. 11A). Justice Stephen Breyer, though new to the highest bench, is seen by some as the most pragmatic of the justices.

Some Court watchers consider Justices Sandra Day O'Connor and Kennedy to be pragmatists also, and swing-voters less driven by ideology. (Of eighteen 5-to-4 votes in the 1996–97 term, these two were on the winning side in all but one vote.) But an examination of the influential votes by these two justices in several diverse cases during the 1995–96 term reflects an overarching principle that explains their votes: It is unconstitutional to treat some groups of people differently from the rest. Examples are their votes in the Colorado gay rights case, the V.M.I. gender segregation case, and the case challenging racially based redistricting in Texas and North Carolina.

Speculation about upcoming votes is inevitable. Lawyers arguing a case before the Court relentlessly count votes (Urofsky, 1997, p. 133, provides an example in one important case). Media mavens do it, law professors do it, and psychologists are not free of such conjecture either. After all, aren't psychologists expected to be able to predict behavior?

Attempting to anticipate outcomes is legitimate, because these decisions have a huge impact on our everyday lives and because the justices' past writings, past decisions, and apparent values and ideologies provide much raw data for prediction. Predicting outcomes is not, however, this book's goal; rather, it is to seek an understanding of not just the "what" but-more importantly— the "how" and the "why" of judicial decision making. *How* do justices form their initial opinions? *Why* do justices differ? "What" is the impact of the opinions of the other justices?

The difficulty of prediction is reflected in a recent case. The *National Law Journal* asked three constitutional law professors to predict the outcome of a case for which the Supreme Court had heard oral arguments in a special session in May 1997. The case, *Raines v. Byrd* (1997), dealt with the constitutionality of the Line-Item Veto Act of 1996 in which Congress gave the president increased budgetary powers; specifically, the act gave the president the right to "cancel in whole" three types of budget items: dollar amounts of discretionary budget authority, new items of direct spending, and limited tax benefits (Coyle, 1997). To veto such specific provisions, the president had to act within 5 calendar days of signing the legislation. The act expires on January 1, 2005.

Six members of Congress challenged the act's constitutionality the day after it became law, creating one of the issues for the Court to decide: Did the persons who challenged the act have standing? That is, could they show that they had an injury or interest that was affected by the law? This issue was raised during the 70 minutes of oral arguments in the May special session. A second issue deals with whether the Court should be required to decide on constitutionality even before the president had exercised the authority granted by the act (Coyle, 1997). President Clinton did not exercise his line-item veto until August 1997.

Needless to say, the president supported the act, and the U.S. solicitor general argued for its constitutionality before the Supreme Court. But the members of Congress who challenged the act contended that it conferred on the president powers of "veto, revision, and repeal of federal law," which violated Article 1 of the Constitution dealing with the separation of powers. They claimed that they had *standing* because the act injured them by altering the "legal and practical effect" of their votes and by "divesting" them of their constitutional role in the repeal of legislation (Coyle, 1997, p. A22). The district court agreed, striking down the law—hence, the appeal to the Supreme Court (*Raines v. Byrd*, 1997).

Three law professors ventured predictions of the outcome:

Peter M. Shane, dean of the University of Pittsburgh law school and author of several treatises on presidential power and public law:

> *Finding standing*: Seven justices-Breyer, Ginsburg, Kennedy, O'Connor, Rehnquist, Souter, Stevens
> *Upholding the statute*: All nine justices
> *Comments*: I do think the executive branch is on very strong ground in defending the law. It is unfortunate Congress has called this a line-item veto. It doesn't at all resemble the constitutional veto power. It does resemble the very routine exercise of delegated authority. The standards prescribed by the statute are as specific as other delegations upheld since the 1930s . . . (quoted in Coyle, 1997, p. A23)

Laurence H. Tribe, professor of constitutional law, Harvard Law School, and author of *American Constitutional Law*:

> *Finding standing*: His response was a question mark, followed by "at least Breyer"
> *Upholding the statute*: Only Breyer
> *Comments*: I think the only difficult question is whether the Court can and should reach the merits or whether the fact that the line-item veto has not yet been wielded and that the challenge is being brought by members of Congress solely in their lawmaking capacities would or should prevent the Court from treating this as a justiciable controversy. The issues of ripeness and standing are much more difficult here than the merits.
>
> If the Court does reach the merits, it should find it quite easy to invalidate the legislation. It is quite a flagrant violation of the separation of powers. Treating this as just one more delegation to the Executive gives delegation a bad name. . . . If the justices reach the merits, I could see a decision striking down the statute, 7-2, 8-1, or possibly 9-0. Justice Breyer, who is very much a pragmatist and less concerned than others with the formal structure of either constitutional doctrine or the government, might be inclined, in the way Justice Byron White once was, to cut through what one would say is mere formalism and treat this as somehow constitutionally acceptable. I hope he won't, but it wouldn't surprise me if he did. For the others, I find it very hard to imagine the other eight finding this acceptable, but predictions are hazardous. (quoted in Coyle, 1997, p. A22)

Thomas O. Sargentich, co-director of the program of law and government at the Washington College of Law and former vice-chair of the Committee on Government Organization and Separation of Powers (American Bar Association's administrative law section):

> *Finding status*: Five justices—Breyer, Ginsburg, O'Connor, Souter. Stevens
> *Upholding the statute*: Four justices—Kennedy, Rehnquist, Scalia, Thomas
> *Comments*: . . . There is a rational basis to say members [of Congress] have a particular interest in their ability to vote, and when an act impinges on that, they have a stake, an injury. The other side of it is, if it goes too far, you are allowing

members to go to court when they lose in Congress. I'm willing to trust the legal process to work with facts of cases to sort out appropriate cases to adjudicate. It would be much more for the Supreme Court to say no, you can never do this. That's the kind of bright-line rule Justice Scalia and others have argued for.

It's possible the Court will never get to the merits of the case. Even if the Court preserves the possibility of congressional standing, it might say this particular case is too premature—the power hasn't been wielded yet. I don't know how to predict it. It comes down to the swing justices.

I could see a 5-4 vote to find standing...But it could easily go the other way. Justice Breyer is the wild card. . . . If the Court does reach the merits, I think you could see the same five justices who found standing vote to strike down the statute. . . . Under the case law so far, I'd say it will fall, if the Court's analysis in *Chadha* [*INS v. Chadha,* 1983] is going to hold, it's very hard to uphold the statute. (quoted in Coyle, 1997, pp. A22–A23)

In a speech before the American Bar Association (ABA), convention, Justice Stevens noted the fallibility of predicting how judges will decide and said that even his predictions about his colleagues' votes were often wrong. For this case, three legal experts have—to use psychological terminology—no *reliability*; their predictions are as inconsistent as a trio of predictions could be. What about their "validity?" The actual decision was announced in late June of 1997; the Court ruled 7 to 2 that the petitioners, in effect, did not have standing because they had not suffered any personal injury (Pear, 1997). Chief Justice Rehnquist wrote the majority opinion; he noted that a private plaintiff who suffered a loss of money or benefits as a result of a line-item veto would probably have the right to sue. The chief justice's opinion was signed by Justices O'Connor, Scalia, Kennedy, Thomas, and Ginsburg. Justice Souter voted with the chief justice but wrote his own opinion. Justice Breyer dissented, as did Justice Stevens, maintaining the reputation we described earlier; Justice Stevens even went so far as to conclude that the act was unconstitutional. Justice Breyer's dissent expressed no opinion on the ultimate issue.

Thus Justice Breyer proved to be the most predictable justice for the panel of experts. For example, Professor Tribe was correct in predicting that Breyer might find that the members of Congress had legal standing because he is "a pragmatist, less concerned than his colleagues with formalism" (Berkman, 1997, p. A10).

The issue came before the Court a second time in April 1998; this time New York City and an Idaho potato growers' group challenged the law. The case, when it went before the Supreme Court, was *Clinton v. City of New York* (1998). In June 1998 the Court announced its decision: by a 6-to-3 vote, it rejected the line-item veto. Justice Stevens, in the majority opinion, concluded that the Constitution prohibited the president from—in effect—rewriting legislation via the veto of single spending items. Voting in the majority with Justice Stevens were Justices Thomas, Souter, Kennedy, Rehnquist, and Ginsburg; in opposition (i.e., supporting the statute) were Justices O'Connor, Scalia, and Breyer.

Thus two of three experts were incorrect in their general prediction that the Line Item Veto Act would be upheld. Predictions of the votes were generally off-base, with the exception of Justice Breyer's vote.

THE PURPOSES OF THIS BOOK

This book has two purposes: First, it seeks to examine from a psychological perspective how judges make decisions. When a panel of appellate judges considers a specific case, is each judge's vote based on precedents and logic, or is it a manifestation of that judge's predispositions and values? Is the panel's eventual ruling a result of reasonable deliberations, or of persuasion and conformity pressures? Chapters 1 through 5 examine competing explanations of judicial decision making and reflect the application of psychological knowledge to the above questions.

I believe that the field of social psychology is the most appropriate discipline for the study of judicial behavior. Not only does social psychology (along with several other social sciences) study decision making, but it is the one discipline that studies both the individual *and* the group as determinants of behavior. Central to this book's analysis is the proposition that a court decision reflects the preferences of its individual members yet is also a group decision that reflects the interactions among its members. A controlling opinion is written by one justice, but it must be acceptable to a majority of the group, whose reactions mold the final draft. Neither the individual nor the group can be neglected as we seek to understand what determines the decision of any appellate court, including the Supreme Court.

The second half of the book explores psychology's relevance to judicial decision making in a different and more precise way. The issue of same-sex marriages was chosen as an introductory example partly because it is an issue about which psychology has something to say. Over the last fifty years, organized psychology has tried to influence the outcome of some decisions by the Supreme Court and other appellate courts, mostly through the use of the *amicus curiae* briefs. How effective have these briefs been? What does the rate of effectiveness tell us about the decision-making criteria of Supreme Court justice? The second half of the book gives detailed examples of successful and unsuccessful *amicus* briefs, and draws conclusions about how psychology and the other social sciences can best have "their day in court."

The focus is on appellate judges rather than on trial judges. The latter have no judicial conference and no need to take other judges' reactions into account (other than considering the possibility of a reversal). Trial judges act as *individual* decision makers, whether presiding over a jury trial, in which they rule on individual motions, or whether finding facts and making decisions in a bench trial. This book concentrates on the process of decision making for a *panel* of judges-how each individual judge forms an opinion, of group discussion process, with its exchange of ideas and attempts to influence, and judges' reactions to pressure to change their opinion. The extended deliberation period is the "hidden middle" in the process, which the public never does see—in fact, most people are not even aware that it occurs. As many as 30 different drafts of a majority opinion may be exchanged among the judges before one emerges for which a majority can agree. This book explores how the group attempts to resolve the conflicts inevitable in the expression of differing, even antagonistic, opinions. Thus, the emphasis is on a *group* process, because all appellate courts make decisions that represent a group consensus.

Though such processes apply to all levels of federal and state appellate courts, almost all of the examples in this book are taken from the U.S. Supreme Court decisions. For decades the decision-making process of the Supreme Court has been secret, but recent access to retired justices' files (those of Brennan and Marshall), plus books by scholars and journalists (including O'Brien, 1993; Schwartz, 1996; Simon, 1995; and Woodward and Armstrong, 1979) who have interviewed justices and law clerks, now provide rich examples of the processes analyzed in this book.

The concentration on the Supreme Court also derives from the fact that it is the ultimate court of our land. As Justice Robert Jackson once said, "We are not final because we are infallible, but we are infalliable only because we are final" (quoted by B. Schwartz, 1996, p. x). The power of the Supreme Court is absolute, at least until Congress passes a law that countermands a Court decision. Furthermore, the breadth of content in the Court's decisions is staggering. Segal and Spaeth (1993) wrote:

> We live in a democracy, but within that democracy we give the nine unelected, virtually unremovable members of the Supreme Court broad discretion to determine, for instance, whether abortions should be allowed, death penalties inflicted, and homosexuality criminally punished. Although the justices might claim for public consumption that they do not make public policy, that they merely interpret the law, the truth is closer to Chief Justice (then Governor) Charles Evans Hughes's declaration: "We are under a Constitution, but the Constitution is what the judges say it is." (p. 1)

Judges do, however, try to minimize decisions that create new policies. Justice Blackmun wrote: "I hesitate to classify judges as policymakers. . . . Although some part of a judge's task may be to fill in the interstices of legislative enactments, the *primary* task of a judicial officer is to apply rules reflecting the policy choices made by, or on behalf of, those elected to legislative and executive positions" (minority opinion in *Gregory v. Ashcroft*, 1991, p. 441, Note 1). But if we accept Segal and Spaeth's interpretation, then "policy making involves choosing among alternative courses of action, where the choice binds the behavior of those subject to the policy-maker's action" (1993, p. 4). Whether the behavior is that of school prayer or physician-assisted suicide or interracial marriage, decisions by the Supreme Court have clearly influenced the actions of a multitude of our compatriots. In fact, a recent book by political scientists Lee Epstein and Jack Knight, *The Choices Judges Make* (1998), concludes that appellate judges frequently make their decisions based on what they consider to be the best policies for the country. The task of the U.S. Supreme Court is to interpret the Constitution, but that means its topics can range from the seemingly unimportant to those of the greatest consequence for society. (Fewer than 20% of the Supreme Court's decisions garner any general media attention.) A justice on the Supreme Court of Canada wrote:

> Reading through an American constitutional law text is like walking through modern human existence in an afternoon. From a woman's control of her own body to the Vietnam war and from desegregation of schools to drunken drivers, it is hard to imagine a facet of American existence that has not been subjected to constitutional scrutiny. (Wilson, 1988, p. 334)

As noted earlier, not every Supreme Court decision is final. With regard to the content of statutes, Congress can overturn judicial decisions. Constitutional amendments can supersede the Supreme Court's interpretation of the Constitution. But on just four occasions in our more than 200-year history has Congress authorized constitutional amendments that overturned Supreme Court decisions. The 11th Amendment in 1798 overturned *Chisholm v. Georgia* (1793) and permitted a nonresident of a state to sue that state in federal court; the 14th Amendment in 1868 overturned *Scott v. Sandford* (1857), which was the dreadful Dred Scott decision that had made Blacks ineligible for U.S. citizenship; the 16th Amendment overturned *Pollock v. Farmer's Loan and Trust Company* (1895), which had previously struck down an earlier federal income tax; and the 26th Amendment (1971) overruled *Oregon v. Mitchell* (1970), which in turn had overruled a federal law granting 18-year-olds the right to vote in state elections.

MODELS OF JUDICIAL DECISION MAKING

The traditional answer to the question "How does a judge decide?" relies on the legal reasoning so valued in law school. This "first wave" of explanation postulates that the judge considers the facts and issues of the current case and relates them to previous decisions, to applicable laws, and to the Constitution. Justice Clarence Thomas in a 1996 public address said: "I always ask myself,

'What is my role in this case as a judge, not as a politician, a citizen, or a policy maker?' " But the first wave explanation does not fully portray the process. In split decisions the nine justices are clearly not emphasizing the *same* precedents; when five justices share a majority opinion and four dissent, a fundamental difference of some sort is present. How to account for such differences?

Consider a recent Supreme Court decision that received little media attention but dealt with a fundamental right. In the case of *Lewis v. United States* (1996), the appellant was a postal worker who had been convicted of two counts of stealing mail; each carried a potential prison sentence of six months. His request for a jury trial had been denied by the federal district court in Brooklyn and by the Second Circuit Court of Appeals.

The Sixth Amendment of the Constitution guarantees defendants the right to a jury trial for serious offenses, which are usually defined as those carrying a potential sentence of more than six months. When the postal worker appealed, the Supreme Court faced the question whether defendants who are prosecuted in a single case for more than one petty offense have a constitutional right to a jury trial. Should the determining factor be the potential sentence for *each* petty offense, or should it be the potential *cumulative* effect, in this case consecutive sentences extending beyond six months? How would the justices interpret the Constitution? What was the intent of the framers?

By a slim (5-to-4) majority, the Court ruled in June 1996 that defendants who are prosecuted in a single case for more than one petty offense do not have the constitutional right to a jury trial. Writing for the majority, Justice O'Connor stated that the determination of whether an offense was petty or serious was up to the legislature. The fact that more than one charge is present "does not revise the legislative judgment as to the gravity of that particular offense, nor does it transform the petty offense into a serious one" (*Lewis v. United States*, 1996, p. 2167).

Chief Justice Rehnquist and Justices Scalia, Souter, O'Connor, and Thomas formed the majority. The four dissenting justices were Breyer, Ginsburg, Stevens, and Kennedy; the latter called the decision "one of the most serious incursions on the right to jury trial in the Court's history (p. 2169)." Such a deep-set difference of reaction makes one wonder if the difference is merely a matter of interpreting the Constitution differently, or if deep-set values about the relative rights of defendants and the purposes of the criminal justice system are the most likely explanation for the often-contrasting votes by justices.

THE ATTITUDINAL MODEL

If we need any further indication that the written opinions of judges involve more than applications of logical analysis, we need only consider the fact that the dissenters sometimes are not satisfied simply to disagree, but that additionally they attack the majority opinion and derogate it in abusive language. The presence of emotionally laden beliefs is apparent in a number of Justice Scalia's dissents—when, for example, he labels a majority opinion by Justice Kennedy as "terminal silliness" and one by Justice Souter as having been created "out of nowhere." Hence the "second wave" of explanation, though first advanced by legal theorists and political scientists, is more psychological in its basis. After World War I, the *legal realism movement*, formulated at the Yale law school, proposed that laws were social constructions. In 1948 political scientist C. Herman Pritchett, in an analysis of Supreme Court decisions during President Franklin D. Roosevelt's administration, showed empirically the consistency over time in the decisions of individual judges and also showed the consistent differences *between* judges. The predictability of particular judges was further documented in the work of Glendon Schubert in *The Judicial Mind* (1965b) and *The Judicial Mind Revisited* (1974). Schubert, also a political scientist, relied on the psychometric framework of mathematical psychologist Clyde Coombs; Schubert proposed that a Supreme Court justice's vote was a function of the relationship between his or her ideological position on the question at hand and the nature of the case stimulus.

Consider, for example, the reaction of Justice Ginsburg when laced with the issue of the men-only policy at the Virginia Military Institute (V.M.I.), a public institution partially financed by tax money (*United States v. Virginia*, 1996). In response to criticisms of blatant sex discrimination, the state had created and funded a separate leadership training program at Mary Baldwin College, a private liberal arts college for women. A lower court had accepted this program as a valid alternative to admitting women to V.M.I. The challenge derived from a suit filed in 1990 by the U.S. Justice Department (while George Bush was President), which itself derived from a complaint filed by a female high-school student who had been denied admission to the military institute (Coyle, 1996b).

By a 7-to-1 vote (Scalia dissented, Thomas recused), the Supreme Court ruled that excluding women from V.M.I. violated the equal protection clause of the Constitution's 14th Amendment. It was not surprising that Justice Ginsburg—a former American Civil Liberties Union litigator and one of the nation's foremost advocates for women's rights—was named to write the majority opinion; in so doing, she concluded that the alternative program at Mary Baldwin College was not an "equal" but a "pale shadow" of V.M.I. In her majority opinion, Ginsburg traced the High Court's position on gender discrimination by citing a number of precedents in cases she had argued before the courts. One observer (Greenhouse, 1996b) concluded that reading her decision in open court must have been "Surely a moment of deep personal satisfaction" for Justice Ginsburg (p. C18).

The attitudinal model proposes that if a challenged behavior is inconsistent with a justice's ideological perspective, that justice will vote to reject the behavior (Rowland & Carp, 1996). According to this model, if the possibility of two persons of the same sex getting married is an insult to the justice's values, he or she will overrule the statute regardless of abstract legal precedents. For example, Chief Justice Rehnquist has throughout his career been a strong supporter of states' rights, as is documented in Chapter 2. But if he were ideologically opposed to two gay persons legitimizing their commitment, the attitudinal model predicts that he would reject the transferability to other states of a marriage license obtained in Hawaii.

Thus the second wave of explanation focused on the judge's attitudes and values. Political scientists have relied on social psychology, concentrating on the concept of social attitude, which has been defined as a relatively enduring, organized reaction. Rohde and Spaeth (1976), influential proponents of this view, extended Schubert's position through transforming his attitudinal model into "an explicitly goal-oriented model by assuming that the goals that motivate justices are policy-based" (Rowland & Carp, 1996, p. 142). The culmination of the position that judges "vote their attitudes" can be found in Jeffrey Segal and Harold Spaeth's 1993 book, *The Supreme Court and the Attitudinal Model*:

> Though attitudes may be said to have cognitive, affective, and behavioral components, our concern is with the votes of justices, and thus the behavioral component of attitudes. These attitudes and the values with which they associate should cause a behaviorally predisposed justice to support certain legal claims and to oppose others, while other justices behave in an opposite fashion. (Segal & Spaeth, 1993, p. 69)

THE COGNITIVE MODEL

The problem with the attitudinal model is that it reflects an outmoded conception of the power of attitudes (Rowland & Carp, 1996). In the 1930s and 1940s, social psychologists viewed attitudes as strongly predictive of behavior, but more recently the one-to-one nature of the relationship has been questioned. The cognitive revolution that has come to dominate social psychology retains the concept of attitudes, but places them in a different light. Attitudes are now conceptualized as "information filters" that influence the cognitive processing of information (Fiske L Taylor, 1991). Thus, the "third wave" of explanation, proposing that decisions are a product of social cognition, emphasizes *process*. It examines the cognitive processes that mediate the relationship between stimulus (a new case) and response (the judge's vote).

Cognitive social psychology seeks to understand how people carry out the difficult task of making complex decisions. As Baum (1997, p. 140) has observed, "Even the relatively simple conceptions of decision making that dominate Supreme Court research imply an intricate set of cognitive processes. A central concept for social cognition theorists is the *schema*, an organized body of knowledge from past experience that is used to interpret a new experience. Each of us possesses *schemas* about many many things—individual people, objects, events, abstract concepts. Introduced to new information we encode, retrieve, and interpret it based on the specific relevant schema. Consider, teenage pregnancy and the right of a teenager to have an abortion. This issue was before the Supreme Court on several occasions during the 1980s. Chapter 9 describes the actions of several states that passed laws requiring adolescents who were contemplating abortions to notify their parents (or even get their parents' permission) before doing so. The constitutionality of these laws was challenged. Also recall that several Supreme Court justices (O'Connor, Scalia, Kennedy, and Rehnquist as chief justice) were appointed by President Reagan, who had pledged to choose strict constructionists, and who attempted to screen appointees to ensure that their attitudes were pro-choice. How would such an appointee proceed when presented with a challenge to the constitutionality of requiring parental notification? A schema about the maturity of such adolescents kicks in, and "no amount of testimony could be expected to overcome [the] schematic perception that pregnancy itself was an indication of immaturity in unmarried teenagers" (Rowland & Carp, 1996, p. 167).

How does a schema differ from an attitude? The attitudinal model of judicial decision making assumed that attitudes and values *directed* behavior, that judicial opinions derived relentlessly from them. The cognitive approach places more emphasis on the perception: through process one's attitudes may play a role as filters or agitators, they are not necessarily one-to-one determinants of behavior.

OVERVIEW

Analysis of judicial decision making focuses both upon each individual judge and upon the group decision that reflects the eventual opinion of the court. At the level of decision making by individual judges, three processes can be distinguished: opinion formation and expression, attempts to influence the opinions of a judge or judges on the panel, and judicial responses to those attempts.

Each of these processes is described in a separate chapter. Chapter 2 concentrates on opinion formation and expression. After identifying the steps in the Supreme Court's procedure in deciding a case, Chapter 2 explores in greater depth the various models of how the Court forms its opinion. The justices's own views on the process are described, as are the contrasting theories of Judge Jerome Frank and former justice Benjamin Cardozo. Chapter 2 elaborates on what social psychology has to offer in the way of explanatory concepts of judicial decision making, including the social cognition approach, the distinction between experts and novices, the person–situation interaction, and the changes in a person over time.

Judges have differing perceptions of the facts and differing interpretations of the law, leading to disagreements about decisions. We examine this in two ways: First, we review the research program described in a book by political scientists C. K. Rowland and Robert A. Carp (1996), which illustrates differences in decisions between federal judges appointed by President Carter and those appointed by President Reagan in regard to several types of issues, including civil rights and abortion rights. Second, we look at a specific Supreme Court decision (*Ake v. Oklahoma*, 1985) to illustrate how two Supreme Court justices (Thurgood Marshall and Rehnquist) chose to process the facts differently in drawing their conclusions.

It is tempting to simply state that justices vote their values, but any model of opinion formation must consider cases in which justices' positions do not reflect their stated values. Specific death penalty cases, in which Justices Harry Blackmun's and Potter Stewart's votes did not reflect their private attitudes, as well as Justice Ginsburg's vote in the Tina Bennis forfeiture case, are some examples. These deviations from the attitudinal model reinforce the more complex approach of social cognition.

Chapter 3 examines the next step in the process, specifically, attempts to influence a justice's decisions. Several types of potential influence are evaluated, including public opinion, briefs and oral arguments, the judicial conference and the postconference negotiations. Again social psychology has something to offer, including conceptualizations of the various types of influence attempts. Examples from judicial decisions are provided.

The place of the chief justice in the influence process is a special one, even though the chief justice has only one vote. The chief justice chairs the judicial conference, summarizing each case and expressing an opinion before the other justices get a chance to speak. Some chief justices have dominated the conferences, barely permitting other justices to speak at all. Some have been extreme in the opposite direction, allowing a laissez-faire atmosphere that dragged each conference out for several days.

What makes for a great chief justice? The most important quality is the ability to shift the views of other justices. Chapter 4 examines the psychological literature on the attributes of effective leadership and relates it to several of the recent chief justices in an attempt to identify the characteristics that made them successful or unsuccessful.

Chapter 5 examines the third phase in the influence process, the responses by appellate judges to attempts to influence them. An extensive social psychology literature exists on attitude change and reactions to conformity pres-

sures. A central distinction is between public compliance and private acceptance, and political scientists have advanced a distinction between strategic
and *sincere* voting (Baum, 1997; Epstein & Knight, 1998; Murphy, 1964). It
may come as a surprise to some that even esteemed Supreme Court justices
will vote in "insincere" ways, but as information has become public regarding
the Court's decision making process, the above phenomena have been shown
to occur. For example, justices—whether conservative or liberal—may occasionally be willing to modify their expressed views in order to maintain a majority.
But person-situation interaction is important here, as these shifts apparently
do not occur in cases of "high principle."

The influence process can also be approached at the group level. Failed
influence attempts lead to conflict in any organization, and the Supreme Court
is no exception. The psychological literature on conflict resolution is applied
to numerous examples of conflict between justices.

Chapter 6 shifts the focus to attempts by psychologists and other social
scientists to the influence decisions of the U.S. Supreme Court and other appellate courts. Formal attempts to use social science research in briefs can be
traced back to the beginning of the twentieth century, but the relationship
between social science and the Court has not been a smooth or congenial one.
This chapter describes high and low points of the relationship and introduces
the theme of conflicting values between psychology and the law.

Following this theme, Chapter 7 details the process of submitting *amicus
curiae* briefs, and illustrates the extensiveness of their use by other organizations with examples from several recent prominent cases. As a case study,
Chapter 7 uses one of the most extensively described and evaluated examples
of the American Psychological Association's involvement with amicus briefs,
Price Waterhouse v. Hopkins (1989). This chapter also describes the history of
the APA's involvement in submitting *amicus* briefs. The distinction between
advocacy briefs and *science-translation briefs* is evaluated, and the question of
how to measure the effectiveness of both types of *amicus* briefs is discussed,
with emphasis on the APA's briefs.

Chapters 8 and 9 consider specific cases in which the American Psychological Association has submitted briefs. Chapter 8 examines those cases in
which the APA was, for want of a better word, "successful." What were APA's
goals? Did the APA brief use logical, constitutional, or empirical bases for its
argument! What was the basis for the Supreme Court's decision? Did the APA
brief have any direct influence?

In about half the cases for which the APA had submitted an *amicus* brief
to the Supreme Court, the Court's eventual majority opinion conflicted with
the APA's position. Chapter 9 reviews examples and makes distinctions between cases in which the APA brief was ignored and those in which the APA's
position was considered but rejected. Of specific interest are cases involving

parental notification for adolescent abortion. The APA's arguments in these cases are examined and evaluated in depth.

In final chapter, Chapter 10, we return to our original focus—the sources of judicial decision making—this time taking another approach. Different appellate judges cite different kinds of sources in their written opinions. An important distinction is made between primary and secondary sources; the latter include social science research findings. The position of individual justices on the types of sources is evaluated, leading to an analysis of the obstacles to psychology's influence on judicial decision making. Given those obstacles, some proposals for improving the relationship are then offered.

2

Opinion Formation
and Expression

As has often been observed, the justices of the Supreme Court operate much like nine individual, autonomous law firms, at least up to the point of the judicial conference to discuss the case. Prior to the conference, each justice has participated in the decision of whether to hear the case, has presumably read the briefs prepared by each side, and has sat through (and perhaps participated in) the oral arguments. Even so, each justice's initial opinion forms largely without input or influence from the other justices.

Judges' orientations reflect their past experiences; they may not approach new cases with a "clean slate," and they often form opinions (even judicial opinions) early in the process. For example, it is said that Chief Justice Earl Warren drew heavily on his own innate sense of justice in reacting to the facts of a case (Gray, 1997). The assumption that reactions may be established upon early exposure does not imply that they cannot or will not change; the important thing to recognize is that the judicial conference is not—as some observers claim—the beginning of the *opinion formation* process (Schwartz, 1996). In some cases, at least, the die may have been cast long before the conference.

THE SUPREME COURT'S PROCEDURE

Some cases come to the Supreme Court on automatic appeal, and a few by statute, but more than 90% are petitions requesting the overturning of a lower court's decision. When a case is submitted to the Supreme Court for resolution, a process is set in motion. This process contains a number of "decision points" (Menez, 1984); judicial decision making occurs at every step in this process. Thus the initial section of this chapter outlines the steps in the process and introduces decision-making issues that are later considered in depth.

CASE SELECTION

Every year approximately six to eight thousand appeals (called "petitions for *certiorari*") are submitted to the Supreme Court; it chooses which to review and resolve. Based on his interviews with Supreme Court justices and their clerks, H. W. Perry, Jr. (1991), concluded that initially the judges disposed of those cases that they saw as frivolous (mostly on the basis of their clerks' recommendations). Next, they asked if there was a doctrinal conflict between the decisions by different circuit courts (Caldeira & Wright, 1988; Ulmer, 1984); an example of such a conflict is the *Harris v. Forklift* (1993) sexual harassment case, described in detail in Chapter 8. Justice Rehnquist has estimated that between 1000 and 2000 petitions each year are "patently without merit" (1987, p. 264). Similarly, Justice William Brennan has estimated that 70 percent of the docketed cases do not merit conference discussion (Stern & Gressman, 1978). The decision to hear a case—colloquially referred to as "granting *cert.*"— means that the appellant's petition has been accepted by the Court for review, which leads to the submission of written briefs and the presentation of oral arguments. In the Court's 1993 term, 7,786 cases were on its docket; of these, the Court agreed to act on only 84. In the 1995 term this dropped to 75; the term ending in June 1997 saw 80 signed opinions. Only a decade before, the Court was acting on 150 or more cases a year.

Many reasons have been offered for the dramatic decrease in granting *certiorari*. Some scholars have even speculated that the justices have gotten lazy. I believe a prominent reason is that, at present, the Court is composed entirely of persons with many years of experience as appellate judges (even before their appointment to the Supreme Court) and that they are more general agreement than in the past as to what constitutes an "appealable" case.

For the Supreme Court to grant *certiorari*, four justices (regardless of how many actually vote) must agree that the case is of sufficient importance to warrant the Court's attention. Fred Vinson, while he was chief justice, wrote:

> The Supreme Court is not, and never has been, primarily concerned with the correction of errors in lower court decisions. . . . The function of the Supreme

> Court is, therefore, to resolve conflicts of opinion in federal questions that
> arisen among lower courts, to pass upon questions of wide import under ..
> Constitution, laws, and treaties of the United States, and to exercise supervisory
> power over lower federal courts. (Vinson, 1961, p. 55)

This "rule of four" is of uncertain origin, but since at least 1924 it has been a matter of public record (Epstein & Knight, 1998). Scholars have noted that "four is the perfect number, striking a sensitive balance between principle and pragmatism" (quoted by Urofsky, 1997, p. 97). If five votes were required, it would, as Urofsky observed, tend to prejudge the case. If only a couple of votes were needed, the docket would be weakened with less-than-significant issues.

The Court rarely indicates why it has denied *cert.*; when a case relevant to an important issue is denied, however, speculation abounds. For example, the case of *Hopwood v. State of Texas* (1996) received extensive publicity because a panel of judges (on the Fifth U.S. Circuit Court of Appeals) rejected a race-based student admission procedure that had been used by the law school at the University of Texas. The school had set lower test score standards for Black and Hispanic applicants than for White applicants and had provided a separate review board for the minority applicants. Thus the law school hoped to achieve a diversified student body, with a goal of about 10% Hispanics and 5% Blacks in the entering class. The school had already scrapped the procedure after being sued by four unsuccessful White applicants, including Cheryl Hopwood, but still the procedure was rejected by the circuit court. Observers were surprised at elements of the circuit court's decision, especially "because it said what the Supreme Court has never explicitly held—that the need for diverse student bodies in higher education can never be compelling justification for racial classifications" (Coyle, 1996c, p. A10). Although the circuit court decision was binding in only three states (Texas, Louisiana, and Mississippi), it could become precedent-setting, especially if it was not overturned by the U.S. Supreme Court. On the final day of its 1995–96 term, the Supreme Court decided not to accept Texas's appeal for review. In addition to the State of Texas, both the Clinton administration and the NAACP Legal Defense and Education Fund had urged the Supreme Court to reverse the Fifth Circuit. Why did the Court shy away from such an important decision? Perhaps because the program was no longer operative (that was the reason given by Justice Ginsburg); perhaps because the matter of affirmative action was too complex or too controversial (but this Court in recent years has not been reluctant to rule on politically sensitive issues). One civil rights scholar, Neal Devins of the College of William and Mary law school, suggested, "With respect to affirmative action in general, my guess is the Court hasn't quite figured out what its position is. I suspect it would just as soon let the lower courts play around with affirmative action to see if some consensus is achieved, or at least wait until it has a better sense of its own feeling" (quoted in Coyle, 1996c, p. A10). This analysis reflects how the Court seeks "rightness" before it agrees to decide; it may want the lower courts to deal with an issue at length before making a final decision. It has even been speculated that in the *Hopwood* case, the liberal justices on the Supreme Court did not push to grant *cert.* because they feared that a Supreme Court decision could rule out affirmative action for the whole country (Burka, 1996). Also, judges may plan ahead and decide to cut their losses rather than force an issue; Epstein and Knight (1998) have labeled this *defensive denial* and have offered it as an example of strategic voting behavior (described further in Chapter 5).

When the Court denies *cert.*, what does it mean? Even the Court's justices have differed on this question. Justice Robert Jackson felt it meant that the lower court decision should stand (and that is the practical effect of denying *cert.*). In contrast, Justice Felix Frankfurter did not believe that it meant approval of a lower court decision at all, but only that the majority of the justices did not think the matter should be adjudicated (Menez, 1984). Chief Justice Rehnquist has been explicit that no conclusions about the merit of a prior decision should be drawn from a denial of *cert.*

What determines whether a specific petition will be chosen? Many of the thousands of appeals that surface annually are from federal prisoners, and most of these are initially processed by the justices' law clerks; it is rare that such an appeal is granted *cert.* (*Gideon v. Wainwright*, 1963, was a noteworthy exception.) The decision to grant certiorari is obviously an important one that needs a more thorough examination; much less has been written about it than about decisions at the judicial conference after the oral arguments. It has been proposed that judges select cases for review in order to achieve their policy goals (Baum, 1997). That is, at this early point in the process appellate judges are already reflecting the phenomenon of strategic voting that becomes more pronounced at the judicial conference and afterward.

Does a vote by an individual justice to grant *cert.* necessarily mean that he or she believes that the earlier decision should be overturned? Clearly not; the vote may reflect a recognition that a constitutional issue is at stake, or it may reflect the fact that two or more different circuit courts of appeal have rendered conflicting derisions on the same question and hence a need for adjudication.

If a petition garners the four votes necessary for the Court to hear the case, the next question is whether an individual justice's vote on the *certiorari* petition is predictive of his or her vote at the judicial conference. This question is difficult to answer, for only rarely are the votes at this initial stage "leaked" to the public. But we know that in least one important case (*Tinker v Des Moines Independent Community School District*, 1969), the justice who eventually wrote the majority opinion in favor of the petitioners initially voted to deny *cert.* Johnson, 1997).

Amicus Briefs

If the Court grants *certiorari*, the two parties—the appellant and the appellee—ordinarily have 90 days to submit written briefs. These legal briefs are made available to the public. Other parties with an interest in the outcome may also be permitted to submit *amicus* briefs. (See Chapter 7.)

Oral Arguments

Fourteen weeks of the Supreme Court's term (which runs from the first Monday in October to the end of May) are allocated to oral arguments; public sessions are usually held on Mondays, Tuesdays, and Wednesdays from 10:00 a.m. to noon and from 1:00 p.m. to 3:00 p.m. (Such a schedule means a maximum of 168 cases could be argued each year.) The Court clerk schedules the opening arguments, which usually take place at least four months after the justices have agreed to review the case.

A century ago, when fewer appeals sought resolution by the Court, virtually unlimited time was allowed for oral arguments (O'Brien, 1993); in the important case of *Gibbons v. Ogden* (1824), the Court heard oral arguments for 20 hours over a 5-day period. But gradually the time allocation became more and more constricted, and since 1970 each side has been permitted only 30 minutes to present its case. Only rarely is additional time given (Rehnquist, 1987). Attorneys are encouraged not to just repeat what is in their written briefs; it is assumed that the justices have read these. Rule 44 of the Supreme Court states: "Oral argument should undertake to emphasize and clarify the written argument appearing in the briefs theretofore filed. The Court looks with disfavor on any oral argument that is read from a prepared text" (Stern & Gressman, 1962, p. 564).

The appellant (also called *the petitioner*) always goes first. It is likely that an oral argument, regardless of which side is making it, will be interrupted by questions from individual justices. (As many as 150 interruptions have been recorded during a single case's oral argument.) For an attorney the experience can be quite disconcerting; the questions are often penetrating, and the justices' observations are sometimes intemperate. The judges can even get into arguments among themselves while the attorney stands there helplessly, watching the 30 minutes evaporate. In a 1982 death-penalty appeal, Justices Rehnquist and Marshall clashed; after Rehnquist pushed the point that execution of a prisoner would be cheaper for the court system than a long imprisonment, Justice Marshall sarcastically interjected, "Well, it would be cheaper just to shoot him when you arrested him, wouldn't it?" (Barbash, 1983). Discussions between justices can even stray from the subject at hand; Justice Rehnquist and Justice Stevens once disagreed about the position played by Hall of Fame baseball player Kiki Cuyler (Mann, 1983).

What are we to make of the justices' questions and comments during the oral arguments? First, individual differences exist as to the frequency of interruption; Justice Scalia is well-known among court watchers for the persistence and zeal of his verbal attacks. He leans back during the presentation, but then his body comes forward and he fires a question at the attorney (C. K. Rowland, personal communication, September 9, 1997). Justice Ginsburg has also developed a reputation for habitual interruptions. In contrast, Justice Thomas has very little to say—in fact, he appears quite immobile throughout the arguments. To some extent, these differences are related to the salience of the particular issue for that justice, but are they also a function of personality style-exuberance versus reticence, for example? Or do they perhaps reflect deep-set, substantive characteristics, such as open-mindedness and need for cognition?

THE JUDICIAL CONFERENCE

A judicial conference is held within 72 hours of the oral arguments. Only the nine justices are present. Sometimes fewer than nine participate.

Whenever judges have a personal, financial, or other conflict of interest in the outcome of a case, they are expected to recuse themselves, but no fixed rules exist for judges' to explain why they absent themselves from granting or disposing of cases. As O'Brien observes, "Some Court watchers find this practice of unexplained judicial disqualification disturbing because of the large number of cases in which one or more justices recuse themselves" (1993, p. 226). For example, in the 1987–88 term, one or more justices refused to participate in evaluating 200 of the approximately 3000 petitions filed.

For me, it is not the number of recusals, but rather the failures to recuse, that are disturbing. Justice Thurgood Marshall recused himself from 98 of the 171 docketed cases that were decided by the Supreme Court during the 1967–68 term, but most of these were cases in which the federal government was a party. Marshall, as the solicitor general of the United States prior to his Supreme Court appointment, had participated in the development of one side's position in these cases (Segal & Spaeth, 1993). In contrast, Justice Rehnquist did not recuse himself with respect to three 1972 cases in which he had been involved as an assistant attorney general before his appointment to the Court. As Rohde and Spaeth (1976) noted, all of these were emotionally charged decisions (they involved the legality of antiwar protests) that were decided favorably for the government, and in each case Justice Rehnquist cast the deciding vote in a 5-to-4 decision. As a result, in 1974 a law was passed that prohibited federal judges from ruling in a case in which they had previously expressed an opinion concerning its merits.

Justice Thomas recused himself from participating in the V.M.I. case described in Chapter 1 because his son was a student there. Thomas was criticized, however, by two legal ethics professors for failing to recuse himself in a case (in which he eventually wrote the majority opinion) involving the pension benefits of an employee at Lockheed Corporation. The issue was how to interpret a law that required Lockheed and other employers to contribute to the pension plans of older workers without discriminating on the basis of age (Mauro, 1996). While chairman of the Equal Employment Opportunity Commission (EEOC) in 1988, Thomas concluded that the law should not be applied retroactively to benefit older workers who had already been the objects of discrimination, saying "We think that substantively, we are absolutely correct" (quoted by Mauro, 1996, p. 3A). The Internal Revenue Service disagreed and instructed companies to make such retroactive payments. In the June 1996 case, Justice Thomas ruled against retroactivity, consistent with his EEOC position eight years before. He was joined in his ruling by six other justices.

Among the current group of justices, the number of recusals varies widely. In the 2½ years, ending in June 1997, Justice Breyer recused himself 105 times, Justice O'Connor 53 times; most of the recusals involved owning stock in ·one of the parties' companies (Mauro, 1997). Half of Justice O'Connor's recusals were related to her ownership of stock from AT&T, a company subject to extensive litigation. The number of recusals for the other judges were quite small (from one by Justice Souter to nine by Justice Scalia).

Experts have noted that the decision to recuse can sometimes impede justice (Lubet, 1995). If the issue before the Court is to decide *certiorari*, the "rule of four" means that an abstention is indistinguishable from a "no" vote. As described in Chapter 1, the recusal of four justices in an appeal involving tax deductions meant the earlier decision had to stand.

Justices are not required to give reasons why they recuse themselves (much less to give reasons why they *don't*), despite a recommendation in 1993 by a federal commission that the Supreme Court establish some mechanism for reviewing justices' ethics.

At the judicial conference, the chief justice presides; he summarizes the case and expresses his opinion. The other justices follow in order of seniority. (Even Oliver Wendell Holmes, when he was a first-year justice at the age of 61, spoke last and had to serve as the doorkeeper at the judicial conference.) This vote—called the "conference vote"—is not the final one, however.

In earlier times, apparently, the vote was taken in the reverse order of seniority, so that the most recently appointed justice would not be unduly influenced by his seniors. This ground rule recognizes the possibility of conformity pressures. Recent accounts of the judicial conference procedure, however, state that it no longer applies; in fact, a formal voting step is not always needed because each justice has made his or her position apparent during the discussion. In his book on the Supreme Court, Chief Justice Rehnquist wrote:

> For many years there has circulated a tale that although the discussion in confer-
> ence proceeds in order from the Chief Justice to the junior justice, the voting
> actually begins with the junior justice and proceeds back to the Chief Justice in
> order of seniority. I can testify that, at least in my fifteen years on the Court, this
> tale is very much a myth. (1987, pp. 289–290)

After it is determined which party's position has received the support of
the majority, an assignment is made as to which justice will draft the majority
or consensus opinion. If the chief justice is in the majority, he assigns the task;
if he is not, the senior associate justice makes the assignment. In actuality, the
chief justice does the major part of the assigning—about 80 percent of the
cases in the Burger and Rehnquist Courts, and about 95 percent when William Howard Taft and Charles Evans Hughes were in charge (Epstein & Knight,
1998). The decision is not a casual one. Epstein and Knight have framed it
well:

> The author of the initial opinion draft can significantly affect the policy the Court
> produces because the opinion writer's first draft establishes the initial position
> over which justices bargain. Depending on the writer's preferences, the first draft
> can be crafted broadly or narrowly can ignore or apply past precedents, and can
> fashion various kinds of policy. Moreover, the opinion writer is in a position to
> accept or reject bargaining offers from [his or her] colleagues. (p. 126)

Some observers have argued that the justice holding the least extreme
position should be the one who writes what serves as a binding opinion for
the Court, but actual reasons for assigning an opinion to a particular judge
depend on a variety of considerations. In highly important cases, the chief
justice (if he is in the majority) assigns himself as the author. Steamer (1986, p.
29) observed that every chief justice since John Marshall (who wrote virtually
all the important opinions of the Court) has assigned to himself the opinion
writing in cases dealing with crucial constitutional issues: Taney on slavery
(*Dred Scott v. Sandford*, 1857), Chase on the nature of the Union (*Texas v. White*,
1869), Waite on state regulation of the economy (*Munn v. Illinois*, 1877), Fuller
on the federal income tax (*Pollock v. Farmer's Loan and Trust Co.*, 1895), White
on the military draft (*Selective Draft Cases*, 1918), Taft on presidential removal
power (*National Labor Relations Board v. Jones and Laughlin Steel Corp.*, 1937),
Stone on the prosecution of Nazi saboteurs during World War II (*Ex parte Quirin*,
1942), Vinson on the conviction of Communist party officials (*Dennis v. United
States*, 1951), Warren on racial desegregation (*Brown v. Board of Education*, 1954),
and Burger on the limits of executive privilege (*United States v. Nixon*, 1974).

What do we know about the writing assignment decision? Do politics
play a role? Many reasons for assigning the job to a particular justice have
been offered (Steamer, 1986; Ulmer, 1970):

- To equalize work load
- To keep this justice in the majority

- To maximize the desired content of the opinion
- To reward a justice who has a particular interest in writing the opinion, *or* to prevent another justice from placing his or her stamp on the opinion
- To give the opinion a political advantage

In an empirical study of assignments made by the three most recent chief justices, Maltzman and Wahlbeck (1996a) concluded that there was a consistent attempt to encourage specialization by assigning opinions to those justices who had expertise on the topic under consideration. Opinion writers were also selected on the basis of their ability to make the majority view palatable to outsiders, such as Congress, the president, and various influential organizations.

The opportunity to select the opinion writer seems to be symbolically important as well. It has been noted that Warren Burger, while he was chief justice, sometimes "passed" at the initial voting or even changed his vote to be in the majority—just so that he could be the one to assign the opinion writing.

Preparing opinion drafts can be time consuming. It is at this point that the Court once again resembles "nine small independent law firms," because the writing of an initial draft is a solitary process, or at least a process done in conjunction with only that justice's own law clerks.

THE DRAFT OPINION

The assigned justice writes a draft, which is circulated to the other justices; they indicate whether they are willing to concur. They may want changes some minor, some major.

NEGOTIATIONS

After the draft opinion is circulated, a period of negotiation—even active lobbying—ensues. Often, many drafts are prepared, because the reasoning behind the decision may be altered to "accommodate other members of a potential majority or [to] win over wavering justices" (Woodward & Armstrong, 1979, p. 3). The attempt to persuade becomes more intense here than in the judicial conference. The situation is rife with the pressures that operate on any group that must form an opinion or take an action, including pressures toward uniformity and opinion change. Baum (1985) observed:

> Once that opinion is completed and circulated, it often becomes a focus of negotiation. Ordinarily the assigned justice wishes to obtain the support of as many colleagues as possible for the opinion. The writer will seek to convince justices in the minority to change positions, and it also may be necessary to discourage allies in the conference from leaving the fold. (p. 115)

Some justices may shift from the majority to the minority; what was origi-
nally the "losing" side may become a winner. Justices who wish to concur in
the direction of the decision may be upset by the rationale of the opinion
drafter. This negotiation process is one of the major topics of Chapters 3, 4,
and 5.

THE MAJORITY OPINION

Eventually an opinion is agreed upon by a majority of the justices (although
some may concur with only certain sections of it). This has been referred to as
the "report vote," to distinguish this final decision from the earlier, tentative
conference vote. Justices who disagree with the majority opinion may prepare
dissents.

Why prepare a dissent, as opposed to simply registering one's vote to
disagree with the majority? One purpose is to try to persuade . . . still. Expressing one's disagreement in writing and in public may also have a cathartic
value for a justice.

Dissents have a tendency to get repeated from one case to another, especially when they reflect a strong ideological viewpoint by the dissenter(s). Both
liberal and conservative justices do this. Justices Marshall and Brennan frequently joined in offering the same dissents in *cert.* decisions regarding capital punishment. For example, in *Witt v. Florida* (1977), they wrote: "Adhering
to our views that the death penalty is in all circumstances cruel and unusual
punishment prohibited by the Eighth and Fourteenth Amendments . . . we
would grant *certiorari* and vacate the death sentence in this case." Two years
later, in their dissent in *Stephens v. Hopper* (1979), their wording was identical.

Some justices and observers are critical of this practice. Justice Stevens,
in *Liles v. Oregon* (1976), wrote: "In the interest of conserving scarce law library space, I shall not repeat this explanation every time I cast such a vote."
Stern and Gressman (1978) are even more critical:

> The repetition of identical language in opinion after opinion would seem to serve
> no useful purpose. Dissenting justices whose strong convictions impel them to
> reiterate their position despite its continued rejection by the minority can do so
> merely by stating that "they dissent for the reasons stated" in prior cases, [and]
> citing them. (p. 352)

ANNOUNCEMENT OF THE DECISION

The decision is announced; the justice who authored the opinion has the option of reading a summary or a portion of it to the press and the public. Those
in the minority may express their dissent. (When the Court began, it followed
the English practice, with every justice delivering an individual opinion on
every case; the custom of joining other justices began about 150 years ago.)

OPINION FORMATION

What is the process when an individual justice contemplates a case scheduled for oral argument? The justice has already been exposed to the case at the *cerliorari* conference, but at that time it was not necessary to form an opinion on the merits of the appeal (nor are the briefs for both sides available.) The fields of psychology and communications, among others, have much to say about attitude formation, and the field of political science offers perspectives on the ways that judges decide cases.

PSYCHOLOGICAL PERSPECTIVES

Any comprehensive explanation of attitude formation must deal with both the "why" and the "how." Why that particular opinion or attitude? How is an attitude or opinion is formed? What is the process? What sources are used? What motivations does the formation of a particular viewpoint satisfy?

An attitude has generally been defined as an evaluative reaction to a denotable object. Here "object" may be specific and tangible or general and abstract. Judges can have attitudes about ideas, arguments, and conclusions. Although conceptual distinctions are sometimes made between the term *attitude* and the term *opinion*, we do not make those distinctions here; by *judicial opinion* we mean essentially the expression of the judge's attitude—his or her evaluative reaction to a stimulus object (legal briefs, in this case). In written form, the judicial opinion becomes the behavioral component of the attitude.

Why do people hold the attitudes they do? The simplest answer is that every attitude serves a function for that person. People hold attitudes that fit their needs; to know the attitudes, we must determine the needs.

Functional Theories of Attitude Formation

Two rather similar functional theories of attitude formation and change have been developed by social psychologists, one by Katz and Stotland (Katz, 1960, 1968; Katz & Stotland, 1959) and one by Smith, Bruner, and White (1956; for a contemporary review of these approaches, see Eagly and Chaiken, 1998, pp. 303–309). Each theory has proposed that attitudes serve one or more functions, as follows:

First, attitudes may serve an instrumental, adjustive, or utilitarian function. According to Katz, a person develops a positive attitude toward objects that are useful in meeting his or her needs. If an object thwarts the person's needs, he or she develops a negative attitude toward it.

Second, attitudes may serve an ego-defensive, or externalization, function. Here, Katz's theory is influenced by psychoanalytic considerations. An attitude may develop or change in order to protect a person "from acknowledging the basic truths about himself or the harsh realities in his external world" (1960, p. 170). For example, derogatory attitudes toward out-groups and minority groups may serve as means of convincing oneself of one's own importance. Without utilizing psychoanalytic supports, Smith, Bruner, and White (1956) see attitudes functioning in a similar way, permitting the externalization of reactions.

For example, with respect to the position of Justice Clarence Thomas on affirmative action, some observers see a paradox. In his professional and career advancement, Justice Thomas benefited from affirmative action policies, yet his Court decisions he have staunchly opposed to these policies. Certainly he does not see affirmative action as the reason why he has achieved his goals. Is it possible that his adamant stance serves an ego defensive function?

Third, there is the knowledge or object appraisal, function. Attitudes may develop or change in order to "give meaning to what would otherwise be an unorganized chaotic universe" (Katz, 1960, p. 175). Particularly, this will happen when a problem cannot be solved without the information associated with the attitude. Smith *et al.* (1956) see this function as a "ready aid in 'sizing up' objects and events in the environment from the point of view of one's major interests and going concerns" (p. 41). Thus, categorizing objects or events is done more efficiently, and no time is spent figuring out afresh how one should respond. Object appraisal thus "stresses the role that gathering information plays in the day-to-day adaptive activities of the individual" (Kiesler, Collins, & Miller, 1969, p. 315).

Put simply, attitudes function to help us with our daily activities. Each of us needs to "size up" relevant stimuli. A judge, when presented with a brief, has a template of attitudes by which to evaluate it: What are the brief's major claims? Are they supported by logic, by precedent, by past experience? Are they articulated clearly? What will the outcome be if they are accepted? Later in this chapter we discuss how experts—and judges are certainly experts in processing appeals—approach their task differently than do novices.

Fourth, there is the value-expression function. Katz theorizes that individuals gain satisfaction from expressing themselves through their attitudes. Beyond this, the expression of attitudes helps to form one's self-concept. Smith *et al.* (1956) diverge most widely from Katz at this point. To them, the expressive nature of attitudes does not mean that any need for expression exists but rather that a person's attitudes "reflect the deeper-lying patterns of his or her life" (p. 38).

Judges on the same court can differ in their deeply held values, and this may help to explain some of the distinctions made between them—for example, whether they are considered "activist" judges or not. Take this statement by Chief Justice Earl Warren: "The beginning of justice is the capacity to generalize and make objective one's private sense of wrong" (quoted by Menez, 1984,

p. 2). Contrast it with the following statements by nonactivist judges sometimes called "strict constructionist" judges):

"The Constitution is not a panacea for every blot upon the public welfare"
(dissenting opinion by Justice John Marshall Harlan in *Reynolds v. Sims*, 1964).

"The Constitution does not provide judicial remedies for every social and
economic ill" (opinion by Justice Lewis Powell in *San Antonio v. Rodriquez*,
1973).

CONSISTENCY OF VALUES

For at least some justices, the expression of judicial opinions seems to reflect
"deeper-lying patterns" of values that have been consistent over time (H.
Schwartz, 1988). The writings of Justice Rehnquist, going back more than 40
years—long before he was appointed a justice—reflect steadfast emphasis on
the values of *property rights* and *states' rights*. For example, Rehnquist has opposed civil rights laws because they infringe on the rights of businesses (S.
Davis, 1989).

Rehnquist has not supported claims of rights by individuals and minorities. Also, as an associate justice, he "consistently denied claims of discrimination brought by women, aliens, and illegitimate children, whether such claims
were based on civil rights statutes or the equal protection clause of the 14th
Amendment. More often than not, he has also denied claims of racial discrimination" (S. Davis, p. 20). For example, he voted to make servicewomen
meet higher standards for obtaining spousal support allotments than service-
men must meet, and he voted to allow the federal government to deny food
stamps to households in which one member is not a blood relative of the others
(H. Schwartz, 1988).

While he was a clerk for Justice Robert Jackson in 1954, Rehnquist drafted
a memorandum in defense of the 1896 *Plessy v. Ferguson* decision that justified racial segregation. He wrote:

> To those who world argue that "personal" rights are more sacrosanct than "prop-
> erty" rights, the short answer is that the Constitution makes no such distinction.
> To the argument made by Thurgood, not John, Marshall that a majority may not
> deprive a minority of its constitutional rights, the answer must be made that while
> this is sound in theory, in the long run it is the majority who all determine what
> the constitutional rights of the minority are. (quoted in Fiss & Krauthammer,
> 1982, pp. 14-15)

In that memorandum Rehnquist also wrote: "I realize that it is an unpopular and unhumanitarian position for which I have been excoriated by
'liberal' colleagues, but I think *Plessy v. Ferguson* was right and should be reaffirmed" (quoted in Adler, 1987, p. 44).

A decade later, when Rehnquist was an attorney in Phoenix during the turbulent 1960s, he opposed a local ordinance designed to prevent discrimination in public accommodations. The issue, as he saw it, was whether it was right to "sacrifice" the freedom of the property owner in order to give minorities the freedom to eat at whatever restaurant they chose. Furthermore, in 1967 he voiced active opposition to a proposal by the Phoenix superintendent of schools for a voluntary exchange of students, developed as a way of reducing racial segregation. "We are no more dedicated to an 'integrated'society," Rehnquist wrote, "than we are to a 'segregated' society" (quoted in H. Schwartz, 1988, p. 114).

Rehnquist values state autonomy and wants states to be free of restrictions, including the restrictions of the Bill of Rights and of later constitutional amendments. Until the Civil War, it was assumed that the Bill of Rights limited the actions of the national government but not those of the separate states. But the 14th Amendment put far-reaching restrictions on states by giving people "due process" and "equal protection." Justice Rehnquist has attempted to impose strict limits on the powers of the federal courts and the U.S. Congress. During the 1995–96 term, Rehnquist authored an opinion that Congress had no basis for outlawing possession of a gun within 1000 feet of a school because it was not a matter of interstate commerce. (Most states already outlaw such possession.)

Another example of Rehnquist's values is the 1976 case of *Rizzo v. Goode,* which involved reform of the Philadelphia police department as result of charges of minority abuse by police. The suit was structured like those of school desegregation cases, which were almost always filed in federal courts. Justice Rehnquist dismissed the proposed reform in Rizzo because "the remedy required a federal institution, a federal court, to reverse the operation of a state agency" (Fiss & Krauthammer, 1982, p. 16). This dismissal was a radical departure from the precedent established in *Brown v. Board of Education* and from subsequent school desegregation cases, that federal courts were the proper avenue for seeking relief. "The *Rizzo* plaintiffs could still seek redress in the state courts," wrote Rehnquist (1976, p. 369).

His opinion here is an example of his view of *stare decisis*; he repudiates precedents frequently and openly, and sometimes prefers to apply precedents that have long since been replaced. Fiss and Krauthammer go so far as to conclude that "in his devotion to state autonomy, . . . [he] does not flinch from using the power of the judiciary to restrict the power of the elected branches, and particularly Congress" (1982, p. 16). Autonomy for the individual states is an even stronger value for Justice Rehnquist than is property rights. For example, he permitted the California State Supreme Court, in interpreting its state constitution, to require a shopping center owner to subordinate his property rights to allow distribution of leaflets on his property. This decision was an important victory for free speech in California and "is a credit to the consistency of Rehnquist's commitment to state autonomy" (Fiss & Krauthammer, p. 21).

Justice Rehnquist wasn't troubled by a Texas law that imposed a life sentence on a man for obtaining $120.75 under false pretenses. (He had accepted payment for repairing an air conditioner but never did the job.) The individual had been convicted twice before, for frauds involving $80 and $28.36, and had received a life sentence under Texas's multiple-offender law. Rehnquist's reaction: "Some state will always bear the distinction of treating particular offenders more severely than any other state" (quoted by Fiss & Krauthammer, 1982, p 21).

Justice Rehnquist seeks to transfer power from the federal government to the states because the states are concerned mainly with preserving property and public order. A typical example of his emphasis on state jurisdiction over the principle of equity is a 1976 decision. Rehnquist wrote for the majority that once a school board had instituted a mandated school desegregation plan, it is not required to change the plan in order to maintain racially desegregated schools when changes in housing patterns resegregated them. At this point, in the view of the Court, the school board had fulfilled its responsibility to correct the *de jure* discrimination (that is, the unlawful segregation) of the past and bore no special burden to correct the *de facto* (that is, actual) racial separation of the present. Recall that a decade before, Rehnquist had stated that integration was no stronger a goal than was segregation.

An analysis by political scientists David Rohde and Harold Spaeth (1989) concluded that the attitudes and values underlying Justice Rehnquist's decisions did not change after he became chief justice in 1986. Similarly, a review of the book that Rehnquist wrote about the history of the Supreme Court (published in 1987) observed that it focused on decisions that have upheld the exercise of governmental power and virtually ignored decisions by the Warren Court (Adler, 1987).

The impressive mass of decisions announced at the end of the 1996–97 term has been interpreted as reflecting Justice Rehnquist's emphasis on the priority of the rights of the states. In an astonishing breadth of decisions, the Supreme Court—in one week—upheld two state laws that prohibited physician-assisted suicide, scolded Congress for instituting federal regulation of what was typically a state-regulated matter (gun sales), and upheld another state law that (in the view of some observers) challenged due process rights of sexual predators. Saying that Congress had unlawfully usurped power from the states and the federal courts, it also struck down the Religious Freedom Restoration Act of 1993 (Carelli, 1997). Perhaps most illustrative of Justice Rehnquist's imprint on the Court was the ruling that invalidated a portion of the 1993 so-called Brady bill, which forced state and local police to make background checks on people seeking to buy handguns. As one expert noted, "This is a Court more skeptical of federal authority than any Court in recent history" (quoted in Carelli, 1997, p. A16). Another longtime Court observer, Professor David O'Brien, author of several influential books on the Supreme Court, said:

"Rehnquist finally got his five solid votes for a strong defense of state powers" (quoted in Mauro, 1997, p. 3A).

THE "HOW" OF INITIAL DECISION MAKING

How do opinions form? More to the point, how do judicial opinions form? Answering questions from a group of students, Justice Breyer had the following straightforward explanation:

> I'm a human being. . . . Because I'm a human being, my own background . . . my own views, will of course shape me. They make a difference. Somebody with different life experiences has different views to a degree; that will influence the way that they look at these things. But that's very different from saying. 'Oh, I decide whatever I want.' I understand that my background, outlook, values, and everything influence me. But I don't feet I'm free to choose any result I happen to think is good. It's a complicated answer because I want you to get a feeling for what I think goes on. (1997, CSPAN television interview)

A psychological analysis of initial decision making would note, for instance, that the process of forming an opinion differs depending on the extent of one's knowledge about the task and the material.

THE EXPERT–NOVICE DISTINCTION

Each of us becomes an expert in categorizing events and objects that are relevant to our jobs. The *expert–novice* distinction has, in the last decade, achieved some prominence in the field of experimental psychology (Chi, Glaser, & Parr, 1988). Experts are described as better able to perceive large, meaningful patterns in their domain of expertise; as faster than newcomers at performing the skills of their domain; and as seeing and presenting a problem in their domain at a deeper level than do novices, who tend to present a problem at a superficial level (Glaser & Chi, 1988).

Political scientists use *cue theory* to describe this process; for example, justices employ cues as a means of separating *certiorari* petitions worthy of further scrutiny from those that may be discarded without further consideration (Ulmer, Hintze, & Kirklosky, 1972). Possible cues include the parties seeking review, the reputation of the attorneys filing the petitions, the reputation of the lower court judge, and the type of conflict involved (Tanenhaus, Schick, Muraskin, & Rosen, 1978).

SOCIAL COGNITION

As subsequent sections of this chapter illustrate, the *how* of judicial opinion formation is often something between using legal reasoning and using personal values as determinants. Chapter 1 introduced the social cognition approach as an attempt to extend such an analysis. After evaluating each of these models, we now attempt to apply some concepts from social cognition theory to explain the *how* of the opinion formation process. One principle of social cognition theory is that persons may differ in the cognitive styles they use in forming opinions. For example, some judges may use a more complex style in processing information. Philip Tetlock and colleagues (Tetlock, Bernzweig, & Gallant, 1985) have used a dimension of cognitive style known as conceptual, or integrative, complexity to make distinctions between different types of judicial decisions.

Conceptual, or *integrative, complexity* is defined on the basis of two cognitive structural variables: differentiation and integration. Tetlock and colleagues explain: "Individuals at the simple end of the complexity continuum tend to rely on rigid, one-dimensional, evaluative rules in interpreting events, and to make decisions on the basis of only a few salient items of information. Individuals at the complex end of the continuum tend to interpret events in multidimensional terms and to integrate a variety of evidence in arriving at decisions" (1985, p. 1228). Thus, a person reflecting differentiation recognizes that multiple perspectives on an issue exist, and the person's use of integration refers to his or her recognition of conceptual relations among differentiated dimensions (Gruenfeld, 1995).

For example, a judge analyzes a case in an undifferentiated manner when he or she focuses all attention on one issue or theme. For Tetlock and colleagues, a more differentiated approach is reflected in a judicial opinion that recognizes the existence of reasonable arguments on both sides of a controversy. They write: "Integration refers to the development of complex connections among differentiated characteristics. Differentiation is thus a necessary condition for integration" (1985, p. 1231).

The published opinions of Supreme Court justices can be "scored" on the basis of integrative complexity, and that is what Tetlock and his associates did. They selected the 25 justices who served on the Court between 1946 and 1978; eight opinions authored by each justice were analyzed. Four dealt with economic issues and four with civil liberties issues. Most of the justices' opinions came from their first term on the Court.

What qualities might be associated with differences in integrative complexity, as reflected in judicial opinions? Two have been suggested:

Political ideology. Tetlock and colleagues leaned toward this explanation. Previous research, using speeches by legislative participants in the U.S. Senate and the British House of Commons, had concluded that advocates of right-wing causes were more likely to think in simple, value-laden, and absolutist patterns than were advocates of moderate or left-wing causes (Tetlock, 1983, 1984). According to this argument, right-wing political beliefs serve one of the functions of attitudes described in this chapter, the ego-defensive function;

they are a means of simplifying things and imposing order on a threatening external world and of dealing with unacceptable inner feelings. Although a tendency existed for extremists at either end of the spectrum to be lower in integrative complexity, the rigidity-of-the-right hypothesis was also verified by Tetlock and colleagues. Both liberals and moderates on the bench wrote more integratively complex judicial opinions than did conservatives, they found. (The differences were substantially greater on economic than on civil rights issues.)

Majority versus minority opinions. Another possible explanation for differences in integrative complexity emphasizes not the qualities of the judge writing the opinion, but the opinion's status. This position argues that, first of all, majority opinions need to be more integratively complex because they must represent viewpoints that may be partially in conflict. Thus, one function is strategic. As we will see in more detail in Chapter 5, the eventual majority opinion is a collaborative enterprise; the opinion writer responds to and incorporates responses from other justices; an implicit goal is to be expansive. Furthermore, a majority position is a policy-making position; the author feels accountable for the positions espoused. In contrast, dissents reflect strongly held beliefs that justice has not been rendered. Writing about senators, but applicable to dissenting justices, Tetlock et al. wrote that those in the minority "had the rhetorical freedom to take strong, unqualified stands in opposition to the majority" (1985, p. 1235).

This analysis found that minority opinions did tend to be less integratively complex; for 198 cases, the correlation was -.21, significant at the .05 level. It also found that political ideology had an impact beyond majority/minority status.

Gruenfeld (1995) has pointed out that during the period from which Tetlock's data were drawn, the Supreme Court was generally dominated by liberals and moderates. In the last two decades the balance has shifted. Would the relationship between ideology and integrative complexity still hold? She sought to control for such factors. In her first study, Gruenfeld examined two majority and two minority opinions authored by each of the eight most liberal and the eight most conservative justices during the period from 1953 to 1990. She found that individual justices expressed lower levels of integrative complexity when writing minority opinions than when writing majority opinions. But contrary to Tetlock et al. (1985), liberal and conservative justices did not differ in overall integrative complexity.

As predicted by our analysis of the function of dissents, more affective intensity (measured by use of verb modifiers, italics, and punctuation) was present in minority opinions, regardless of ideology.

The function of inclusiveness in majority opinions was examined in Gruenfeld's second study, which compared majority opinions in unanimous versus nonunanimous cases. The latter had a higher level of integrative complexity. Unanimous decisions, as expected, were lower in complexity than nonunanimous decisions; the lack of dissent rendered differentiated cognitive processing less necessary. Overall, Gruenfeld's analysis found support for the conclusion that opinion status (majority vs. minority) was more strongly related to integrative complexity than was political ideology.

The Salience of Attitudes

In some cases a judge's attitudes or values may be quite salient, playing a major role in the judge's formation of a judicial pronouncement. In other cases values may be less so, making the judge less ready to form a definitive opinion, more open to agreement with other justices, and more likely to change his or her vote. For example, Justice Scalia tends to expresses his opinions with vigor and sometimes shows no tolerance for opposing viewpoints, but other times he concedes to the majority. Any theory seeking to explain how a judge's opinion is formed must reflect the variable influence of these internal qualities.

ATTITUDES AND JUDICIAL DECISION MAKING

When forming a judicial opinion, does a judge dispassionately and objectively consider the issues, or is the opinion formed on the basis of background attitudes and values that are part of the judge's personality? This question is one that divides expert opinion on judicial decision making. In this section we review two models of judicial decision making from the field of political science, then apply them to accounts by actual judges of how judicial decisions are made.

The Legal Model versus the Attitudinal Model

Chapter 1 introduced contrasting viewpoints about the determinants of judicial decision-making. Segal and Spaeth (1993) made a distinction between two models of the process. The traditional view reflects what they called the legal model. This conception assumes that the Court's decisions are based on the facts, and that the justices consider these facts "in light of the plain meaning of statutes and the Constitution, the intent of the framers, precedent, and a balancing of societal interests" (p. 32). In this theory, judges begin with a rule or principle of law as their premise; they apply this premise to the facts and thus arrive at a decision (Frank, 1930). When William Rehnquist testified before a Senate committee at his confirmation hearings, he said: "My fundamental commitment, if I am confirmed, will be to totally disregard my own personal beliefs" (quoted by Baum, 1997, p. 57).

Political conservatives believe that the legal model should be the determinant of judicial opinions, especially the "plain meaning" of the laws and the original intent of the authors of the Constitution. They fear that judges have come to substitute their own values for legal determinations. Agreeing with a dissent by Justice Scalia, George Will (1996) sees only two choices in interpreting the Constitution: "The meaning given it must either be decisively shaped by history—by the framers' intent, as illuminated by national traditions—or it must be determined by something other than the Constitution, meaning the justices' personal preferences" (p. C11). In response to the majority opinion in *Romer v. Evans* (1996), described in Chapter 1, Mona Charen wrote that "six members of the Court have obviously decided that they are free to legislate their preferences in the guise of applying legal principles. . . . [but] courts are not supposed to interpret the law based on changing political and social fashions" (p. 7B).

Justice Cardozo's Analysis

Benjamin Cardozo (1921), a Supreme Court justice from 1932 to 1938, wrote a book-length classification of factors that determine an individual judge's ruling. The main factors that he identified serve to illustrate those postulated by Segal and Spaeth to be ingredients of the legal model.

THE USE OF RULE OR ANALOGY AND THE USE OF PRECEDENTS.   Some judges may ask: How does this case resemble past cases? What principle or rule applies? By studying rulings in previous cases, the judge may see something analogous in the case at hand. In such an approach, the place of precedent is central; according to Justice Cardozo, judges continually reaffirm the legal doctrine of *stare decisis*. Many are reluctant to overturn precedent—that is, to take completely new directions. Especially with regard to traditional topics, such as property and contracts, British and U.S. law "developed primarily through the aggregation of judicial decisions rather than through constitutions and statutes, and the only law to be interpreted was precedent" (Baum, 1985, p. 123).

SOCIETAL EVOLUTION.   Cardozo notes that in some cases precedents can be found to support both sides of a case. For this and other reasons, justices rely on additional factors for their decisions. For example, they recognize that society changes, and that these changes may make precedents inappropriate. The Congressional Research Service (1982) found that the Court overruled precedent in 75 decisions between 1961 and 1980. To varying degrees, judges acknowledge that law and society interact and that one purpose of the law is to meet the needs of society (Kadish & Kadish, 1971). As our characteristic ways of behaving change, new interpretations of the law arise. Recall that in Segal and Spaeth's analysis of the legal model, one of the considerations was "a balancing of societal interests."

SOCIOLOGICAL CONSIDERATIONS. Justice Cardozo's third major determinant of judicial decisions was what he termed sociological concerns. By this he meant an awareness of changes in predominant societal values that demand reinterpretations of the laws. For example, only in the decade of the 1990s was a right articulated for physically disabled people to have access to public buildings. Although conservatives like George Will and Mona Charen decry legal decisions that are based on changes in society's goals and values, such decisions occur.

The Attitudinal Model

Segal and Spaeth's second model—which they endorse over the legal model— is much more congruent with a psychological approach. In the *attitudinal model*, judges' decisions are viewed as based on the facts of the case "in light of the ideological attitudes and values of the justices" (1993, p. 32). The genesis of the attitudinal model was the "legal realist" movement that dominated the teaching in some law schools, beginning in the 1920s. In this view judicial opinions that contained legal rules used them as rationalizations for personal preferences (Pritchett, 1947). That is, legal rules expressed social policies, and a judge's conception of such policies reflected his or her social, economic, and political outlook, which usually derived from the judge's education and social environment (Frank, 1949, pp. 147–148). According to this view, most judges do not recognize the impact of their own values. Segal and Spaeth write: "Justices . . . do not admit the validity of [the attitudinal model] as an explanation of their decisions. To do so would give the lie to the mythology that the justices, their lower court colleagues, and off-the-bench apologists have so insistently and persistently verbalized: that judges . . . do not speak; rather, the Constitution and laws speak through them" (p. 33). Clarence Thomas is apparently an example. In a speech at the University of Kansas simply titled "Judging" (1996), he stated, "There are right and wrong answers to legal questions." Attacking the approach of legal realism, he concluded that "bright-line rules" exist, and furthermore, that "federal judges do not make law or policy."

But some judges are not so sanguine. Justice Douglas (1980) reported that Chief Justice Hughes once told him: "You must remember one thing. At the constitutional level where we work, ninety percent of any decision is emotional. The rational part of us supplies the reasons for supporting our predilections" (p. 8).

In summary, the attitudinal model rejects the claim that judges merely apply the law (rather than make it) and that they do so objectively, dispassionately, and impartially.

JUDGE JEROME FRANK'S VIEW.   Another prominent judge, Jerome Frank (1930), strongly disagreed with Justice Cardozo regarding the way that judges form opinions. He wrote:

> Since the judge is a human being and since no human being in his normal thinking processes arrives at decision (except in dealing with a limited number of simple situations) by the route of any such syllogistic reasoning it is fair to assume that the judge, merely by putting on the judicial ermine, will not acquire so artificial a method of reasoning. Judicial judgments, like other judgments, doubtless, in most cases, are worked out backward from conclusions tentatively formulated. (p. 101)

As an example, Felitti's 1995 article about a California judge, Jacqueline Taber, noted her complaint about attorneys' failure to supply her with good legal arguments for their viewpoints. She said, "Many times I'd like to get where they were going but they wouldn't spout law to show me how to get there" (p. 110; cited by Baum, 1997, p. 65).

That is, a judge may first arrive at a decision intuitively and only then "work backward to a major 'rule' premise and a minor 'fact' premise to see whether or not that decision is logically defective" (Frank, 1949, p. 184). Judge Frank did not consider such a procedure as improper or unusual. That intuition has chronological priority does not mean that subsequent logical analysis is without value.

LEGAL PRECEDENTS AND THE ATTITUDINAL MODEL.   In the matter of legal precedents, so central to the legal model of judicial decision making, Segal and Spaeth concluded that the citation of precedents is only a justification for previously formed opinions:

> As further evidence that precedents exist to support the contentions of both parties, merely consult any appellate court case containing a dissenting opinion. This, as well as the majority opinion, will likely contain a substantial number of references to previously decided cases. Reference to these cases will undoubtedly show that those cited by the majority support its decision, whereas those specified by the dissent bolster its contrary judgment. (1993, p. 46)

The frequency with which important cases are settled by 5-to-4 or 6-to-3 votes indicates that not all the justices are reading the precedents the same way. Even Justice Thurgood Marshall acknowledged this; in the *Payne v. Tennessee* (1991) decision, he wrote: "The continued vitality of literally scores of decisions must be understood to depend on nothing more than the proclivities of the individuals who *now* comprise a majority of this Court" (p. 753, italics in original).

LIMITS OF THE ATTITUDINAL MODEL.   Segal and Spaeth note that there are limits to which attitudes determine behavior; if an appeal has no merit to it, for example, "no self-respecting judge would decide [it] solely on the basis of his or her policy preferences" (1993, p. 70). Their example is, perhaps deliberately, rather extreme: "If Michael Dukakis filed a suit arguing that he should be declared the winner of the 1988 presidential election, and if the Supreme Court had to decide the case, we would not expect the votes in the case to depend upon whom the justices voted for in the election" (p. 70).

DO JUDGES' VALUES AND ATTITUDES COLOR THEIR OPINIONS?

Theories aside, what evidence is there that judges' values and attitudes affect their judicial opinions? If such evidence exists, are there limits on these characteristics as determinants? In this section, we bring to bear several types of evidence. First, we look at anecdotal evidence of extreme or rare decisions made by trial judges, for which a strong attitude or value is a likely explanation. Second, we review the literature on the differences between Democratic and Republican appointees in decisions they have rendered. Third, we shift to the Supreme Court specifically and consider how two justices, Marshall and Rehnquist, perceived the facts of one case (*Ake v. Oklahoma,* 1985) in different ways, leading them to form two contrasting judicial opinions. We end by introducing the social cognition theory of *motivated reasoning,* as an example of a "third wave" attempt to reconcile such contrasting viewpoints.

Judges' Values and Their Pronouncements

Occasionally we read in our newspapers of outrageous or idiosyncratic decisions made by trial judges in the evaluation of evidence or their pronouncing of a sentence. For example:

• In a custody battle between John—a convicted killer (of his first wife), an accused child molester, a racist, and deadbeat $1400 behind in his child support payments—and his ex-wife, Mary—a lesbian—which parent was awarded the custody of their 11-year-old daughter by a Pensacola, Florida, judge? The father. The judge was quoted as saying, with respect to homosexuality, "I'm opposed to it, and that's my beliefs" (Pitts, 1996, p. C13).

• A judge in Harrisburg, Pennsylvania, faced the decision of how to punish a man who beat up another man he caught in bed with his girlfriend. Michael Fulkroad punched Greg Allen Cook in the mouth, threw him against a wall, and chased him out of the house. Cook needed 32 stitches; Fulkroad pled guilty to assault. The judge's sentence: 5 minutes' probation (Associated Press, 1966b).

What is the foundation for such decisions? To gain publicity? To win reelection? Perhaps so, but often they reflect underlying biases that the judge, like every human being, possesses.

JUDGES' VALUES AND PRESIDENTIAL APPOINTMENTS

One of the responsibilities of the president is to send to the Senate for ratification of persons to fill vacancies on the federal bench. At present there are 835 federal judgeships (federal district judges plus the appellate judges on the 13 circuit courts of appeals and on the U.S. Supreme Court). About 9 of every 10 federal judicial appointments are of the same political party as the incumbent president. It appears that presidents seek to appoint federal judges who reflect their goals and policies. If so, is this goal successful?

Certain presidents have been explicit about the values they wanted—or wanted to avoid. President Nixon opposed the "liberal jurisprudence" of the Court while Earl Warren was chief justice, and President Reagan, as mentioned previously, sought judges who passed an ideological litmus test on certain issues central to his policy goals. In campaigning, Reagan charged the Democrats with "placing a bunch of sociology majors on the bench" (quoted in H. Schwartz, 1988, p. 119). Both President Nixon and President Reagan named only those judges whom they believed shared their "strict constructionist" judicial philosophy and conservative position on deregulating business, and who agreed with them on various social policies, such as abortion and affirmative action (O'Brien, 1993). Franklin Roosevelt, as detailed in Chapter 3, sought to appoint Supreme Court justices who opposed the conservative economic policies of the Court that he inherited in 1933.

Perhaps the most widely cited example of a presidential appointee whose values did *not* conform to those of the president who appointed him was Earl Warren as chief justice, appointed by President Eisenhower. Warren had no previous experience as a judge, but was a highly regarded governor of California. The president was "convinced that the prestige of the Supreme Court had suffered severely . . . and that the only way it could be restored was by the appointment to it of men (sic) of nationwide reputation, of integrity, competence in the law, and statesmanship" (quoted in O'Brien, 1993, p. 102). Warren had national stature, unimpeachable integrity, middle-of-the-road views, and a "splendid record during his years of active law work" as attorney general of the state of California (O'Brien, 1993, p. 102). After his appointment, however, Warren led the Court in a number of legal decisions that went against Eisenhower's values. Much has been made of Eisenhower's reaction to the *Brown v. Board of Education* (1954) decision; it led Eisenhower (long after he left office) to call his appointment of Warren "the biggest damn-fooled mistake" he had ever made (O'Brien, 1993, p. 106). But when we discuss Earl Warren in Chapter 4, (which deals with chief justices) we argue that Warren was a very complicated person who reflected a number of contradictory values, making it difficult for anyone to have predicted very far in advance his position on specific Court challenges.

Political scientists C. K. Rowland and Robert A. Carp (1996) have spearheaded a scholarly effort to answer questions about the impact of presidential appointments. They have studied federal district judges (trial judges) rather than appellate judges, and it is true that the fact-finding function of such judges is different from that of appellate judges, who decide the applicability of the law. In examining trial judges' decision making between 1933 and 1988, Rowland and Carp conclude that 48% of the decisions rendered by Democratic appointees were in the liberal direction, compared with only 39% of the rulings by Republican appointees. The effect was even greater in cases involving civil rights and civil liberties.

Rowland and Carp (1996, p. 47) analyzed the published decisions made by federal district court judges appointed by each president; clearly, the president's party has an effect:

President	% Liberal Decisions
Roosevelt	47%
Truman	40%
Eisenhower	38%
Kennedy	41%
Johnson	52%
Nixon	39%
Ford	44%
Carter	53%
Reagan	36%
Bush	33%

The effect is more pronounced in appointees of certain presidents. For example, a comparison of Carter appointees with Reagan appointees shows striking differences in some types of cases. On race discrimination cases, 78% of the decisions of Carter appointees were liberal, as compared with only 18% for Reagan appointees; for right-to-privacy cases, the difference was 78% to 45%; for women's rights issues, 56% to 36%.

What of the appointments of President Clinton? By the end of his first term, Clinton had appointed 204 judges, including more than 25% of the federal trial judges and nearly that many circuit courts judges, he also appointed two of the nine Supreme Court justices. By the end of his second term, Clinton could end up naming more than half the federal bench, exceeding President Reagan's 375 appointments. Despite Republican claims during the 1996 presidential election campaign that Clinton's appointees were soft on crime (for example, see Bolick, 1996), his nominees have generally tended to be moderate and nonideological (Berkman & MacLachlan 1996). The most obvious difference from the appointees of previous presidents is in race and gender.

Clinton has named more women and minorities—53% of his appointments—than any other president. For the first time in history, White males constituted less than half of the appointments (40.8% of 125 nominees confirmed by the Senate, according to research by Sheldon Goldman, cited by Berkman & MacLachman, 1996).

In a major empirical study in examining 330 criminal justice decisions by Clinton's district court appointees, Robert Carp classified 34% of them as "liberal" (i.e., siding with the defendant), as compared with 23% by President Reagan's appointees and 38% by President Carter's appointees (cited by Berkman & MacLachman, 1996, p. A21). In civil liberties cases, the percentage of "liberal" decisions (i.e., decisions that broadened individual rights) was as follows: Clinton appointees, 39%; Reagan appointees, 33%; Carter appointees, 52%.

Professor Carp has likened Clinton's judicial nominees to those of President Eisenhower: "Both Ike and Clinton made an effort to get people who are well-thought-of locally, who are top-quality people, but without much interest in their ideology. When you don't consider ideology as a factor, then you are going to get some who are fairly liberal and some who are fairly conservative" (quoted by Berkman & MacLachlan, 1996, p. A21). The "top quality" appellation is confirmed by Professor Goldman's analysis; two thirds of Clinton's judges received the American Bar Association's highest rating, compared with slightly more than half of the appointees of Reagan and Bush—the best record of any president since the ABA began evaluating appointees in the 1950s. (But three of Clinton's appointees were rated "not qualified," a label not given to any Reagan or Bush appointee.)

JUDGES' ATTITUDES AND PERCEPTION OF THE FACTS

Chapter 1 described the cognitive revolution in psychology as one that emphasized the central nature of the process of taking information from the outside world and interpreting it in light of one's internal characteristics. Do values serve as filters for the way that "facts" are perceived? The social cognition approach argues that one's expectations, motivations, attitudes, and values color how one perceives even straightforward matters. Appellate briefs present a variety of "facts"; we use quotation marks because some of these facts are matters of dispute, and others are testimony, which may or may not be reliable. Each judge must choose—though not necessarily consciously—which "facts" to use. No clearer demonstration can be made than how Justices Marshall and Rehnquist differed in their selection of "facts" in the case of *Ake v. Oklahoma* (1985).

The Case

Glen Burton Ake had been convicted in the 1979 murder of an Oklahoma minister and his wife. Ake and an accomplice, Steven Hatch, had gained entrance to the rural home on the pretext of using the phone. They immediately pulled out guns, bound the family members with heavy twine, and terrorized them for several hours. As Mrs. Douglass begged for mercy, Ake shot and killed both her and her husband. He also wounded their two children, shooting each in the back. Although the prosecution had been permitted to introduce testimony by a psychiatrist who concluded that Ake was sane, Ake had been denied a court-appointed psychiatrist for his defense. He appealed to the Supreme Court, claiming that due process required that the state provide access to a psychiatrist if the defendant could not afford one.

Justice Marshall's "Facts"

At the judicial conference, Thurgood Marshall was assigned the task of writing the Court's opinion. Here is his description of the facts of the case, drawn from the various briefs submitted to the Court:

> Late in 1979, Glen Burton Ake was arrested and charged with murdering a couple and wounding their two children. . . . His behavior at arraignment, and in other prearraignment incidents at the jail, was so bizarre that the trial judge, *sua sponte*, ordered him to be examined by a psychiatrist "for the purpose of advising with the Court as to [the psychiatrist's] impressions of whether the Defendant may need an extended period of mental observation." The examining psychiatrist reported: "At times [Ake[appears to be frankly delusional. . . . He claims to be the 'sword of vengeance' of the Lord and that he will 'sit at the left hand of God in heaven.' [The psychiatrist] diagnosed Ake as a probable paranoid schizophrenic and recommended a prolonged psychiatric evaluation to determine whether Ake was competent to stand trial.
>
> In March, Ake was committed to a state hospital to be examined with respect to his "present sanity," i.e., his competency to stand trial. On April 10, less than six months after the incidents for which Ake was indicted, the chief forensic psychiatrist at the state hospital informed the court that Ake was not competent to stand trial. The court then held a competency hearing, at which a psychiatrist testified: "[Ake] is a psychotic . . . his psychiatric diagnosis was that of paranoid schizophrenia-chronic, with exacerbation, that is with current upset, and that in addition . . .he is dangerous. . . . [B]ecause of the severity of his mental illness and because of the intensities of his rage, his poor control, his delusions, he requires a maximum security facility within—I believe—the State Psychiatric Hospital system." The court found Ake to be a "mentally ill person in need of care and treatment" and ordered him committed to the state mental hospital.
>
> Six weeks later, the chief forensic psychiatrist informed the court that Ake had become competent to stand trial. At the time, Ake was receiving 200 milligrams of Thorazine, an antipsychotic drug, three times daily, and the psychiatrist indicated that, if Ake continued to receive that dosage, his condition would remain stable. The State then resumed proceedings against Ake. (*Ake v. Oklahoma*, 1985, p. 1090, italics in original, citations deleted)

Nothing in this description suggests the possibility that Ake was faking or malingering. We are led to believe that his symptoms are genuine, and the opinion cites the diagnosis, prior to medication, of Ake as a paranoid schizophrenic. Justice Marshall's view, concurred with by the majority of justices, was that Ake had deserved the assistance of a state-paid psychiatrist when he raised the insanity defense at his trial.

Justice Rehnquist "Facts"

Justice Rehnquist wrote a dissenting opinion in which he questioned both the breadth of the decision and the majority's interpretation of the facts: "I do not think the facts of this case warrant the establishment of such a principle; and I think that even if the factual predicate of the Court's statement were established, the constitutional rule announced by the Court is far too broad" (p. 1098). Here is Justice Rehnquist's description of the facts:

> Petitioner Ake and his codefendant Hatch quit their jobs on an oil field rig in October 1979, borrowed a car, and went looking for a location to burglarize. They drove to the rural home of Reverend and Mrs. Richard Douglass, and gained entrance to the home by a ruse. Holding Reverend and Mrs. Douglass and their children, Brooks and Leslie, at gunpoint, they ransacked the home; then they bound and gagged the mother, father, and son, and forced them to lie on the living room floor. Ake and Hatch then took turns attempting to rape 12-year-old Leslie Douglass in a nearby bedroom. Having failed in these efforts, they forced her to lie on the living room floor with the other members of her family.
>
> Ake then shot Reverend Douglass and Leslie each twice, and Mrs. Douglass and Brooks once, with a .357 magnum pistol, and fled. Mrs. Douglass died almost immediately as a result of a gunshot wound; Reverend Douglass' death was caused by a combination of the gunshots he received, and strangulation from the manner in which he was bound. Leslie and Brooks managed to untie themselves and to drive to the home of a nearby doctor. Ake and his accomplice were apprehended in Colorado following a month-long crime spree that took them through Arkansas, Louisiana, Texas and other States in the western half of the United States. (pp. 1098–1099)

Even Justice Rehnquist's description does not reflect the full extent of the "crime spree" by Ake and Hatch. They stole $1500 at gunpoint from another Oklahoma family, and two weeks after the Douglass murders, Ake shot two Texas surveyors in cold blood after Hatch refused to do so. They were finally captured in northwest Colorado after they had driven a stolen car into a snowdrift (Jerome, 1996).

In contrast to Justice Marshall's opinion (which did not even mention the attempted rape), Justice Rehnquist gives a description of the actual crime; he names the victims, thus personalizing them; and he later uses emotion-laden words such as "brutal murders" and "month-long crime spree" (p. 1100). Later in his dissenting opinion, Justice Rehnquist expresses his doubt about the validity of Ake's insanity claim, noting that:

- Three days after he was extradited from Colorado to Oklahoma on November 20, 1979, Ake gave the local sheriff a detailed statement about the crime which, when typed, ran to 44 pages. No suggestion of insanity is present in this detailed confession.

- Ake again appeared in court, along with his co-defendant, on December 11; at that time, Hatch, the other defendant, was transferred to the state hospital for a 60-day observation period to determine his competence to stand trial. No such request was made by Ake or his attorney.
- It was not until the formal arraignment on February 14, 1980—almost three months after the extradition—that Ake began to be, in Rehnquist's description, "disruptive."
- During Ake's June 23, 1980 trial, the prosecution produced the testimony of a cellmate of Ake's, who testified that Ake had told him that he was going to try to "play crazy." The jury was not allowed to hear this testimony.

Justice Rehnquist concluded his review by stating: "The evidence . . . would not seem to raise any question of sanity unless one were to adopt the dubious doctrine that no one in his right mind would commit murder" (p. 1100). But no justices concurred in Justice Rehnquist's dissent, and Ake was given a second trial. At this trial, in 1986, a court-appointed psychiatrist testified that he diagnosed Ake as a paranoid schizophrenic who had been hearing voices since 1973. He said that Ake had gone to the victims' home in an attempt to find the source of the voices and make them stop. Despite this testimony, the jury in the second trial also found the defendant guilty, and Ake was sentenced to life in prison. Paradoxically, the other defendant, Steven Hatch—who did not commit the murders—was sentenced to death and executed in August 1996.

In describing their attitudinal explanation of judicial decision making, Segal and Spaeth wrote: "Simply put, Rehnquist votes the way he does because he is extremely conservative; Marshall voted the way he did because he is extremely liberal" (1993, p. 65). Though the labels fit, we need to move beyond them in order to understand the determinants of opinion formation. Social cognition theory emphasizes the differences in processing information.

INTEGRATING APPROACHES TO OPINION FORMATION: MOTIVATED REASONING

How can two justices see one case in such different ways? The concept of *motivated reasoning* offers an explanation. Psychologist Ziva Kunda (1990) has proposed that motivation may affect reasoning through reliance on what she calls a biased set of cognitive processes. Thus, motivation—defined as "any wish, desire, or preference that concerns the outcome of a given reasoning task" (p. 480)—can affect the forming of impressions, the evaluating of evidence, and the making of decisions. That is, "People rely on cognitive processes and representations to arrive at their desired conclusions, but motivation plays a role in determining which of these will be used on a given occasion" (p. 480). Kunda's conception is consistent with Justice Breyer's description of some of the bases for judging:

> People do not seem to be at liberty to conclude whatever they want to conclude merely because they want to. Rather, I propose that people motivated to arrive at a particular conclusion attempt to be rational and to construct a justification of their desired conclusion that would persuade a dispassionate observer. They draw the desired conclusion only if they can muster up the evidence necessary to support it (cf. Diuley & Gross, 1983). In other words, they maintain an "illusion of objectivity" (Pyszuynski & Greenberg, 1987; cf.. Kruglanski, 1980). To this end, they search memory for those beliefs and rules that could support their desired conclusion. It is this process of memory search and belief construction that is biased by directional goals (cf. Greenwald, 1980). The objectivity of this justification construction process is illusory because people do not realize that the process is biased by their goals, but they are accessing only a subset of their relevant knowledge, that they would probably access different beliefs and rules in the presence of different directional goals, and that they might even be capable of justifying opposite conclusions on different occasions. (1990, pp. 482–483)

Can such an analysis apply to even Supreme Court justices, who are experts on their topic and very involved in their task? Kunda's review concludes that people can process information in depth and yet be biased at the same time (1990, p. 490). Justice Breyer acknowledged that different justices come from different backgrounds, with different values. Confronted with the briefs in the *Ake* case, Justice Marshall drew upon his lifelong commitment to the rights of defendants and minorities; he was influenced by the fact that the prosecution had a psychiatrist whereas the defendant did not. In contrast, Justice Rehnquist has long subscribed to a crime-control model, which emphasizes the likelihood of wrongdoing by defendants and suspects. Furthermore, Rehnquist values deference to police power and has a strong need for order. The "facts" about Ake's "crime spree" and his reported confession of intent to fake psychosis thus jumped out at Justice Rehnquist as he read the briefs.

CONCLUSIONS

Application of the motivated reasoning theory means that there are limits to the kinds of decisions judges can make. Baum commented on this perspective:

> Judges are unlikely to reach a decision consistent with their policy preferences when they would have great difficulty justifying it in legal terms. In contrast, the very hard case gives judges free rein to justify whatever decision best accords with their policy views. (1997, p. 66)

3

Attempts to Influence Judges

While on the faculty of the Harvard Law School almost 100 years ago, Roscoe Pound (1912) wrote that judges are influenced by, and must take account of, the world around them. They can be influenced in at least three respects—in what decisions they make, in *why* they make them, and in the *sources* they use to justify the decisions. For example, in declaring racial segregation in the public schools to be illegal in 1954, Earl Warren and the other Supreme Court justices knew that their decision would be quite unpopular in parts of the country. In their effort to give every support and justification for the legitimacy of their action, they were willing to include in their decision a footnote citing contemporary psychological research that concluded that segregation diminished the self-esteem of Black children (see Chapter 6). Whether the psychological research that they cited was truly a *reason* for their decision is debatable.

In some cases public opinion may be cited as a support for both the majority opinion and the dissent. When the Supreme Court reinstituted the death penalty in 1976 in *Gregg v. Georgia*, the plurality decision by Justice Potter Stewart concluded that public opinion reflected a desire to impose the death penalty (a Gallup poll showed 65% of respondents in favor of it), but Justice Thurgood Marshall, in a strong dissent, argued that Americans were uninformed about the death penalty and would hold different opinions if they had more knowledge of capital punishment's consequences (*Gregg v. Georgia*, 1976, p. 152).

The possible sources of influence on judicial decisions can be studied from several disciplinary perspectives. The perspective of the sociology of law might emphasize the writings of Emile Durkheim, who illustrated how legal institutions directly reflect their host community, or perhaps those of Max Weber on the role of the courts as agents of social change (McIntosh, 1990). Class conflict is one pressure on the courts. As McIntosh (1990) observes, most litigation involves interclass disputes, such as landlords versus tenants, debtors versus creditors, employers versus employees, and insurance companies versus accident victims.

Karl Marx's writings led to a conclusion that the courts, in response to ongoing class conflict, support those social and economic interests that are powerful, and some legal philosophies have built on Marxian principles to argue that the agenda of the Supreme Court is highly influenced by the dominant economic forces, especially during periods of socioeconomic change and dislocation (Llewellyn, 1925; Twiss, 1942).

This chapter focuses on specific types of environmental pressures and demands. Do judges' decisions conform to the wishes, of the populace, or to the wishes of the powerful? Do certain kinds of interest group carry more clout? We will examine four possible sources of influence and seek to determine the effect of each. These are: (1) public opinion, (2) oral arguments, (3) judicial conferences, and (4) postconference interactions. The role of the chief justice in the influence process is reviewed in the next chapter.

PUBLIC OPINION

Are judges immune to public opinion? If a consensus exists with regard to the public's wishes, do judges capitulate to such wishes? No general answer exists. To say that judges capitulate frequently is too strong, but at the same time they are certainly not immune to public opinion pressures. Chief Justice Rehnquist (1987), in his book on the Supreme Court, described a case in which he believed that public opinion played an "appreciable" part in the Court's decision.

It was the case of *Youngstown Sheet & Tube Co., et at. v. Sawyer* (1952), the famous "steel seizure case." In the midst of the United States' involvement in the Korean War, the United Steel Workers of America, a labor union, gave notice of a nationwide strike scheduled to begin on April 9, 1952. President Truman's response was to issue an executive order instructing Secretary of Commerce John Sawyer to take possession of the country's steel mills. The steel companies protested, claiming that Congress had to approve such an act, and the Supreme Court agreed to hear the case. By a 6-to-3 vote, the Court ruled that the president did not have the power to take over the steel mills without the authorization of Congress. As Justice Rehnquist noted, "This was a case that unfurled in the newspapers before the very eyes of the justices long before any papers were filed in the Supreme Court. . . . The government's litigation strategy in the district court, reported blow by blow in the Washington newspapers, undoubtedly had an effect on how the case was finally decided by the Supreme Court" (1987, pp. 95–96). Rehnquist also concluded that the ambivalence of the public toward the "police action" in Korea (President Truman never asked Congress for a declaration of war) and the negative reaction to Truman as president played "a considerable part" (p. 97) in the way that the steel seizure case was decided.

The impact of public opinion varies from case to case and from judge to judge, but it is always a possible factor. Justice Rehnquist offered this summary:

> I was recently asked at a meeting with some people in Washington, who were spending a year studying various aspects of the government, whether the justices were able to isolate themselves from the tides of public opinion. My answer was that we are not able to do so, and it probably would be unwise to try. We read newspapers and magazines, we watch news on television, we talk to our friends about current events. No judge worthy of his salt would ever cast his vote in a particular case because he thought the majority of the public wanted him to vote that way, but that is quite a different thing from saying that no judge is ever influenced by the great tides of public opinion that run in a country such as ours. (1987, p. 98)

ELECTED VERSUS APPOINTED JUDGES

It should be recognized that in many states, judgeships are elected positions and thus judges are subject to the whims of the electorate. Some of the idiosyncratic or even outrageous sentencing decisions by trial judges may reflect "playing to the grandstand" to increase the likelihood of reelection. Also, some state judges, like some legislators, may adopt a "blame avoidance" strategy that leads to cautious decisions and decreases the chances of attack from potential opponents (Baum, 1997).

Unlike many state judges, federal judges are appointed for life and are thus free from the fear of being voted out of office. Furthermore, their salaries offer financial security; in 1998 the salary of each of the 647 federal district judges was increased to approximately $140,000, and the salary of each of the 179 circuit court judges was raised to $148,000. U.S. Supreme Court justices, as of January 1998, receive approximately $172,000 per year (with the chief justice's salary slightly higher, almost $180,000).

Federal judges do sometimes succumb to public opinion, however. The example of New York Judge Harold Baer, Jr. is an example of this.

In April 1995 several New York City police officers pulled Carol Bayless's car over because of suspicious behavior. The car, which had Michigan license plates, had stopped and double-parked in a drug-infested part of the city at 5:00 a.m.; two men then placed duffle bags in the trunk. According to later testimony by the officers, when the police approached the car, the men ran away (*United States v. Bayless*, 1996).

The police believed that Ms. Bayless fit the profile of a drug courier, because it was common for people in cars with out-of-state license plates to come to Washington Heights to obtain drugs. Upon opening the trunk, the police found 80 pounds of heroin and cocaine; after arrest, Ms. Bayless confessed to being a drug courier. Her videotaped confession detailed how she rented the 1995 Chevrolet Caprice in Michigan and had driven to New York expressly to pick up drugs and bring them back to Detroit:

An open-and-shut case? In January 1996, Judge Harold Baer, Jr., a federal district judge in Manhattan, threw the evidence out of court, invoking the exclusionary rule by concluding that the police did not have the reasonable grounds required by the Fourth Amendment to justify stopping the car, obtaining the keys, and opening the trunk to search the bags. In *Florida v. Royer* (1983), the Supreme Court had held that when a suspect fitting a "drug courier profile" was asked by police to produce a key to one of his suitcases, their subsequent search of the suitcase was illegal; it exceeded the limited degree of intrusion that the Court was willing to impose on the privacy of an individual without probable cause (Mirsky, 1996). Judge Baer applied this decision to the *Bayless* case.

The public was outraged. Both the mayor and the state governor excoriated Judge Baer, castigating him for coddling criminals and calling him "soft on crime" (Mirsky, 1996). Senator Daniel Patrick Moynihan suggested that the judge be sentenced to a year in Washington Heights. House Speaker Newt Gingrich went so far as to conclude that Judge Baer's ruling was "the perfect reason why we are losing our civilization." What most upset these critics was Judge Baer's conclusion that it was plausible for the men to flee from the police in a neighborhood where police were viewed as "corrupt, abusive, and violent" (quoted by Van Natta, 1996, p. A10).

President Clinton, who had appointed Judge Baer in 1994, joined in the criticism; a White House spokesperson called the decision "wrongheaded" and suggested that if the judge did not change his mind, the president might ask for his resignation. As result of the chorus of criticism, the judge made the extraordinary decision to hold a second hearing on the case, which included testimony from a second arresting officer. After doing so, Baer reversed his decision, concluding that new evidence buttressed the police officers' version of the disputed search and questioned the credibility of the defendant's story (Van Natta, 1996). He reinstated the seized drugs as evidence and, apologized for his earlier remarks disparaging the police.

Did the pressure cause the change? Observers, including an editorial writer in the *New York Times,* found him "caving in" to politicians and thus sacrificing the concept of judicial independence. Not only was he considered "spineless" but his reversal was viewed as being based on questionable procedures. No one came out looking good in this matter—not the judge, not the president, not the critics who used the issue for political gain. After Judge Baer reversed his decision, President Clinton said: "I support the independence of the Federal judiciary. I do not believe that means that those of us who disagree with particular decisions should refrain from saying we disagree" (quoted by Mitchell, 1996, p. C18).

When considering the impact of public opinion upon appellate judges' decisions, we should distinguish between short-run and long-run considerations. Occasionally, the Supreme Court has rendered decisions that—in the short-run—clearly are in opposition to public sentiment. In 1989, for example, the Court struck down a Texas criminal statute against flag desecration (*Texas v. Johnson,* 1989), despite the public's outrage over television portrayals of antiwar protesters burning the U.S. flag. In *Reno v. American Civil Liberties Union* (1997), the Court also declared as unconstitutional the Communications Decency Act, which Congress had passed and which the media had portrayed as a response to the dangers of exposing children to "cyberporn" on the Internet.

But in the long run, public opinion may be more generally influential. Even Justice Scalia, in a 1988 speech at the University of Kentucky, concluded that public opinion inevitably influences the Court (Caldeira, 1990), if only for the reason that judges come from among the public. Another perspective on the difference between short-run and long-run effects of public opinion takes into account the lag in the normal attrition in Court membership through retirements and deaths. New justices can reflect the goals of the incumbent president and the current wishes of the public (Schubert, 1965a), but it took President Roosevelt, for example, years to attain a majority of justices whose values were congenial with the country's mood.

In a review of the research on this issue, Caldeira concluded that it is "difficult to speak with precision about the impact of public opinion on the courts in the short run. The truth is, we know virtually nothing systematically about the effect of public opinion on the Supreme Court" (1990, p. 313). One reason for this is that it is difficult to achieve the proper statistical controls for research of this sort. Barnum (1985) examined some of the most emotional issues that the Court faced between 1940 and 1970—including racial integration of the schools, birth control, interracial marriage, and the rights of women—and concluded that Supreme Court decisions usually did reflect trends in public opinion, but this study failed to evaluate alternative explanations.

As Caldeira (1990) observes, the causal linkage between Court decisions and public opinion is probably more complicated. For example, Page and Shapiro's (1983) survey of the relationship between public opinion and public-policy decisions between 1935 and 1980 found greater congruence for "salient and large-scale social issues" than for economic or welfare policies. But they acknowledge that it is difficult to separate cause and effect; in about half the cases of congruence, they concluded that "policy may [have] affect[ed] opinion" (Page & Shapiro, 1983, p. 187) rather than the opposite.

Further documentation of complexity is found in the results of a 1989 study by Marshall, who matched results from national opinion polls with decisions by the Supreme Court in 146 cases from 1935 through 1986. His general conclusion: "The modern Court appears neither markedly more or less consistent with the polls than are other policy makers" (p. 80). More specific conclusions are:

- In times of crisis, the Supreme Court reflected public opinion more accurately than at other times.
- If a federal law was in conflict with public opinion, the Court was more likely to agree with the latter.
- "State and local policies usually did not agree with national opinion; when the Court confronted a conflict with public views, the justices chose public opinion over the decisions of state and local government" (Caldeira, 1990, p. 315).

Despite this degree of specificity, we still lack understanding of *why* linkage exists. How does public opinion exert an influence? Caldeira's 1990 summary of a review of relevant research, though helpful, does not answer this question:

Does the Supreme Court represent public opinion? The answer, I think, is that we do not yet have sufficient evidence on which we can place much confidence. The extant studies, although intriguing and suggestive, lack the conceptualization and measurement to permit us to make a well-considered judgment on this issue. This should not reflect poorly on the scholars working in this arena; the problems of data are severe, perhaps insuperable, and the enterprise remains young enough to justify exploratory efforts. (p. 316)

INTEREST GROUPS

One way public opinion often gets transmitted to appellate judges is through lobbying by interest groups, and the pressure to decide certain cases in certain ways can be immense. For example, when considering the *Webster v. Reproductive Health Services* case concerning restrictions on abortion rights in 1989, the Supreme Court received more than 40,000 letters—most of them by members of organized groups—and 300,000 people marched in support of women's rights. As Epstein (1991) points out, after the Court announced its intention to hear the case, groups representing each view held vigils outside the Supreme Court building; that is, they "treated the Court as if it were Congress considering a piece of legislation, not a judicial body deliberating points of law" (Epstein, 1990, p. 349). In the spring of 1992, when *Planned Parenthood v. Casey* was being considered, some 750,000 pro-choice supporters rallied on the Washington Mall in support of abortion rights legislation, on the assumption that the Court would use *Casey* as an opportunity to overturn *Roe v. Wade* (1973).

Another means of expressing public opinion-at least that of designated groups-is the submission of *amicus curiae* briefs. The effectiveness of such briefs in general is reviewed in Chapter 7; at this point, however, we note the dramatic increase in the percentage of Supreme Court cases that included at least one anticus brief, from less than 2% in the 1930s and 1940s to 80% a decade ago (Epstein, 1990).

Justices know that the acceptance of their decisions rests in part with the public. Shifts in their decisions may be related to—if not based on-changes in the political climate. An example is the "saluting the flag" case, which began in 1935 when two children, ages 10 and 12, were expelled from the public schools of Minersville, Pennsylvania, because they refused to participate in the daily school exercise of saluting the flag. Their reason was that their parents, members of Jehovah's Witnesses, considered saluting the flag as worship of a "graven image," a practice forbidden by the Bible. The appeal of the childrens' expulsion from school reached the U.S. Supreme Court in 1940 as *Minersville School District v. Gobitis*. With only one justice dissenting (Harlan Fiske Stone), the Court decided that the action of the school board did not deny the constitutional rights of the Gobitis children. The Court did so despite the First Amendment's statement that "Congress shall make no law respecting an establishment of religion, or prohibiting the free exercise thereof."

The *Gobitis* decision is a good example of how Court opinions sometimes reflect the mood of the country. A 1940 Gallup poll had found that 65% of American citizens believed that Germany would soon attack the United States. The nation became flag-conscious, as the flag was the symbol of America. In some small towns people began to suspect members of the Jehovah's Witness sect of being Nazi agents. In the words of one observer, "The Court, swayed by popular emotions and prejudices of Americans against any group that seemed different, ignored the constitutional guarantees that were the foundation of democracy" (Ball, 1978, p. 77).

Just three years later, in *West Virginia State Board of Education v. Barnette* (1943), the Supreme Court reversed its position. The facts of the case were similar to those of *Gobitis*. West Virginia required its schoolchildren to salute the flag; to refuse meant expulsion, with readmission denied until the child agreed to comply. The child's parents could even be prosecuted and penalized with a $50 fine and/or 30 days in jail. In a 6-to-3 vote, the Court concluded that such regulations were in conflict with constitutional rights to free speech. In concurring opinions several justices (including Hugo Black and William O. Douglas), tried to explain their change of view.

Change in world conditions may have been a factor. Though in 1943 World War II was still in progress, the fear of foreigners and the fear of impending attack by Germany did not motivate public behavior as they had three years before (Ball, 1978).

"Never for a very long period is the Court out of touch with the populace," states Thomas G. Krattenmaker, associate dean of the Georgetown University law school; "They are always sensitive to what they perceive to be the shared values of Americans" (quoted in Rubin, 1989, p. 7A). In fact, the wife of current justice Clarence Thomas is the top aide to U.S. Representative Dick Armey, one of the most powerful members of Congress. Do they talk at home about their work and her boss's legislative goals?

On the question of whether Supreme Court justices are interested in audiences outside the Court, Baum (1997) offers a distinction between Justice Thomas and Justice Souter; Thomas, he notes, has given several speeches to conservative organizations and received an award from one of them; he has defended his position before several groups of African Americans. In contrast, Baum observes that Souter's outside activities are quite limited. Baum thus concludes that "external audiences might be only moderately salient to him" (p. 54).

On occasion—on a *rare* occasion—judges will even acknowledge that the weight of public opinion is consistent with their decision. In March of 1996, the Ninth Circuit Court of Appeals struck down a Washington state law that prohibited physician-assisted suicide. Judge Stephen Reinhardt, in the opinion, cited a Harris pull from 1994 that showed that 73% of respondents supported the legalization of physician-assisted suicides under certain conditions. The judge wrote: "Polls have repeatedly shown that a large majority of Americans—sometimes nearing 90%—fully endorse recent legal changes granting terminally ill patients, and sometimes their families, the prerogative to accelerate their death by refusing or terminating treatment" (cited by Rosen, 1996, pp. 30–31).

Of course, the approval of a *passive* decision not to maintain life by curtailing life-sustaining measures (the example the judge gave in the above quotation) is different from the *active* termination of life, as practiced by Dr. Jack Kevorkian. With regard to the latter—which is commonly thought of as physician-assisted suicide—the poll results do not show anywhere near the 90% approval rate suggested by Judge Reinhardt (Rosen, 1996). Voters in two states— Washington and California—rejected proposals to permit physician-assisted suicide for the terminally ill by margins of about 54% to 46%. In Oregon the proposal was endorsed, but by a narrow 51-to-49% margin. As Rosen notes, no state legislature has passed a bill that would decriminalize physician-assisted suicide; six state legislatures recently considered and rejected such bills. And in June 1997, the Supreme Court unanimously overturned the decision of Judge Reinhardt's court.

Some justices have a personal investment in the popularity of their actions. Charles Evans Hughes left the Court to run for president in 1916; he narrowly lost to Woodrow Wilson. He later returned to the Court, having been appointed chief justice by President Herbert Hoover in 1930. Justice William O. Douglas, Jr., was discussed as a possible vice presidential running mate for Franklin Roosevelt in the 1940s and apparently had ambitions for the presidency. Some of his colleagues felt that his political aspirations affected his judicial decisions (Lash, 1975). More recently, speculation about Justice O'Connor's interest in the vice presidency has surfaced (Davis, 1994).

Perhaps the most extreme example of a justice with explicit political aspirations was Salmon Chase, chief justice from 1864 to 1873. Earlier in his life, he told a friend that he would like to hold two offices: President of the United States and Chief Justice. He unrelentingly sought the first after having been named to the second (Steamer, 1986). According to his biographers, he considered himself better qualified to be president than any of his contemporaries, including Abraham Lincoln (who appointed him first as the secretary of the Treasury and later to the Court). Chase sought the nomination of his party as its presidential candidate five times, including for the election of 1864, when he "in an undoubted act of personal disloyalty encouraged the organization and expenditure of funds in his behalf in order to secure the Republican nomination for president" (Steamer, p. 239)—against Lincoln, in the middle of the Civil War!

THE MEDIA AND LEGAL COLLEAGUES

Justices' decisions can be subtly but significantly influenced by the opinions of two other groups: the mass media and the legal community (Baum, 1985). Some justices are sensitive to criticism by the press, and they are aware of the media's role in communicating their decisions to the public. Epstein and Knight wrote:

> During our examination of the files of Justices Marshall, Brennan, and Powell, we came across many clippings of newspaper stories and editorials about specific cases those the Court had decided and those awaiting action. Occasionally justices even circulate copies of newspaper stories, with commentary, to their colleagues. . . . These . . . suggest that justices pay attention to how the press reports on issues on their docket and on their activities; and we do not imagine that the clippings found in their files are the only articles they read. (1998, pp. 145–146)

In at least one case, *Richmond Newspapers, Inc. v. Virginia* (1980), the Court's decision was affected by severe media criticism of a related decision it had made a year earlier (Lewis, 1981). Both decisions dealt with the right of the media, during a trial, to have information about jurors, including their names and addresses, and access to those jurors after the trial.

The legal profession is especially important to some justices because it serves as a reference group (Baum, 1985). Judges interact socially with other lawyers. More relevant to their professional activity, articles in law reviews are useful in forming decisions, as Chapter 10 discusses in more detail.

The relationship between appellate judges and their law clerks also cannot be ignored as a possible source of influence. As Hoeflich (1996) noted, judges and their clerks come to form close professional and personal ties. The clerks do legal research on pending cases; many draft opinions for their judges. All the current justices except Justice Stevens participate in a *"cert.* pool" in which their clerks review the numerous *certiorari* petitions and draft summaries of them for judicial review.

The phenomenon of the judicial clerkship was given prominence by Justice Oliver Wendell Holmes, Jr. Each year he would invite a new graduate of Harvard Law School to work with him as a combination of secretary, research assistant, and personal assistant (Hoeflich, 1996). The idea caught on; now almost all federal judges and some state judges have such clerks. Each Supreme Court justice has four, if he or she wishes to.

As Posner (1996) noted, observers wondered exactly what, if anything, Justice Holmes' clerks did "besides balancing his checkbook, listening to his anecdotes, reading to him at night and doing other valet-like services for this elderly and eventually quite infirm man (Holmes retired at age 90)" (Hoeflich, 1996, p. 16). But the recent publication of Justice Holmes's voluminous correspondence with Justice Frankfurter (edited by Mennel & Compston, 1996) proves that Holmes sought out and occasionally followed the clerks' criticisms of his opinion drafts. Judge Posner notes in his review: "There was more give and take between Justice and clerk than I had suspected, even on matters far from the law" (p. 16).

The relationship between judge and clerk is individualized, and no general statement of degree of influence can be made. But the workload of judges, especially federal judges, where currently there are 100 vacancies (Rowley, 1997), means that their clerks certainly provide important input beyond the review of the massive number of petitions sent to the Court. A book published in 1998 by a former Supreme Court clerk claims a more insidious influence, however. Edward Lazarus served as one of the four clerks to Justice Harry Blackmun during the Court's 1988–89 term; he concluded that in the Court, "Justices yield great and excessive power to immature, ideologically driven clerks, who in turn use that power to manipulate their bosses and the institution they ostensibly serve" (p. 6). What was most disturbing to Lazarus was an influential "cabal" (his term) of conservative law clerks driven to use proximity to their judges to achieve certain politically conservative goals: elimination of abortion rights and affirmative action and a more expeditious review of death penalty appeals. Lazarus also described "the guerilla war that liberal and conservative clerks conducted, largely out of the sight of those Justices, to control the course of constitutional law" (p. 261).

Lazarus wrote of the process as follows:

> Every year the behind-the-scenes commencement of the new fall term is a cocktail party for Justices, clerks, and senior Court staff held roughly two weeks before the first oral argument in October. As clerks, we had already been at work for two months when Chief Justice Rehnquist, partway through the evening, gave us an official welcome and admonished us about our clerkly duties. . . .
>
> I remember looking around the room and thinking how quaint such lofty abstractions sounded. By the time that Rehnquist spoke to us, the clerks of October 1988 Term already were divided into two well-entrenched and hostile camps. Across the room we glared at each other, eyes hooded with distrust or outright contempt. . . . We had been through one execution and nearly came to blows over others narrowly averted. Preparation of the first set of argued cases was far enough along for us to know each other's policies and how cleverly we could pursue our respective views. Our thoughts were not of the "public trust" but of private strategies for the coming battle over the future of the Court. (p. 263)

Lazarus's book makes two major claims about clerks: that they come to the Court with political biases and self-serving goals, and that their actions significantly influence decisions purportedly made by their mentors. The first is easier to evaluate; certainly many clerks have already developed political orientations and, in fact, have been socialized to a particular point of view by having served as a clerk for a federal district judge or circuit court judge before clerking at the Supreme Court. Justices often get recommendations from other judges, and a certain kind of "farm system" develops.) But do clerks "spoon-feed" opinions to their justices, or do they merely suffer from an exaggerated sense of their own importance? It is true that clerks spend huge amounts of time on drafts that are acted upon by their justices, and often a first draft—in its selection of words, materials, and structure—sets the tone for the final one. Lazarus repeats the oft-told tale that during his last years on the Court, Justice Thurgood Marshall watched soap operas while in his chambers and let his clerks do almost everything other than cast his votes. And it is no secret that current Justice Stevens spends much of the winter at his Florida condominium; Lazarus says he has come to be known as the "FedEx Justice." Eight of the nine current justices allow their clerks to write first drafts of opinions, and eight of the nine also participate in a "*cert.* pool," in which their clerks divide the review of submitted appeals. The one justice who does not is Lazarus's "FedEx judge," Justice Stevens—although it is claimed that on occasion key parts of even his rulings have been written by his clerks (see Mauro, 1998, p. 2A). Lazarus claims that "rarely do the Justices disassemble the drafts they've been given to examine" and some judges function as nothing more than "editorial Justices" (p. 273). However, many justices have already given detailed instructions to their clerks about what should go into these drafts, and as Chapter 5 details, negotiation and back-and-forth memoranda between justices during the opinion-drafting period reflect how involved each justice is on a day-to-day basis. Do clerks affect decisions? We fall back on our original answer: it depends. It depends on the justice (some do less supervision than others), the clerk, and the case.

CONGRESS

Does Congress have an influence on Supreme Court decisions? The U. S. Congress can impeach Supreme Court justices; does this power coerce the Court? (The one actual case of impeachment involved Justice Samuel Chase, a Federalist, whom the Jeffersonian Democrats sought to remove from the Court in 1804; the effort failed.) Segal and Spaeth (1993) noted: "There is some evidence that two justices, Roberts in 1937 and Harlan in 1959, reversed previously unpopular decisions in the face of threats by Congress" (p. 71) but they conclude that this is rare.

THE PRESIDENT

The president appoints the justices to the Supreme Court, subject to the approval of the Senate, but the president has no direct authority over them once they are confirmed. Does this mean that the potential for influence is nonexistent? The most direct examples—cases in which the president had a vital interest in the outcome—lead us to conclude that the Court remains free of presidential influence. We refer to two cases, *United States v. Nixon* (1974) and *Clinton v. Jones* (1996) to delay any trial resulting from Paula Jones' allegations until after his term ended.

When President Nixon refused to relinquish the Watergate tapes to the independent counsel investigating the Watergate break-in and alleged coverup, he claimed the principle of executive privilege. Whether he had this right was quickly sent to the Supreme Court to decide. Three of the justices had been appointed by President Nixon (Rehnquist, Blackmun, and Chief Justice Burger); they joined the other justices in a unanimous ruling, authored by the Burger, that the claim of executive privilege was not applicable in this matter. The subsequent release of these tapes led to the recommendation to impeach President Nixon. He resigned soon after. President Clinton sought to delay the Jones trial until his term was over. His two appointees to the Court voted along with the other justices that there is no constitutionally based presidential immunity that requires delaying court actions beyond the term of office. The Court's decision was quite popular when it was announced on May 27, 1997; media commentators were in virtual agreement that no one, not even the president of the United States, is "above the law." But during the rest of 1997 and the first three months of 1998, as the case dragged on and consumed more and more of the Clinton's time and concentration, people began to wonder if the decision was such a wise one. Furthermore, the Supreme Court came under stinging criticism from trial attorney Vincent Bugliosi (1998), who argued that the Court had made an incorrect decision. Rather than relying on the argument of President Clinton's attorneys that this was a separation-of powers case, Bugliosi said that the central issue was public interest versus private interests, "whether or not the American public's interest in the effective functioning of the office of the president outweighed the private interest of Paula Jones in having the lawsuit go forward without delay" (p. 45). The issue never was—contrary to the media's analyses—whether the president was above the law; it was agreed that Ms. Jones had the right to bring charges. The only question was whether or not to postpone their resolution. But regardless of the reasons for the Court's decision, the justices certainly did not conform to the president's wishes.

An attempt to "pack the Court" in 1937 leads to a less clear-cut conclusion about presidential influence (Kull, 1996). When Franklin Roosevelt assumed the presidency in March 1933, his primary task was to deal with the nationwide economic depression. With public opinion strongly behind him, he introduced a number of bills that created agencies and other mechanisms to improve the economy. Congress quickly passed them. But the Supreme Court, following its tradition of limiting the power of the federal government, struck the laws down as unconstitutional.

The issue of child labor regulation serves as an example. The shift from agricultural to factory work near the beginning of the twentieth century meant that many children were forced to work long hours in unhealthy conditions. Abuses were commonplace. The first effort to curtail such abuses was a series of laws passed by state legislatures; by 1910 most states had restrictions on the employment of children, although many of these statutes were narrowly drawn and riddled with loopholes. Progress in the next few decades was erratic. In 1916 the federal government took over; Congress passed the Keating–Owen bill that banned certain types of child labor. Homer Dagenhart, the father of two sons employed in a cotton mill—one younger than age 14—filed suit, asking the North Carolina district court to enjoin enforcement of the act. Two years later, in the *Hammer v. Dagenhart* (1918) decision, the Supreme Court nullified this act, concluding that Congress had exceeded its authority to regulate interstate commerce (Ball, 1978). The next year Congress passed a law that put an excise tax on any goods manufactured with child labor; three years later the Supreme Court found it an unconstitutional intrusion on states' rights (in *Bailey v. Drexel Furniture Co.*, 1922). Another approach by Congress—in 1924—was a proposed constitutional amendment to establish protections for child labor; despite widespread popular approval, only 20 of the required 36 states approved the proposal. As the Great Depression intensified, Congress saw the need to protect adult workers from being replaced by children and again adopted restrictions on children's work as a part of the Roosevelt-initiated National Industrial Recovery Act. Again the Supreme Court interceded; in a highly unpopular decision, *Schechter Poultry Corporation v. United States* (1935), the Court ruled unanimously that Congress had once more exceeded its authority to regulate business within a state's borders. (The *Schechter* appeal has been called the "sick chicken" case because the Schechter Corporation was alleged to have been successfully shipping diseased poultry to unsuspecting buyers because no effective inspection occurred *within* the state.) Congress, at Roosevelt's urging, had passed a law creating the National Recovery Administration (NRA), which was granted the power to regulate wages and working hours. The Court ruled that the Brooklyn-based kosher poultry business run by the Schechter brothers was exclusively intrastate in character; thus their violation of the NRA regulations could not be punished by the federal government (Kennedy, 1995). Even their sale of diseased poultry was beyond the federal government's reach—the government regulated *interstate* commerce only. In fact, on a single day, May 27, 1935, which came to be labeled "Black Monday," the Supreme Court announced three decisions that eviscerated important aspects of the president's New Deal; "We have been relegated to the horse-and-buggy definition of interstate commerce," Roosevelt complained (quoted by Kennedy, 1995, p. 88).

Even though it became obvious by the middle of 1936 that the Supreme Court was not going to let Roosevelt initiate legislation aimed at relief of the economic hard times, the president did not make the Court much of an issue in his reelection-campaign. But after his overwhelming victory in November of 1936 he made a bold move, proposing a court reform bill under the guise of improving judicial efficiency. His proposal—made only two weeks after his second-term inauguration—was that the president would appoint one new justice for every justice over the age of 70 who chose not to resign. The language of his message to Congress reflected his exasperation. "Aged or infirm justices [are inclined to avoid an examination of complicated and changed conditions. . . . older men, assuming that the scene is the same as it was in the past, cease to explore or inquire into the present or the future" (quoted in Kennedy, 1995, p. 88). (Ironically, the New Deal's most consistent ally on the Court was Louis Brandeis, who was 80 years old.) Six of the nine currently obstinate justices were beyond the age of 70, so Roosevelt's proposal, if passed, would have significantly altered the Court's composition, increasing the number of justices from 9 to 15. But what came to be called the "court-packing" proposal was in itself widely disliked; public, press, and Congress all rejected it (Caldeira, 1987). As Segal and Spaeth put it, "Though many of the Court's decisions were unpopular, the notion of judicial independence was not" (1993, p. 96).

Though the legislation was never adopted, President Roosevelt got what he wanted (Leuchtenburg, 1995). For it wasn't just the president who was being criticized; the Court was feeling pressure from the public for impeding the president's program of reform. For whatever reason, Justice Owen Roberts shifted his vote-the so-called switch in time that saved nine. In a decision announced only a month after the proposal's dissemination, the Court, in a 5-to-4 vote, overturned 40 years of doctrine that had guaranteed the freedom of a contract (*West Coast Hotel Co. v. Parrish*, 1937). Two weeks later, the Court upheld the National Labor Relations Act; it granted the right of labor to bargain collectively and provided government intervention to prevent unfair labor practices (*National Labor Relations Board v. Jones and Laughlin Steel Corporation*, 1937). Then, within the next month, the Supreme Court concluded that it was constitutional for Congress to establish a tax that would generate income to fund the payment of Social Security benefits.

With respect to the regulation of child labor, the "Nine Old Men" of the Court also did an about face. Congress in 1938 had passed the Fair Labor Standards Act that included child labor protections among the multitude of wage and hour provisions. For example, the law prohibited manufacturers, producers, and dealers from shipping goods that were the product of "oppressive" child labor. The Supreme Court, in *United States v. F. W. Darby Lumber Co.* (1941), expressly overruled *Hammer v. Dagenhart* and concluded that the Fair Labor Standards Act was a valid exercise of Congress's authority to regulate commerce.

In May 1937 one of the justices (Willis Van Devanter) resigned, permitting the president, five years into his administration, to make his first appointment and shift the balance of the Court. (By the time of President Roosevelt's death in 1945, eight of the nine justices then on the bench were his appointees.) Roosevelt lost the battle to expand the Court, but he won the war (Pritchett, 1948; Segal & Spaeth, 1993).

BRIEFS AND ORAL ARGUMENTS

Chapter 2 described the procedure in the oral argument phase of judicial decision making. Can we draw conclusions about the future vote of a justice from his or her questions during oral arguments? Frequently, newspaper reports of the oral arguments for a specific case will describe a justice's questions as reflecting "skepticism" or "doubt" about the claims of one side—are such reactions manifested in the judge's eventual vote? Anecdotal evidence drawn from specific cases indicates that a relationship exists. For example, in the oral arguments on the line item veto case (see Chapter 1), several justices raised questions about whether the legislators had "standing" to appeal. But systematic research is urgently needed; the work of Stephen Wasby and his colleagues provides only tentative support for the idea that "oral argument at times—but certainly not always—has been directly relevant to the Court's disposition of a case—and at times determinative of the outcome" (Wasby, Peterson, Schubert, & Schubert, 1992, p. 30).

Such questions cannot be thoroughly answered without a consideration of the justices' motivations for asking questions during oral arguments, and these motivations can be diverse and hard to discern. A question may reflect hostility more than it reflects a genuine desire to know the answer, and justices may also use questions to clarify their thoughts on an issue. Additionally, questions may reveal that a justice has a misunderstanding about an important fact of the case, or has read a precedent differently from the way in which one of the attorneys thinks it should be read (Rehnquist, 1987). Aaron Hull (1997) has suggested that justices' questions during oral arguments fall into three major categories:

- *Affirming questions* are those asked to aid an attorney in answering a question, or to provide a new direction of thought. They are "generally signaled by a calm voice tone of the justice, and an enthusiastic affirmative response by the attorney" (p. 28).
- *Inquisitive questions* regarding case facts alone, as in case-framing at the beginning of the oral argument; for example, "Mr. Smith, isn't this case about . . . ?"
- *Challenges,* or abrupt interruptions of attorneys in a harsh tone of voice, the net result of which is often to corner attorneys into saying things that are potentially damaging to their case.

Systematic study of the impact of oral arguments on attitude change is in its infancy. (As an aside, I note that the Supreme Court does not completely aid scholars who want to analyze oral arguments. When you receive a copy of the official transcript of the oral arguments from the Alderson Reporting Company of Washington, D.C., you will find that when a justice speaks or asks a question, the justice's name is not given. You must obtain tape recordings of the session to link the question with the questioner.)

Segal and Spaeth cite two papers as examples of empirical research on the topic (Peterson, Schubert, Schubert, & Wasby, 1991; Wasby *et al.*, 1992). In their review, they conclude that the extent to which oral arguments affect the justices' votes is "problematic" (1993, p. 208). Chief Justice Warren, similarly, found oral arguments "not highly persuasive" (quoted by O'Brien, 1997, p. 43). After all, the justices have previously read the extensive briefs and reviewed the relevant decisions. Most have probably discussed the case with their law clerks. Justice Holmes considered oral arguments so unimportant that he often took catnaps while on the bench (O'Brien, 1997).

Despite all the prior activity, oral arguments are not simply a formality, claims Chief Justice Rehnquist. He wrote: "I think that in a significant minority of the cases in which I have heard oral arguments, I have left the bench feeling different about the case than I did when I came on the bench. The change is seldom a full 180-degree swing, and I find it most likely to occur in cases involving areas of law with which I am least familiar" (1987, p. 176). On this matter, Justice Brennan agreed with his frequent adversary, saying, "Often my idea of how a case shapes up is changed by oral argument" (quoted in O'Brien, 1993, p. 285).

A more extensive claim that oral arguments are influential comes from Justice John M. Harlan II: "The view is widespread that when court comes to the hard business of decision, it is the briefs, and not the oral argument, which count. I think that view is a greatly mistaken one" (1955, p. 6). Justice Harlan went on to write:

First of all, judges have different work habits. There are judges who listen better than they read and who are more receptive to the spoken word than the written word.

Secondly, the first impressions that a judge gets of a case are very tenacious. They frequently persist into the conference room. And those impressions are usually gained from the oral argument, if it is an effective job. While I was on the court of appeals, I kept a sort of informal scoreboard of the cases in which I sat, so as to match up the initial reactions which I had to the cases after the close of the oral argument with the final conclusions that I reached when it came time to vote at the conference on the decision of those cases. I was astonished to find during the year I sat on that court how frequently—in fact, more times than not—the views which I had at the end of the day's session jibed with the final views that I formed after the more careful study of the briefs which, under our system in the Second Circuit, came in the period between the closing of the arguments and the voting at the conference.

Thirdly, the decisional process in many courts places a special burden on the oral argument. I am giving away no secrets, I am sure, when I say that in one of the courts of appeal where I was assigned to sit temporarily the voting on the cases took place each day following the close of arguments. In the Supreme Court, our practice, as is well known, has been to hold our conferences at the end of each week of arguments. They have been on Saturdays up until now, but under a more enlightened schedule they will be on Fridays next term, because beginning October we are going to sit four days a week. Under either of those systems you can see the importance which the oral argument assumes.

> Fourth, and to me this is one of the most important things, the job of courts
> is not merely one of an umpire in disputes between litigants. Their job is to search
> out the truth, both as to the facts and the law, and that is ultimately the job of the
> lawyers, too. And in that joint effort, the oral argument gives an opportunity for
> interchange between court and counsel which the briefs do not give. For my part,
> there is no substitute, even within the time limits afforded by the busy calendars
> of modern appellate courts, for the Socratic method of procedure in getting at the
> real heart of an issue and in finding where the truth lies. (1955, pp. 6–7)

A survey by Wasby (1982) of Ninth Circuit judges also reflects the opinion that in cases that are complex or deal with novel issues of the law, it is especially helpful to have the opportunity to question attorneys orally. It is less helpful in simple cases, in "frivolous" ones, and—as one would expect—in "run-of-the-mill" cases.

These comments reflect a fundamental psychological contribution to understanding judicial decision making: the phenomenon of the person-situation interaction. The influential social psychologist Kurt Lewin (1951) proposed that behavior is a function of both the person *and* the environment Similarly, Justice Rehnquist's statement can be read as saying, "On many issues, I already know enough about the case before hearing the oral arguments to form a firm opinion, but on those topics for which I am least knowledgeable, it is the environment (i.e., the points made in the oral arguments) that affects my behavior." Thus from a psychological perspective, the effectiveness of any given oral argument is interactionally determined. For some judges with strongly held positions, the best oral argument possible is still doomed to be ineffective. For others, whose opinions are not so solid or who may be less informed on the topic, the quality of oral argument may make a difference. However, Justice Harlan is reported to have said that the opportunity to argue a case before the Supreme Court is "an opportunity to lose, not win, a case" (quoted by O'Brien, 1997, p. 42).

Judges also differ in how well prepared they are for the oral arguments. O'Brien (1997) reports that most of the current Supreme Court justices come armed with "bench memos" that note central facts, issues, and potential questions. Thus prepared, a judge is much more capable of probing the factual basis and the logical support for each side's oral arguments than is a judge who has only casually read the briefs.

THE JUDICIAL CONFERENCE

As noted earlier, the chief justice initiates discussion of each case at the conference, and every justice expresses an opinion. The voting may be quite informal. Our information about what happens at case conferences—all of which comes from those judges' notes that are public and from reports by their law clerks of what the judges told them—leads to a conclusion that direct efforts to persuade others are not so much in evidence at this stage as are justifications for why each justice sees a case as he or she does.

Does the discussion at the judicial conference change opinions? Not much, according to Chief Justice Rehnquist. One reason for Rehnquist's belief is the fact that each justice has already been dealing extensively with the case before arriving at the conference (O'Brien, 1987, p. 295). Rehnquist's conclusion supports our assumption that judicial opinions are formed early in the process.

POSTCONFERENCE INFLUENCE ATTEMPTS

Although the oral arguments on a given appeal may be held in October or November, the Court's decision is not announced until the following May or June. What transpires during this long interim? The first draft of a majority opinion may take only a few weeks (though some justices are quicker at this than others); from then on, the exchange of reactions and suggestions for change may take months. How can we conceptualize this process?

PSYCHOLOGICAL ANALYSIS OF THE INFLUENCE PROCESS

COMPLIANCE-GAINING STRATEGIES

Communication theorists have used the term *compliance-gaining* to refer to the process of trying to get others to act in ways they desire; one definition refers to it as "the attempt of some actor—the source of communication—to affect a particular, preconceived response from some target—the receiver of the persuasive effort" (Schenck-Hamlin, Wiseman, & Georgacarakos, 1982, p. 92). To apply concepts from this body of theory and research to the process by which one justice seeks to influence another to his or her way of thinking, we will rely on a review by Perloff (1993). Influence attempts can occur during oral arguments (infrequently), during the judicial conference (still infrequently, as previously noted), or during the postconference period, in which the exchange of memos or hallway conversations reflects compliance-gaining attempts.

Compliance-gaining is obviously sought frequently in ordinary life. Marwell and Schmitt (1967) posed a question: How do people generally go about trying to gain compliance? A list of 16 different tactics was generated that were later reconceptualized by Miller and Parks (1982) along two dimensions:

- *Reward versus Punishment.* For example, did the persuader try to use rewarding or punishing techniques to gain compliance?

- *Communicator-recipient onus.* That is, did the persuader try to manipulate rewards directly (the "communicator onus") or did he or she try to stimulate positive or negative self-persuasion techniques, or the "recipient onus" (Perloff, 1993). The latter dimension, exemplified by such statements as "you owe me one" or "you'll feel better about yourself if you vote my way," seem less applicable to Supreme Court negotiations.

TYPES OF POWER AND INFLUENCE

Another set of dimensions, potentially more applicable, emerged from the research of psychologist Toni Falbo (1977), who asked respondents to write a paragraph on "How I Get My Way." Again, 16 strategies emerged:

TABLE 3.1. POWER STRATEGIES

Strategy	Definition	Example
Assertion	Forcefully asserting one's way.	I voice my wishes loudly.
Bargaining	Explicit statement about reciprocating favors and making other two-way exchanges.	I tell her that I'll do something for her if she'll do something for me.
Compromise	Both agent and target give up part of their desired goals in order to obtain some of them.	More often than not we come to some sort of compromise, if there is a disagreement.
Deceit	Attempts to fool the target into agreeing by the use of flattery or lies.	I get my way by doing a good amount of fast talking and sometimes by white lies.
Emotion-agent	Agent alters own facial expression.	I put on a sweet face. I try to look sincere.
Emotion-target	Agent attempts to alter emotions of target.	I try to put him in a good mood.
Evasion	Doing what one wants by avoiding the person who would disapprove.	I get to read novels at work as long as the boss never sees me doing it.
Expertise	Claiming to have superior knowledge or skill.	I tell them I have a lot of experience with such matters.
Fait accompli	Openly doing what one wants without avoiding the target.	I do what I want anyway.
Hinting	Not openly stating what one wants; indirect attempts at influencing others.	I drop hints. I subtly bring up a point.
Persistence	Continuing in one's influence attempts or repeating one's point	I reiterate my point. I keep going despite obstacles.
Persuasion	Simple statements about using persuasion, convincing, or coaxing	I get my way by convincing others that my way is best.

(Continued)

(Continued)

Reason	Any statement about using reason or rational argument to influence others.	I argue logically. I tell all the reasons why my plan is best.
Simple statement	Without supporting evidence or threats, a matter-of-fact statement of one's desires.	I simply tell him what I want.
Thought manipulation	Making the target think that the agent's way is the target's own idea.	I usually try to get my way by making the other person feel that it is his idea.
Threat	Stating that negative consequences will occur if the agent's plan is not accepted.	I'll tell him I will never speak to him again if he doesn't do what I want.

(From Falbo, 1977).

The factors that emerged from an analysis of responses are the following:

- Direct versus indirect (e.g., assertions and simple statements vs. hinting and bargaining)
- Rational versus irrational (e.g., by use of reason and compromise or by use of evasion and threat).

It is important to realize that the seen as two independent -dimensions, such that a tactic could be:

- Both direct and rational; *persistence*
- Both direct and nonrational; *threat*
- Both indirect and rational; *bargaining*
- Both indirect and nonrational; *deceit*

Persuasion is context-bound, and different influence strategies are used in different situations (Perloff, 1993; Wiseman & Schenck-Hamlin, 1981). Situations differ with respect to intimacy level between parties, relationship status (equal vs. superior–subordinate), and degree of resistance encountered (Perloff, 1993). A later section of this chapter illustrates the claim that many of these strategies-including nonrational strategies-can be found in exchanges between Supreme Court justices.

Individual differences are also reflected in the process of compliance gaining. In general, women employ polite or negotiable compliance-gaining tactics more often than do men (Baxter, 1984; Fitzpatrick & Winke, 1979). Some people rely on manipulation and deceit; others avoid such tactics. *Machiavellianism* as a measurable interpersonal orientation was a concept developed by social psychologists Richard Christie and Florence L. Gels (1970) to reflect the ideology of a person who has a zest for manipulating others and will use any tactic to gain their compliance.

In recent years research on compliance-gaining has reflected the influence of social cognition theory; for example, Berger (1985) defined compliance-gaining strategies as "cognitive schemata that are abstract and provide general guidelines for action" (quoted by Perloff, 1993, p. 275).

NORMATIVE VERSUS INFORMATIONAL INFLUENCE

Social psychologists Morton Deutsch and Harold Gerard (1955) made a distinction between two types of influence that can operate in decision-making groups, a distinction certainly applicable to any appellate court's deliberations. *Informational influence* is reflected by the behavior of a group member who uses facts, logic, and data to try to persuade; *normative influence* is demonstrated when a group member appeals to someone in the minority to conform because implicitly, the majority must be right because it *is* the majority. Emotional appeals that disparage the minority are also considered examples of normative influence. The courts assume that informational influence predominates, but the following shows examples of justices attempting normative influence to persuade other justices.

JUSTICES' ATTEMPTS TO INFLUENCE OTHER JUSTICES

Despite the three decades of conceptualizing and researching compliance-gaining strategics, we still know little about how frequency the different tactics are used, because "the overwhelming majority of compliance-gaining studies do not measure actual behavior, but, rather, a choice of a particular message strategy (Boster & Stiff, 1984; Dillard & Burgeon, 1985). We do not know if an individual would actually translate his or her choice into action" (Perloff, 1993, p. 275). Access to the files of several justices has, however, permitted scholars to find examples in the correspondence that reflect various tactics.

Furthermore, it is impressive that the treatises by political scientists on influence attempts within the Court refer to these compliance-gaining strategies, though not by that term. For example, Waiter Murphy's 1964 groundbreaking book *Elements of Judicial Strategy* spends a chapter on such procedures. Murphy wrote:

> A justice has considerable opportunity to try to exercise influence over his colleagues. He could attempt: to appeal to their interests—to convince them that their interests would gain from furthering his interests or that their interests would suffer injury if they opposed his; to . . . appeal to their personal and professional

esteem for him; and to appeal to their concepts of duty and moral obligation. (pp. 39–40).

Muryhy went on to describe the range of procedures a judge might use, even including the Machiavellian ones:

First, he might try by force of . . . intellect and will to convince his colleagues not only that what he wanted was in the best interests of themselves, the Court, the country, humanity, or whatever goals they might wish to foster, but also that it was morally incumbent upon them to act in the manner that he was proposing. Second, a justice might plan to endear himself to the other justices that they would be reluctant to vote against him in matters he considered to be vital. Conversely, he might try to capitalize on fear rather than affection and try to bludgeon his colleagues into agreement by threatening them with the sanctions available to him. Fourth, he might conclude that the only viable way to come near achieving his goal would be to negotiate: to compromise with those who were less intensely opposed to his policies. (1964, p. 40)

BARGAINING AND NEGOTIATION

Influence attempts are commonplace during the period between case conference and announcement of a decision. The act of attempting to win over another and the other's reaction to this attempt serve as a unit, so extended examples of the process are deferred until Chapter 5, which deals with responses by the judges. Bargaining, however, is so common that an example is provided here.

In a 1941 case involving an injunction against picketing by milk delivery drivers, Justice Frankfurter sought the support of Justice Frank Murphy; he wrote to Murphy:

1. You know how eager I have been—and am—to have our Milk opinion reflect your specifically qualified expert views. You also know how anxious I am to add not one extra word, and especially not to say anything that is absolutely avoidable by way of creating a heated atmosphere. So here is my effort to translate the various suggestions into terms that would fit into, and truly strengthen our opinion.
2. *Of course* I am open to any further suggestion.
3. I am sending this to you, and not circulating it to others. (quoted by Murphy, 1964, p. 59)

Notice that in this brief message, Justice Frankfurter displays ingratiation, flattery, and deceit. He notes Justice Murphy's "expert views" and points out that Murphy is the only recipient of this memo. He further indicates he is open to Justice Murphy's suggestions for revision. To place this influence attempt in context, Justice Frankfurter had little respect for Justice Murphy. Frankfurter, a former Harvard Law School professor, valued legal craftsmanship; Murphy was an ex-politician (a former governor of Michigan) who had been appointed by President Roosevelt to the Court's so-called Catholic seat. Murphy had neither the critical legal skills nor the writing ability that Frankfurter considered essential for a justice.

JUSTICE DOUGLAS AND *ROE V. WADE*

Is blackmail of another judge beyond the pale for appellate judges? Apparently not. When the conference on the case of *Roe v. Wade* was completed in late December of 1971, Chief Justice Burger asked Justice Blackmun to write the opinion, even though the chief justice was not then a part of the majority. In a strongly worded but brief memorandum, Justice Douglas protested this assignment, saying that because the chief justice had represented the minority view, he should have asked him—as the Senior Associate Justice in the majority—to assign the opinion. Douglas threatened to publish a dissent noting that Burger's decision was "an action no Chief Justice in my time would ever have taken. For the tradition is a longstanding one that the senior Justice in the majority makes the assignment. . . . When, however, the minority seeks to control the assignment, there is a destructive force at work in the Court. When a Chief Justice tries to bend the Court to his will by manipulating assignments, the integrity of the institution is imperiled" (quoted by Schwartz, 1996, p. 46)

Justice Burger was not persuaded; he replied that "there were, literally, not enough columns to mark up an accurate reflection of the voting" in his docket book, and therefore he had marked down no vote (quoted by O'Brien, 1993, p. 30). He told Douglas that this was a case that would stand or fall on the writing, apparently meaning that the issues were so complex or fundamental or emotional that a majority opinion would not be decided until after a further exchange of drafts.

The assignment of the case remains shrouded in some mystery. It is possible that the chief justice did not see this as an assignment to write an opinion, but as merely a memorandum dealing with the multitude of issues. At any rate, Justice Blackmun found it no small task. It was only his second year on the Court, he was already known for being notoriously slow in preparing drafts, and this was his first major case and hence his biggest challenge. He did not circulate a first draft until May 18, 1972, almost five months later. Although his draft supported striking down the Texas antiabortion law—and Douglas was pleased with that—the senior justice was quite unhappy with the rationale, for it said nothing about a woman's constitutional right to privacy, which Douglas, along with Justice Brennan, pointed out was the *basis* of the majority's view at the December conference.

Meanwhile, another problem for Douglas had surfaced. When the oral arguments were held the Previous December, two new appointees to the Supreme Court. Powell and Rehnquist, had not yet been confirmed by the Senate, and hence they did not vote. But now they were on the Court, and there a was movement to delay the decision and rehear the oral arguments next term, before a full Court. Justice Douglas saw his majority slipping away. He sent Chief Justice Burger another inflammatory message, threatening to publicize the way that Burger had handled the matter and to document "the tragedy it entails" (quoted by O'Brien, 1993, p. 31). He would make public the secret inner workings of the Court and embarrass the chief justice, whose public image was of great importance. He sent to Justice Brennan a draft of his dissent, which said:

> The plea that the cases be reargued is merely a strategy by a minority somehow to suppress the majority view with the hope that exigencies of time will change the result. That might be achieved, of course, by death or conceivably retirement. But that kind of strategy dilutes the integrity of the Court and makes the decisions here depend on the manipulative skills of a Chief Justice. (quoted by Simon, 1995, p. 103)

The threat did not materialize; cooler heads prevailed. Justice Brennan realized that the Douglas dissent, in that form, could do grievous damage to the Court. He urged Douglas to remove all references to the chief justice's motivations. Douglas—when time came to decide whether to hold arguments anew the next term—noted his dissent from the majority but did not express what he had shared with the other justices in private. However, he insisted that Blackmun personally assure him that he would not change his position after the reargument. The decision to delay might in actuality have been consistent with Douglas's goals it gave Blackmun a summer to research the complex issues in the case, and after the second round of oral arguments in October 1972, Blackmun produced a draft opinion in keeping with the rationale advanced by Douglas and Brennan at the initial conference. That rationale persisted in the final opinion that Blackmun read from the bench on January 22, 1973.

Did Douglas's threat succeed? Court observer James Simon believes it did. He wrote:

> As it turned out. Justice Douglas was the biggest winner of all. His prolonged tantrum had produced a firm commitment from Justice Blackmun to hold to his original position of voting to strike down the Texas and Georgia statutes. And seven members of the Court eventually endorsed a woman's fundamental right to privacy that was broad enough to cover her decision to have an abortion in the early stages of her pregnancy—a position Douglas had taken in his original draft in December 1971. (Simon, 1995, p. 104)

CONCLUSIONS

The attempts to influence judges are muitifaceted; they are both blatant and subtle. One purpose of this chapter is to illustrate and evaluate some of the sources of influence, including the interest groups that lobby their viewpoints, the ideology of the president who appointed the judge, and the procedures that the courts use to identify issues for consideration. The social sciences, especially communication studies and psychology, have useful theoretical concepts for understanding various types of influence attempts.

The role of the chief justice is a central one in the influence process; therefore, the next chapter is devoted to the impact of the Court's leader upon judicial decision making.

4

The Role of the Chief Justice

In more than 200 years, fewer than 20 persons have held the title Chief Justice of the United States. It has become commonplace to identify the Court at different times by the name of its chief justice (e.g., "the Warren Court," "the Rehnquist Court") implying that the chief justice exceeds his brethren in power as well as in prestige—but does the chief really have a heightened ability to persuade the other justices? This chapter examines the influence of the chief justice on the other judges.

WHAT MAKES A "GREAT" CHIEF JUSTICE?

Legal scholars consider 3 of our 16 chief justices as deserving of the label "great"—John Marshall, Charles Evans Hughes, and Earl Warren. When President Eisenhower appointed Warren chief justice in the fall of 1953, few expected Warren to become one of the most influential ever to hold this position. He was not even the president's first choice John Foster Dulles and Thomas E. Dewey, among others, received earlier consideration). It is true that Warren possessed a distinguished career in public service, first as district attorney, then as attorney general, and later governor, of California. He ran for vice president of the United States (unsuccessfully) on a ticket with Thomas E.

Dewey in 1948. But Warren was not considered an intellect; he had never authored any law review articles or significant policy analyses. Furthermore, he had not engaged in legal practice, or even been in a courtroom, in many years. When John Gunther, a prominent journalist, published his widely read 1947 chronicle of political life, *Inside U.S.A.*, he said of then-governor Warren: "He will never set the world on fire or even make it smoke; he has the limitations of all Americans of his type with little intellectual background, little genuine depth or coherent political philosophy; a man who probably never bothered with abstract thought twice in his life" (1947, p. 18). Warren came to the Court "with no judicial experience, limited exposure to the world of ideas, no easily characterizable social attributes and no evidence of literary talent" (White, 1976, p. 337). Even his biographer saw him mainly as a healer of quarrels, a competent but colorless manager thrown among prima donnas such as Felix Frankfurter and William O. Douglas, who dominated the Supreme Court at that time (Steamer, 1986, p. 49).

As mentioned in Chapter 3, the president who appointed him later (much later—after his presidency ended) told associates that the appointment was the "biggest damned fool mistake" he had ever made as president, because he had expected Warren to be a moderate Republican like himself who would not rock the boat. Yet for some observers, the appointment was the most important act of Eisenhower's presidency. Earl Warren was a "great" chief justice because he shaped Supreme Court decisions that continue to influence American life today. In doing so, he created a unified court and capitalized on the strengths of each justice. Yet Warren could not have done what he did if other justices on that Court (first, William O. Douglas and later William Brennan) had not provided a combination of intellectual content and liberal conviction to endorse Warren's emerging values.

Before Warren's appointment, the Court was split on the issue of school desegregation. Fred Vinson, the chief justice who died suddenly and was replaced by Warren, had polled the justices and found the three Southerners to have strong reservations. A fourth justice, Felix Frankfurter, had expressed concerns about the activist nature of any such decision, writing: "However passionately any of us may believe that such a policy of segregation . . . [is] both unjust and short-sighted, he travels outside his judicial authority if for this private reason alone he declares unconstitutional the policy of segregation" (quoted by Cray, 1997, p. 282). Despite his intellectual limitations, Warren had a sense of himself, an ability to communicate his authority that generated loyalty and respect from his colleagues. Within two years he brought this contentious group of justices to a position of unanimous agreement on one of the most momentous decisions in Supreme Court history. In this chapter, we seek to understand the combination of internal and external factors that permits a chief justice to excel.

We can generate a kind of checklist against which to evaluate the leadership success of the various chief justices. Seven qualities stand out. We now examine each in detail.

Willingness and Ability to Work Hard

The ability to work hard includes being ready for the conferences that discuss the *cert.* petitions and briefs accepted for oral argument, as well as writing at least share of the majority opinions. Chief Justice Charles Evans Hughes came to the *cert.* conferences fully prepared, having read all the petitions and weeded out those he considered without merit. He allowed only 3½ minutes of discussion on each petition. His "blacklist" of meritless petitions was rarely questioned. In contrast, when Harlan Fiske Stone was chief justice, he encouraged extensive discussion of the *cert.* petitions, and his own analysis of them was offered in a most diffident manner (White, 1978). As a result, the Stone-led conferences went on relentlessly, often extending into the weekend.

Intellectual Capability

Experts look to a leader to provide a perspective, a "vision." In the case of the chief justice, this includes putting a stamp on his opinions, or persuading the other justices to adopt some ground-breaking principles. Effectiveness as chief justice means displaying a coherent jurisprudence that gives the lower courts reliable guidance. Chief Justice Warren is an excellent example. Despite the disclaimers about his intellect, Warren had a consistent judicial philosophy that he implemented in a program of decisions with long-reaching effects on the criminal justice system and on social policy in general. Similarly, though not the first chief justice, John Marshall (he was fourth, serving from 1801 to 1835) established the Court's role as a result of his vision that the provincialism of state legislatures required the discipline of federal laws if the American republic was to survive (Smith, 1996). Chief Justice Marshall's perspective led to the establishment of guidelines for the challenging task of allocating power between the federal government and the states.

Sensible Assignment of Opinions

We are aware that the chief justice has great discretion in the assignment of opinion writing. Playing favorites or attempting to sabotage the process are to be avoided. Chief Justice Warren once stated that "if assigning opinions wasn't done with regard to fairness, it could well lead to great disruption in the Court.

During all the years I was there . . . I did try to see that we had an equal work load . . . Everybody, regardless of the length of time they were on the Court, had a fair opportunity to write important cases" (quoted by Rohde & Spaeth, 1976, p. 173). (However, an analysis by Ulmer, 1970, indicated that Frankfurter was consistently slighted by Warren, perhaps because of his argumentative nature.)

It is said that Chief Justice William Howard Taft, in making his assignments, relied heavily on three factors: his estimate of the judge's ability, his concern for the judge's views, and his knowledge of the judge's temperament and state of health (Steamer, 1986). When one of the other justices was ill, Taft would lighten his load and take on the extra writing assignments himself.

Some chief justices, including Fuller, Taft, Hughes, and Warren, would assign the dullest and most boring cases to themselves (Menez, 1984). Also, assignments were often made on the basis of expertise. Taft assigned to Justice Brandeis the tax and rate litigation cases, to Justice Van Devanter land claims and Indian litigation, and to Justice Sutherland cases involving boundary lines, water rights, and irrigation projects. Patent cases were especially burdensome because they were so technical and complicated, and justices sought to avoid them (Mason, 1965). Tax cases have apparently replaced patent cases as the current "dogs" of the Court; Baum (1997, p. 114) noted Justice Souter's joke that he willingly responded to Chief Justice Rehnquist's request to sing carols at the Court's Christmas party because "I have to. Otherwise, I get all the tax cases."

Running an Organized Ship

One of the major goals of the Court is disposing of cases. This can be done efficiently, or in a too-casual or leisurely manner. Chief Justice Edward Douglass White had an easygoing nature that allowed for prolonged debate; this elevated tension between the justices as well as delayed case disposition. Noted above was the opposite extreme: Chief Justice Charles Evans Hughes, whose skill as a presiding officer of the Court has never been equaled, allowed just minutes for discussion. Paul Freund wrote of Hughes:

> His Jovian figure seemed to occupy the central seat by natural right. His powers of concentration were total; he transfixed counsel with a piercing stare, at intervals betraying his purpose to intervene by a quickening movement of the eyelids. When he did intervene, he showed a remarkable capacity to bring an argument into focus, to go for the jugular. Not infrequently he rescued counsel as they suffered repetitive assaults from vantage points along the bench. (1967, p. 13)

Sensitivity to Others

Designated leaders are expected not only to be task leaders but to be concerned about the welfare of other members of the group and about the maintenance of a continued positive group atmosphere. When Earl Warren was suddenly named a chief justice, he realized that he lacked appellate experience, whereas the other justices were veterans at it. He therefore asked Associate Justice Hugo Black to chair the judicial conferences until he learned the procedures. Warren also recognized that Justice Frankfurter was an inveterate law professor and thus was willing to let Frankfurter treat him as a promising but untutored student who needed to be brought up to speed (Howard, 1997).

Development and Maintenance of a Collegial Atmosphere

Before they begin a day of oral arguments or a judicial conference, the nine justices on the Supreme Court shake hands with each other, a tradition begun by Chief Justice Melville Fuller in the late 1800s. This act recognizes the ties between them despite whatever ideological conflicts may be present. But chief justices differ in the degree to which they implement this appearance of collegiality; an example of Chief Justice Burger's impetuous procedures will be described to illustrate one type of obstacle to the maintenance of collegiality.

Spirit of Conciliation

In seeking to maintain an atmosphere of good will between participants, the chief justice must often take the lead in reducing tensions—that is, he must go more than halfway—when conflict emerges. After Morrison Waite became chief justice in 1877, his assignment of an opinion writer in one of the first major cases drew the ire of another justice, who had expected to be given the task. Chief Justice Waite answered in a conciliatory manner, leading the upset justice, Stephen Field, to retract some of his original harsh language, though Field still held that the assignment should have been given to him. At that point, Waite responded:

> No one appreciates your vigorous style more than I do, and, but for these considerations [that the opinion should be written by a justice who was not so close to one of the parties involved in the case], I should have been glad to have had its use in the case—And while I regret that you do not look on the matter as I do, I cannot but think that my judgment was for the best interest of us all. . . . I certainly intend to treat all my brethren fairly in this most delicate and at the same time important part of my work. If I do not, it is the fault of the head and not the heart. I am glad to know that I misunderstood some of the expressions in your former note, and that I may hope to retain your friendship and respect if my conduct shall be such as to merit it. (quoted by Steamer, 1986, p. 131)

POWER TO PERSUADE

The position of chief justice carries enormous prestige; former Justice Fortas is only one of many advocates of this view: "This prestige not only affects the public, the bar, and the bench generally, but it also makes it possible for the Chief Justice to influence the output of the Court, to a much greater degree than colleagues of equal or superior personal and professional calibre" (1975, p. 405). Steamer (1986) notes that "it has been almost routinely accepted among the scholarly fraternity of Court watchers to refer to the chief justice as *primus inter pares*, or first among equals" (p. 10), but then he asks: Is this really so? True, the chief justice has duties beyond the administration of the Court, and true, he speaks first (and usually longest) at the judicial conference, and he also assigns the writing of opinions for cases for which he is in the majority. (In the latter role he can certainly reward his cooperative colleagues and punish miscreants by his assignment choices), but does this grant him any greater power to persuade?

I believe the short answer is no, and that chief justices can be distinguished on the basis of success in overcoming their limited power over their colleagues. Chief Justices Marshall, Hughes, and Warren were all able to persuade, leading to Court decisions of immeasurable importance. Some of the other chief justices saw decisions made *despite* their efforts to lead. Before expanding on this claim and providing further examples of the effectiveness of various chief justices, it is desirable to consider the psychological approach to leadership, because it provides a useful theoretical framework for considering why some chief justices are effective despite their limited power.

LEADERSHIP THEORIES

What makes one person a successful leader, while another person fails in the same position? Early efforts in the scientific study of leadership sought to discover traits that were present in all leaders to a greater degree than in those who did not become leaders. This approach was of limited value in understanding what made a particular chief justice "great". First, every chief justice was designated a "leader" by his appointment to that office. Second, this approach did not produce much in the way of consistent findings; only a few traits steadfastly surfaced. Just four—intelligence, initiative, extroversion, and a sense of humor—appeared often enough to be labeled "general traits of leadership" (Bird, 1940, p. 380).

Still, it is illuminating to compare these traits with those shared by the most eminent chief justices. Although the three designated "great" chief justices lived at different times and came from different backgrounds, they did have traits in common. Steamer (1986) evaluated the traits shared by Chief Justices Marshall, Hughes, and Warren as follows:

> All had a commanding physical appearance; all had robust health and all were capable of hard work, Hughes by nature, Warren and Marshall by necessity, the

latter only in spurts. All were exemplary patriots with a deep respect for the American system and a mission to preserve it. They were basically conservative in outlook, but all were wilting to stretch judging—in different degrees—to accommodate their own convictions, a not uncommon trait in American appellate judges generally. All had a certain natural dignity. Marshall and Warren liked most people and were liked in return, but each had a reserve which only the intimate might penetrate. Hughes' reserve was closer to the surface, very much so in fact, and he was generally characterized as personally aloof, a human icicle, but many of those close to him found him charming and warm and not at all like the public image he projected.

All were strong self-disciplinarians, Hughes sternly so, Marshall and Warren less rigid than Hughes but concerned with regulating their lives in order to accomplish the tasks at hand. All had an ability to see the irony and fate in life; they were serious men who did not take themselves seriously, men who were never impressed with any self-importance, a trait that enabled them to discern the superficial and shallow among them. John Randolph wrote that John Marshall was the "most unpretending and unassuming of men" and the same can be said of Earl Warren and Charles Evans Hughes. Perhaps more important, all were straightforward, moral men, personally, professionally and publicly incorruptible. Justice Story said of Marshall that he could never be in "intriguer," and again the same may be said of Hughes and Warren. None of them was a scheming, petty politician; none was an aggressive office seeker. Although there is a difference in degree from the reluctant participation of Marshall in public affairs to the seeking of the presidency by both Hughes and Warren, neither of the latter was an enthusiastic political self-starter but was borne on the winds of circumstance in pursuing elective office. (Steamer, 1986, pp. 37–38)

There are several likely explanations for the small number of demonstrable "leadership traits." Situational factors can override personality factors in influencing how effective a leader is; by situational factors we mean resources available to the group, difficulty of the task, nature of the working relationship between group members, and the like. We explore the issue first by looking at psychological approaches that take into account the quality of the environment in which the leader operates, and second by applying the concept of person–situation interaction to different chief justices.

LEADERSHIP FUNCTIONS

Leadership is composed of a mixture of functions, and refinements in the definition of leadership reflect this awareness. In the 1950s studies began centering on the functions of a leader; influential work was done by R. F. Bales at Harvard University and by John Hemphill, Ralph Stogdill, Carroll Shartle, and others at Ohio State University. The result of these efforts was a new focus upon influence as the main aspect of leadership. For example, Stogdill defined leadership as "the process (act) of influencing the activities of an organized group in its efforts toward goal setting and goal achievement" (1950, p. 3). An emphasis on goal-oriented leadership functions led to various analyses of the

group's tasks and the leader's tasks. Lists of the dimensions of a leader's behavior were generated, sometimes seven dimensions, sometimes nine or another number. A factor analysis of leaders' actions, however, eventually led to
a conclusion that two qualities accounted for most of the variance between
successful and unsuccessful leaders (Halpin & Winer, 1952). The first quality
was labeled *consideration*, which means the extent to which a leader shows
behavior that is "indicative of friendship, mutual trust, respect, and warmth"
in interactions with the other group members (Halpin, 1966, p. 86). Genuine
consideration by a leader reflects an awareness of the needs of each group
member. In Halpin and Winer's 1952 analysis, consideration accounted for
almost half of the variance in leaders' behaviors.

The second quality was called *initiating structure*, later defined as "the
leader's behavior in delineating the relationship between himself and members of the work group, and in endeavoring to establish well-defined patterns
of organization, channels of communication, and methods of procedure"
(Halpin, 1966, p. 86). Thus, initiating structure refers to the leader's task of
getting the group moving toward its designated goal. This quality accounted
for almost a third of the variance in leaders' behaviors.

The focus on leadership functions produced other, similar divisions into
two primary dimensions. Bales (1953) concluded that leadership functions may
be differentiated into *task orientation* (achievement of the group's goals) and
group-maintenance (or *relationship*) orientation, in which a leader is concerned
with maintaining the group's morale and cohesiveness. Independent confir-
mations by Bales (1958) and others (Fleishman, Harris, & Burtt, 1955) allow
one to conclude that initiating structure and consideration are two major dimensions of leadership behavior, not mutually exclusive leadership styles (Gibb,
1969).

Can a leader to be skilled in both dimensions? Yes, but some leaders
cannot fulfill both functions simultaneously, pressures from the job situation
may preclude it. The work load of a chief justice is tremendous. The Chief is
not, incidentally, Chief Justice of the Supreme Court, but Chief Justice of the
United States. In addition to presiding over the Court, a chief's duties include
chairing the Judicial Conference of the United States, the governing body for
the federal judicial system that includes all federal judges; chairing the board
of the Federal Judicial Center, a research and training agency with four meetings annually; supervising the administrative office of the U.S. courts; and
serving as a member of the boards for trustees of the National Gallery of Art,
the Hirschhorn Museum and Sculpture Garden, and the Smithsonian Institution.

The memoirs of Chief Justice Warren describe his schedule and workload:

> We accepted practically no invitations to private homes because that called for
> reciprocation, and that would crowd our evenings and so could not be accommo-

dated to my work. I worked almost every night to some extent, even on nights when we attended a White House or embassy dinner. Even at that pace, I never felt that I was abreast of my reading. I am not a fast reader of important materials, and the amount of such reading at the Court is colossal. When I first came to Washington, I wondered how I would ever get through it. At that time the Court met at noon, recessed for lunch for thirty minutes at 2:00 p.m. and then sat until 4:30. This was the procedure Monday through Friday while hearing the cases argued. Then on Saturday morning at ten o'clock, we would convene in conference and, with the exception of thirty minutes for lunch, would continue until our work was completed—until five, six, or even seven o'clock. (Warren, 1977, p. 345)

Although Justice Warren was able to simultaneously accomplish the goals of initiating structure and of consideration, his personal life and family time were sacrificed to do so. In his memoirs, Warren also described his schedule as "backbreaking"; his mornings were consumed with administrative tasks, including the management and board activities listed above. He took briefs and memoranda to his home every evening, usually reading them until midnight. He awakened early and read for another 90 minutes before departing for the Court. In his 16 years as chief justice, he missed only one day at work because of illness.

If a chief justice is only able to achieve one function, initiating structure, another justice may emerge as the relationship-oriented leader, sometimes called the *socio-emotional* leader. This might be the best-liked judge; it is usually someone who seeks to avoid conflict on the court (Danelski, 1979). On rare occasions it is the chief justice who becomes the socio-emotional leader and another judge who takes on the role of task leader. Danelski's analysis of the Supreme Court leads him to conclude that this was the case during William Howard Taft's chief judgeship:

Taft was the social leader and his good friend and appointee, Van Devanter, was task leader. Evidence of Van Devanter's esteem and task leadership is abundant. Taft, time and time again, asserted that Van Devanter was the most able justice on the court. . . . At times, Van Devanter's ability actually embarrassed Taft, and the Chief Justice wondered if it might not be better to have Van Devanter run the conference himself. (1979, p. 510)

Some leaders have difficulty achieving both goals because they find achievement and consideration to be in competition. A task-oriented leader must often be critical of the ideas or activities of other group members; constantly turning their attention toward the goal whenever they digress into some diversionary activity or discussion. Leaders often report that it is difficult to be task-oriented and considerate at the same time, hence the phenomenon of another member's becoming the socio-emotional leader, concerned with arbitrating disputes, relieving tension, and giving each member a chance to be heard or a pat on the back. Yet sometimes an action may facilitate both functions; a leader who helps the group solve a difficult problem may in so doing develop solidarity and better group morale (Cartwright & Zander, 1960, p. 496).

APPLICATIONS TO THE CHIEF JUSTICE

Chief justices can be contrasted with respect to their degree of success on the two functions. Consider the difference between Hughes and Stone in their approach to processing *certiorari* petitions: Charles Evans Hughes came to the conference fully prepared. He barely tolerated debate and discouraged efforts by the other justices to have more time to study the matter (White, 1978). In contrast, Harlan Fiske Stone presented his ideas in a casual manner and encouraged full discussion and debate; he "allowed himself to be freely interrupted, and invariably granted extensions [of time]" (White, pp. 226–227).

Chief justices can demonstrate their skill in initiating structure and their concern for consideration in numerous ways. With regard to initiating structure, one indication—as shown in the above contrast between Hughes and Stone—is the ability to move the justices expeditiously through the agenda of cases. Steamer has noted that although Chief Justices Edward Douglass White and Harlan Fiske Stone were the intellectual equals of other justices, each was incapable of orchestrating a cohesive Court. He wrote:

> Chaos is the only word to describe the Court after Stone succeeded Hughes. The conference became a debating society with tempers out of control and tensions running high as the justices bickered almost endlessly, with honest intellectual differences escalating into personal antagonisms. Rather than concluding the conference in a few hours, Stone permitted it to go on for days. White, a genial, well-liked man, did not [and] could not give the conference firm leadership. Encountering a difficult case, he was known to say: "Here's a baffling case. I don't know what to do with it. God help us!" Clearly such prefatory remarks to the discussion of a case give wide berth to the brethren to debate ad *infinitum* until one of them assumes the leadership role abandoned by the chief. (Steamer, 1986, p. 28)

One possible reason that Stone was ineffective in initiating structure was that, after becoming chief justice, he continued to behave like an associate justice (Danelski, 1979). Not only did he seem to be struggling for a solution when presenting cases, he also participated in the evaluative reactions of the other associate justices during discussion; he would say, "Jackson, that's damned nonsense" or "Douglas, *you* know better than that" (Danelski, 1978, p. 512). Eventually, it fell upon Associate Justice Hugo Black to provide task structure during the period of Stone's chief judgeship.

Another possible indication of success in initiating structure is the degree to which the other justices concur with the chief justice's view of a case. According to this conception, the more frequently the chief justice is in the minority, the less effective he is. If dissents indicate an inability to lead, once again Chief Justice Stone has the worst record, having disagreed with the majority in almost half the cases. John Marshall was the opposite, with only six dissents in his 34-year term. (Marshall authored more than half of the thousand opinions written during his time on the Court.) As chief justice, Earl Warren dissented, either with or without a written opinion, about a quarter of the time, but on major cases he was almost always in the majority (Steamer, 1986).

It is dangerous, however, to put too much emphasis on dissent rate as an indicator of ability to initiate structure, because this fails to recognize the situation in which the chief justice operates. Steamer observes:

> The chief is always a prisoner of the times in the sense that some issues are so controversial—affirmative action, abortion, integration of the schools through busing, capital punishment—that the most charismatic leader in the nation could not persuade eight independent colleagues to adopt a single view'. (p. 8)

Increasingly, the Court is divided; during the last 25 years, the Court was unable to produce a majority opinion in more than 100 cases, as compared with only 45 such *plurality opinions* between 1801 and 1956 (Novak, 1980). (A plurality opinion a decision with less than a majority of the justices supporting it.) The split court may have reached the ultimate in complexity at the end of the 1995–96 term, as exemplified by two decisions in June 1996. One struck down as unconstitutional three Texas congressional districts. The vote was recorded as 5 to 4. Justice Sandra Day O'Connor wrote the main opinion, but only two other justices (Rehnquist and Kennedy) joined. Justices Thomas and Scalia voted for the same result but for different reasons, as expressed in a concurring opinion by Thomas.

The second decision, dealing with "indecent programming" on cable television, produced 6 separate opinions and generated 118 pages. The vote may be summarized as follows: Justice Breyer announced the judgment of the Court and delivered the Court's opinion with respect to Part III (in which Stevens, Kennedy, Souter, and Ginsburg joined), an opinion with respect to Parts I, II, and V (in which Stevens, O'Connor, and Souter joined), and an opinion with respect to Parts IV and VI (in which Stevens and Souter joined). Stevens and Souter filed concurring opinions. O'Connor filed an opinion concurring in part and dissenting in part. Kennedy filed an opinion concurring in part, in which Ginsburg joined. Thomas filed an opinion concurring in part and dissenting in part, in which Rehnquist and Scalia joined.

An important aspect of initiating structure is the chief justice's intellectual leadership. Effective as he was in rallying justices to his view, Earl Warren—as noted earlier—was not seen as an intellectual giant. Rather than analyzing the legalistic ramifications of an issue, he simply asked: "What is fair?" Basic principles of justice guided his decisions; he deferred to the intellect of

Justice Black or Justice Frankfurter. A colleague, Justice Potter Stewart, described Warren as deciding cases in favor of "widows or orphans or the underprivileged" (Howard, 1997, p. 33).

Robert Steamer's comprehensive review of chief justices concludes that only two, John Marshall and Charles Evans Hughes, were able to "approximate the ideal in the simultaneous exertion of personal and intellectual leadership" (1986, p. 27). He stated:

> We do not know the precise ways in which John Marshall dealt with his Court, but we do know of his warmth, his magnetism, the respect, affection and esteem in which he was held by his colleagues, and of, course, the brilliant results of his labors. The Hughes record is well documented. At one time or another, virtually all of the brethren paid tribute to Hughes' leadership generally and to his conduct of the conference specifically. Hughes' penchant for order and his photographic memory brought him to each conference almost formidably prepared. After summarizing a case accurately and comprehensively, he would then suggest how the case ought to be decided, and in some instances that was the only discussion the case received as the justices proceeded to vote for the disposition suggested by the chief. When a justice did want to speak, he did so in order of seniority and without interruption, which meant that interchange of views was with the chief and not with the other justices. (1986, pp. 27–28)

The second leadership quality, consideration, can be manifested in many ways. The chief justice, like any leader, has to settle petty disputes and make everyday decisions in a manner that avoids charges of favoritism or arbitrariness. When Justice Reed retired in 1957, Chief Justice Warren was informed that Justice Frankfurter wanted Reed's office. Before acceding to this request, Warren consulted with Justice Black, who was senior to Frankfurter. He then wrote the other justices that he had assigned Reed's office to Frankfurter, adding: "Unless one of you wishes to move into the rooms vacated by Justice Frankfurter, that suite will be assigned to the new justice" (February 8, 1957, memorandum, quoted by Steamer, 1986, p. 21).

Sometimes the "little things" that a chief justice does are the strongest indicators of his degree of consideration. According to one of his law clerks, Warren had an operating principle: "If you want to talk to somebody, don't ask them to come to your office. . . Go to theirs" (quoted by Cray, 1997, p. 283). This policy of relinquishing power and the willingness to meet on the other's "turf" reflected Warren's sensitivity to the needs of others. Also, for several years Warren tried to persuade Congress to appropriate the money for cars and drivers for each of the justices (the chief is the only justice with this "perk"). Warren argued that Frankfurter, at age 70, and Reed, Black, Burton, Minton, and Jackson, in their 60s, should not have to negotiate the traffic congestion of Washington. Although his efforts were not successful, they were appreciated by his colleagues, who recognized the basic concern for their needs.

Similarly, when Justice Douglas was in the hospital in 1947 but insisted on doing his share of work, newly appointed chief justice Fred Vinson tried to accommodate Douglas's workaholic tendencies but still act in his better interests, as noted in this letter:

> Dear Bill:
>
> Received your note relative to No. 715, State of Oklahoma vs. The United States.
>
> I also have your note of the 11th, insisting on some more work. I am saving some cases without assignment, but with the understanding that they will be ready for you if you are ready for them. Actually, old-timer, I hesitate to assign any cases to you for a week or so unless you are dead certain that you can do it without the slightest danger from it. So, hold your horses and get well. That bug innervates, and not a one of the Brethren wants to retard your speedy recovery.
>
> Missed you at Tom Clark's party, and Mildred didn't act like she was having a good time at all.
>
> Harold [Burton] did a good job for you in the rate case. . . .
>
> So, again, hold your horses, and get back in trim. If you are in fit form, we will enter you for the home stretch; otherwise, you will not even get to the paddock.
>
> Affectionately,
> Fred (quoted by Steamer, 1986, p. 20)

FIEDLER'S CONTINGENCY THEORY

The search for basic personality traits of "leaders" having produced little in the way of consistent results, researchers shifted to a functional analysis of leadership toward analyzing behavior, along with documenting the relationship between a leader's effectiveness and the ratings he or she received from supervisors, co-workers, and subordinates. But functional analysis alone was insufficient. Fred E. Fiedler (1967, 1969, 1971) later meaningfully combined the trait approach with functional analysis.

Fiedler defines a leader as the individual who is given the job of directing and coordinating task-relevant activities. His theory is called a *contingency theory of leadership* because it relates the leader's effectiveness to aspects of the environment in which the group operates. The contingency theory predicts that a leader's contribution to group effectiveness is dependent upon both the characteristics of the leader and the favorableness of the situation for the leader. To Fiedler, there is no one successful type of leader; task-oriented leaders may be effective under some circumstances but not others. Relationship-oriented leaders who have been successful in one group may not be successful in another group where the situation differs.

What does Fiedler mean by "the favorableness of the situation for the leader"? He proposes that three qualities are central in determining favorableness: a leader's *personal relations* with the members of the group, a leader's *position power*, and the degree of *structure* in the group task. Each is examined below.

The Leader's Personal Relations with Members of the Group

This first situational determinant refers to the atmosphere within the group and the degree of confidence and attraction the group members have for the leader (Northouse, 1997). Relationships between the leader and the group members can range from very good to very poor; they are partially determined, of course, by the leader's personality, but there may be aspects of the relationship beyond the leader's control. The leader may have been a replacement for someone who was quite popular and well liked by the group; resentment over the replacement may be directed at the new leader: Fiedler finds that the leader-group relationship is the single most important factor in determining the leader's influence in a small group (1964, p. 159). If the atmosphere is positive and members trust and get along with the leader, leader-member relations are defined as good; to some extent, leaders with good relationships can overcome the limitation of being weak in the second component, degree of position power.

Recent chief justices have certainly differed in their relationships with the other justices. Earl Warren was a considerate and diplomatic leader; one of his colleagues noted that he "was never divisive, impatient, short-tempered or abusive. He created an atmosphere of comradeship, even within strongly felt and sometimes sharply stated disagreements" (Fortas, 1975, p. 412). He was so highly esteemed that the label "Super-Chief"—bestowed on him by Justice Douglas—reflected a genuine respect and admiration from his colleagues (Fortas, 1975).

In contrast, Warren Burger had—in Fiedler's framework—poor relationships with the other justices. He replaced the highly regarded Warren, he made some early decisions (such as converting the justices' conference room into his office) that were quite unpopular, and furthermore, some justices viewed him as an intellectual lightweight.

Chief Justice Burger's way of running case conferences and assigning opinions reflected a lack of consideration for his colleagues, and his actions sometimes drew rebuke from the other justices. For example, Justice Thurgood Marshall wrote in April 1972 to his colleagues:

> I am deeply disturbed as a result of the conference on argued cases being held in my absence. I know that this has not occurred during my few years here except where the justice involved was ill and unable to be present and, even then, it was with the consent of the justice involved. I had assumed that this was the usual practice here.
>
> I am not worried so much about this particular conference as I am that it may become a precedent for some future time. Like the late John Harlan, I, for one, am worried about changing some of the time-honored practices of the Court. (quoted by Cooper, 1995, p. 43)

Burger's way of assigning opinions was unique. On several occasions Justice Douglas asserted that the chief justice miscounted conference votes so that he could determine the opinion assignment (Cooper, 1995, p. 43). On one occasion, Douglas—who was the senior justice in the majority at the conference—found that Burger had assigned the opinion on his own, to another justice. Douglas chided the chief justice as follows:

> You apparently misunderstand. *Lloyd* is already assigned to Thurgood and he's at work on an opinion. Whether he will command a majority, no one knows.
>
> You led the conference battle against affirmance and that is your privilege. But it is also the privilege of the majority, absent the Chief justice, to make the assignment. Hence, *Lloyd* was assigned and is assigned.
>
> The tragedy of compromising on this simple procedure is illustrated by last term's *Swann* [decision]. You who were a minority of two kept the opinion for yourself and faithfully wrote the minority opinion which the majority could not accept. Potter wrote the majority view and a majority agreed to it. It was not circulated because we thought you should see it. After much effort your minority opinion was transformed, the majority view prevailed, and the result was unanimous.
>
> But *Swann* illustrated the wasted time and effort and the frayed relations which result when the traditional assignment procedure is not followed.
>
> If the conference wants to authorize you to assign all the opinions, that will be a new procedure. Though opposed to it, I will acquiesce. But unless we make a frank reversal in our policy, any group in the majority should and must make the assignment.
>
> This is a two-edge sword. Byron might well head up five members of the Court, you, Bill Brennan, Potter Stewart and I being the minority; and we might feel strongly about it. But in that event it is for Byron to make the assignment. It is not for us in the minority to try to outwit Byron by saying "I reserve my vote and then recast it to control the assignment." That only leads to a frayed and bitter Court full of needless strains and quarrels.
>
> *Lloyd* stays assigned to Thurgood. (quoted by Cooper, 1995, pp. 44–45)

(Neither Congress nor the Constitution provides for the assignment of opinions. Historically, the chief justice has made the assignment if he is in the majority, and if he is not, the assignment is made by the senior justice in the majority.)

Later we will see other examples of how chief justices differ on the relationship dimension. Not only do we note Fiedler's conclusion that it is the most important of the three factors in determining the leader's influence, but we observe that it is the most variable factor among chief justices. There is little room for variation in the second situational component, position power.

Position Power

How much power and authority does the leader have by virtue of the position he or she holds? Does the leader have the authority to hire and fire? Can the leader reward persons by giving raises in pay or status? Or is the leader limited in regulating the behavior of other members? Leaders with high position power carry some kind of separate rank or status and have "clout," whereas leaders low in position power cannot reward or punish their members by altering rank or status. Fiedler considers position power as the least important of the three components of effectiveness, because group success can often result from a structured task or a popular leader even if the leader lacks authority and power.

How much position power does a chief justice have? With respect to regulating the behavior of the other justices, not much. Steamer has speculated that if an advertisement were to appear in the help wanted section of *The New York Times* with a job description for chief justice, it would include:

> Although the Chief Justice will be responsible for assigning the writing of opinions among eight associate justices, he will have no legal authority to discharge or take minimal disciplinary action against any of the associates for any reason what so ever. If any of them is slothful, senile, abrasive, or downright impossible, the Chief's ability to cope with such an exigency must depend solely on his powers of persuasion. (1986, p. 3)

The chief justice neither hires nor fires. Associate justices have ultimate job security and a salary fixed by Congress. They choose their own law clerks and office staff. Once, when Justice James McReynolds was sent a request from Chief Justice Hughes, he instructed the messenger: "Tell the chief justice that I don't work for him" (quoted by Steamer, 1986, p. 21).

When it comes to making judicial decisions, the chief justice's vote counts no more than any other justice's. About the only discernible example of the leader's position power is the chief justice's prerogative in assigning authorship of opinions when he is in the majority. Although a chief justice can use this power to reward or punish other justices (as we saw in Chapter 3 and earlier in this chapter in the example of Justice Douglas's reactions to a writing assignment) the chief justice can been seen by other justices as abusing even this limited power.

Task Structure

The amount of structure in the task that the group has been assigned to perform is Fiedler's third situational determinant of the leader's effectiveness. Does the leader know how to proceed? Some types of tasks possess a great deal of *goal clarity*; the requirements of the task are clearly known or programmed. In contrast, tasks of ad hoc committees, policy-making bodies, and creative groups often lack goal clarity and structure—no one knows what the group's purposes are, much less how to proceed A second element of task structure is its degree of *solution specificity* (Shaw, 1963); that is, there may or may not be more than one correct solution for the group's task. A third aspect is the degree of *decision verifiability*: Once a decision has been made, how clearly does the group know that it is a correct one? All these aspects of a task's structure play a role in determining the effectiveness of different types of leaders. The contingency theory proposes that completely structured tasks tend to give more control to the leader (Northouse, 1997). However, task structure interacts with position power. If the task is clearly structured, the leader does not need as much position power to get the job done, because everybody's role has already been specified.

How much structure is there to the task of appellate judges? The task requirements are clearly stated and known to the individuals in the group, the path to accomplishing the task has few alternatives, and only a limited number of correct solutions exist. Furthermore, in the case of the Supreme Court, or any appellate court, the group has been in operation for a long time, procedures have been developed to handle the process, and group members are aware of how to proceed. The one aspect that varies from the definition of a highly structured task is verifiability, in that there is no *one* correct solution. *Decision verifiability* can vary from case to case. Sometimes the language of the Constitution is clear; some cases are settled by a 9-to-0 vote, but in cases that result in a 5-to-4 or 6-to-3 vote, it would seem that decision verifiability is lower.

An established way of doing things can, however, work to the leader's detriment. Leaders who try to change firmly established procedures find out how just much position power they have. Shortly after William Rehnquist became chief justice, he let an oral argument extend 15 minutes beyond its allotted time, so that it cut into the justices' lunch hour. Two of the justices walked out while the attorney was still making her oral argument, and the others grumbled about the deviation in procedure. Rehnquist later let his colleagues know that he would never permit intrusions on their lunch hour again (O'Brien, 1993).

For the purposes of simplification and analysis, Fiedler has viewed each of these three aspects as a dichotomy. Leader-member relationships were either good or poor; position power was either strong or weak; and task structure was either clear or unclear. As there are two categories in each of three aspects, this yields, a system of eight classifications (2 × 2 × 2) which would encompassing all possible combinations of these aspects. Fiedler has done this to see which leadership style works best in each situation, although he has added a ninth category to cover instances in which the leader-member relationships are *extremely* poor.

The major hypothesis of Fiedler's contingency model is that the leader's effectiveness is a function of both the leader's style and the three situational components. With regard to style, he distinguishes between *task-oriented* and *relationship-oriented* leaders. Task-oriented leaders get satisfaction and self-esteem from the group's completion of its tasks, even if the leader must suffer poor interpersonal relationships to achieve this. In contrast, for relationship-oriented leaders, satisfaction comes from happy group relationships.

Fiedler hypothesized that the degree to which the conditions are favorable for the leader interacts with leadership style. Favorable conditions emerge from situations that permit the leader to exert a great deal of influence on the group. Fiedler proposed that task-oriented leaders are most effective under conditions that are either very favorable or very unfavorable, that is, in cases in which the leader has a great deal of influence and power or in cases in which the leader has no influence and power. On the other hand, relationship-oriented leaders are most effective under moderately favorable or unfavorable conditions, wherein the leader's influence and power are mixed and moderate as well.

Several meta-analyses have generally supported the validity of Fiedler's contingency theory, and Fiedler has extended it to cognitive factors of leadership and to additional situational factors, such as job stress (Fiedler & Garcia, 1987; Peters, Hartke, & Pohlmann, 1985; Strube & Garcia, 1981). The conditions under which task-oriented versus relationship-oriented leaders were most effective were more apparent in studies of groups created in the laboratory; in real-life groups the relationship was less clear-cut. However, the contingency theory perspective is currently the main one by which to evaluate leadership effectiveness (Chemers, 1997). In a subsequent section we explore the theory's heuristic value for the courts.

APPLICATIONS TO THE SUPREME COURT

How may a contingency theory of leadership be applied to the Supreme Court! With regard to the three situational characteristics, the following conclusions seem warranted: The position power of the chief justice is poor; he has no "clout" to get other justices to behave as he wishes. The group's task structure is mostly clear. There is a long-standing tradition about how to proceed, the agenda for the group is generated by the petitions submitted to the Court, and the outcome is determined by a vote of the group members. As noted earlier, decision verifiability is the only ingredient clouding the clarity of task structure and in fact, the correctness of the Court's decision is the major issue of dispute. Occasionally, a justice will later disclose that he or she erred in an earlier decision. Four years after voting with the 5-to-4 majority in the case of *Bowers v. Hardwick* (1986), Justice Lewis F. Powell announced that he "probably made a mistake" to have done so (Jeffries, 1994, p. 530).

It is mainly the leader-member relations dimension for which variability can exist from one chief justice to another. If we can say that the chief justice's job is one where the leader's position power is weak, the task structure is clear, and the leader-member relations can range from good to poor depending on the chief justice, we find that the Supreme Court reflects Fiedler's combinations of factors that create situations wherein Fiedler finds the task-oriented leader more effective than the relationship-oriented leader.

TASK ORIENTATION

Aren't all chief justices task-oriented? Would a person attain such a prestigious position without demanding productivity and outcomes in his work? Yes, but only to a point. Variations exist in the backgrounds, eminence, and probably even task orientation of the 16 persons who have become chief justice. We mentioned Earl Warren's record as a political office holder; clearly, he was innovative and task-oriented in his behavior. His background seems to contrast with that of Morrison Waite. When Waite was appointed chief justice by President Grant in 1874, he was a national nonentity, unknown outside his home state of Ohio. He had held only three minor elected positions within that state, he had never sat on a court of any kind, and he was mostly content to be a successful Toledo lawyer. When a then-current justice on the Supreme Court, Stephen Field, heard of Waite's's appointment, he wrote: "He is a new man that never would have been thought of for the position by any person except President Grant" (quoted by Steamer, 1986, p. 115). Ironically, only because he was President Grant's seventh choice was he confirmed by the Senate; Grant first offered the job to two of his closest friends and associates, but the Senate opposed them. After four prominent politicians—including three senators and the secretary of state—declined the offer, President Grant in desperation turned to Waite, and the Senate confirmed him with relief (Steamer, 1986).

Morrison Waite served as chief justice from 1874 to 1888. His entry into the job reflects perhaps the nadir in leader-member relations. As Steamer (1986) observes, he came to the Court with three strikes against him: He was appointed by President Grant, known for cronyism and for the mediocrity of his appointments; he had no national reputation; and he joined a Court to which several of the incumbent justices had themselves sought the appointment as chief justice, and they clearly considered themselves superior to the new appointee.

Despite the tough entry, Waite became a good chief justice—not a great one, but a generally effective one. He was not brilliant, nor especially talented, but he worked hard, he assigned opinions fairly and sensibly, and he wrote more than his share of opinions. Even though at least one associate justice, Samuel Miller, never quite accepted being passed over for chief, Waite showed diplomatic skill in achieving a smoothly running court.

What seems to differentiate the chief justices most is relationship orientation. As noted earlier, Warren Burger, when he became chief justice, made a number of decisions about Supreme Court procedure without consulting the other justices: He took over the judicial conference room as his own office, he changed the structure of the courtroom table from rectangular to boomerang-shaped, and he even tried to standardize the justices' chairs. This pattern of unilateral decision making does not imply concern for relationships. In contrast, Chief Justice Taft was more the socio-emotional leader of the Court. He wanted to be liked, and he valued the friendship of each justice with whom he served—even that of Justice James McReynolds, whom he described as a "grouch." Taft wrote to one of his sons, after an altercation with McReynolds, that "the best way to get along with people with whom you have to live always is to restrain your impatience and consider that doubtless you have peculiarities that try other people" (quoted by Danelski, 1979, p. 510).

The Taft court illustrates the conclusion that the chief justice does not have to be the task-oriented leader if he is successful at being the relationship oriented leader and there is someone else to provide structure and task leadership. Even critical justices such as Brandeis were pleased with the conferences: "The judges go home less tired emotionally and less weary physically than in White's day," he reported (quoted by Danelski, 1979, p. 511). And the tasks got done; for the first time in more than 50 years, the court came close to clearing its docket.

CONCLUSIONS

In a speech before the American Bar Association, Chief Justice Rehnquist recalled being told of a Canadian chief justice who, during oral arguments, would tap his pencil on the bench whenever he wanted his fellow judges to stop asking so many questions. Rehnquist wistfully confided, "I have occasionally wished that I had similar authority in our court" (Associated Press, 1996, p. 7A).

The contingency theory of leadership is sensitive to just such complaints by a leader. As applied to the role of chief justice, the theory makes two contributions to understanding his or her effectiveness:

1. Some types of leaders are more effective in certain situations; other types are more effective in other situations. With a clear task structure and limited position power, the leader's relationships with the group members largely determine effectiveness.

2. Leaders who are liked and respected do not need formal position power; they can achieve compliance even under challenging circumstances.

Thus although, to use the terminology of psychological theory, the position power of a chief justice is limited, the chief remains a designated leader with sizable prestige; with the right mix of character and qualifications, the chief can be more persuasive than might be expected from the weak position power of the office.

5

Responses to Influence

This chapter focuses on the time between the judicial conference and the announcement of the Court's opinion. What takes place during this period (which usually lasts several months but can even traverse court terms) is not public, although the willingness of some justices to release their conference dockets, notes, and memoranda has provided a degree of information about what takes place during this interval. At the conference only the participating judges are present, and no public record is made of the vote—if there is a vote. Recall that any decision made about the disposition of the case at the case conference is a tentative one; allegiances can shift, and slippage can develop in what appeared to be a firm majority.

The procedure can be summarized. The judge designated to draft the majority opinion circulates a draft to the other judges on the Court; they respond by: agreeing with the opinion as drafted (signaled by stating "join me to this opinion); indicating what they want to see changed, or indicating their decision to dissent. Revisions continue to be made, circulated, and responded to until a stable majority is achieved. The decision is then announced by the judge who authored the final majority opinion. But this summary disguises the extensive and often tense interactions, occurring mostly in writing but occasionally in the form of lunchtime discussions, hallway conversations, and even exchanges between the clerks of one justice and another.

The one-word description of what happens in this interval is "influence." How does a justice write an opinion that will stabilize a majority to his or her position? How do swing voters respond to the draft, and to the exchange of memos between one side and the other? Do they feel pressures to conform, and if so, do they acquiesce? Do dissenters continue to try to convince the majority, or do they give up? What we do know about this process causes us to relinquish any assumption that it is always free of passion, or that the reasons for an agreement or a dissent are always rational.

Consider the decision-making process in a "real-world" group. We recognize that the individuals in such groups sometimes advocate a position for emotional rather than rational reasons. When forced to choose whether to go along with a colleague's conclusion, some will succumb to conformity pressures and acquiesce for the wrong reasons, or apparently, for no reason at all. Conflict may result over issues that are legitimate and central to the goals of the organization, but often conflict reflects other, more personal concerns, and some conflict is the result of a single group member who is bellicose or individualistic. We recognize also that real-world groups must make compromises; individual preferences cannot always be ratified or accommodated. Solutions to the task facing the group may reflect more of a mutual concession than an achievement of the "ideal" solution.

Is the nine-person working group that is the Supreme Court different from any other nine-person working group? Yes and no. Some groups (for example, juries) are temporary; they don't have either the past or the future together that the Court has. Some groups have an hierarchy of power and leadership, or separate tasks for each group member so that disagreements may defer to individual expertise and hence are more easily resolved, at least on the surface. Few groups face tasks as important as those faced by an appellate court, and most do not possess the capabilities or support staff of the Supreme Court. In certain basic ways, however, the justices on the Supreme Court face the same problems and the same potential conflicts that are faced by any small, working group, and their reactions to the task at hand may reflect irrational or less-than-ideal solutions.

Might a justice's vote in a particular case reflect his or her allegiance to another justice rather than to the merits of the case? Consider the following: The issue was whether a man sentenced to life in prison deserved a new trial. Justice Brennan's vote would have been the fifth vote needed to permit Lyman A. "Slick" Moore a second chance.

Woodward and Armstrong's 1979 book *The Brethren* described the situation:

> One of [Justice] Brennan's clerks thought that if Brennan had seen the facts as (justice) Marshall presented them, he would not have voted the other way. He went to talk to Brennan, and thirty minutes later, returned shaken. Brennan un-

derstood that Marshall's position was correct, but he was not going to switch sides now, the clerk said. This was not just-a-run-of-the-mill case for [Justice] Blackmun. Blackmun had spent a lot of time on it, giving the trial record a close reading. He prided himself on his objectivity. If Brennan switched, Blackmun would be personally offended. That would be unfortunate, because Blackmun had lately seemed more assertive, more independent of the Chief [Burger]. Brennan felt that if he voted against Blackmun now, it might make it more difficult to reach him in the abortion cases or even the obscenity case. (1979, p. 225)

Like any group, the votes and decisions of the Supreme Court can be affected by the personalities of the participants and their attitudes toward each other. Like any group, the Supreme Court has, on occasion, been composed of members who dislike some of their associates.

Phillip J. Cooper's 1995 book *Battles on the Bench* describes some interactions in which justices attributed undesirable qualities to other justices. For example, Justice Frankfurter once wrote to Justice Jackson that Justice Douglas "is the most cynical, immoral character I've ever known" (p. 26), and he dismissed Justice Reed's intellect as "largely vegetable."

In another case Justice Burger had taken two footnotes (virtually verbatim) from a draft by Justice Powell and used them in his own majority opinion. Powell's clerk suggested a rebuke, to which Powell responded: "It's no time to get into a pissing contest with a skunk" (p. 42).

Justice Scalia, in dissents, has described one of Justice O'Connor's opinions as "irrational" and one of Justice Kennedy's as "terminal silliness." Once, as Scalia dominated oral arguments—as is his custom—Justice Powell turned to Justice Marshall and asked: "Do you think he knows that the rest of us are here?" (p. 47).

Certainly a justice can have personality characteristics that impede the smooth resolution of conflicts. Consider what court-watcher Rodney Smolla says about Antonin Scalia:

In the end, his color and candor may at once define Justice Scalia's strengths and limitations. He does not appear to build coalitions easily among his colleagues. With the possible exception of Justice Clarence Thomas, who often does join with him, Scalia has not formed lasting or consistent alliances with others on the Court who might be thought to share his general inclination toward conservatism, such as Chief Justice Rehnquist or Justice Kennedy. His willingness to attack his colleagues in dissenting opinions with bitter derision might, some Court watchers argue, interfere with his ability to work behind the scenes to create solid voting blocs on the Court. (1995, p. 11)

WHAT HAPPENS PSYCHOLOGICALLY?

An objective description has been provided of the decision-making process, but what happens psychologically? It is clear that influence attempts and the reactions to them reflect the operation of basic psychological concepts. What are the goals of the individual judges? How do we characterize the group process? Is their discussion on an intellectual plane, or do power plays surface? Do justices use emotion and bargaining to get other justices to go along, and do recipients of influence attempts change for less-than-desirable reasons? Our analysis, an extension of the approach from Chapter 3, begins by dealing with methods of attempted influence. Later in this chapter, we consider how justices respond to such methods.

MOTIVATIONS FOR ASSIGNING OPINIONS

As noted, the chief justice or the senior associate justice in the majority assigns the task of drafting an opinion. Although a number of reasons may exist for the choice, the potential influence of the draft on the votes of other justices in closely contested cases is certainly a considerable factor. When an initial vote is only 5 to 4, the opinion writer plays a crucial role in maintaining this majority or even strengthening it. Furthermore, the assignment of opinions is one of the few ways that a chief justice exerts position power and a degree of leverage on the other judges (Baum, 1992). Waiter Murphy (1964) has described several possible reasons for the assignment choice.

First, the chief justice might assign an opinion to the most moderate justice in hopes that the resulting mild statement of doctrine will prevent defections or even gain adherents. In the controversial case *McCleskey v. Kemp* (1987), which involved whether it was constitutional to give death sentences more frequently to Blacks than to Whites, Chief Justice Rehnquist asked Lewis Powell to draft the majority opinion rather than asking Justice White, who had verbally attacked the petitioner's reasoning during the oral argument and who wanted to write the opinion himself (Lazarus, 1998). Justice Powell was seen as a centrist and a skilled arbiter who could maintain a majority for the opinion desired by the chief justice. The slender 5-to-4 majority held.

Furthermore, Chief Justice Rehnquist knew that Justice Powell had a well-developed view of the case. When Warren McCleskey's attorneys appealed his death sentence, one of their strongest arguments used a survey of the race of convicted murderers and their victims in Georgia cases. This survey, by Professor David Baldus and his associates, showed that Black murderers were much more likely to be sentenced to death than were White murderers, and that those who killed Whites were much more likely to receive such a penalty than those who killed Blacks. Justice Powell had made his opinion known to his colleagues back at the *cert.* hearing on *McCleskey v. Kemp*. In a memorandum at that point, he urged them not to take the case. One reason he gave was that it was hard to know what to make of the survey's statistics: "Sentencing judges and juries are constitutionally *required* to consider a host of individual-specific circumstances in deciding whether to impose capital punishment. No study can take all of these individual circumstances into account, precisely because they are fact-specific as to each defendant" (quoted by Jeffries, 1994, p. 439, italics in original). But Powell was not sympathetic to statistically based arguments in general, once commenting, "My understanding of statistical analysis . . . ranges from limited to zero" (quoted by Jeffries, p. 439).

A second reason might be to assign the opinion to a wavering justice in hope that this task will strengthen the justice's resolve and perhaps sway the minority. For example, Chief Justice Rehnquist, in an important civil rights case (*Patterson v. McLean Credit Union*, 1989), assigned Justice Kennedy to write the majority opinion, even though the latter had not yet completed one term on the bench. In the opinion of an observer, the chief justice "needed Kennedy's vote to capture the Court for his conservative position and the assignment could help reinforce the junior justice's commitment" (Simon, 1995, p. 67).

Another reason is to use the assignment as a reward. For example, a "chief justice may use the opinion-writing power to reward his coalition within the Court. He can assign the opinions in interesting and important cases to those justices who tend to vote with him, leaving the dregs to those who vote against him on issues that he thinks important" (Murphy, 1964, p. 84).

Murphy observed that a chief justice might even use his opinion assignment authority to encourage an elderly or failing colleague to retire. Chief Justice Fuller did so, withholding opinions from Justice Stephen Field "to help nudge him off the bench" (p. 84), and Chief Justice Taft tried the same tactic with Justice Joseph McKenna.

Since the publication of Murphy's groundbreaking book on judicial strategy more than 30 years ago, research has confirmed his basic assumption that opinion assignment is a form of strategic behavior, in that its goal is the achievement of an outcome consistent with the assigner's policy preferences (Baum, 1997). Summarizing this research, Baum concluded that justices "tend to assign opinions to themselves and their ideological allies in more important cases" (p. 110) and then achieve a kind of balance in assignments by giving the less important cases to the other justices. For example, Chief Justice Warren overassigned civil liberties cases to himself and to the justices with whom he was closest, but he did not do so in economic cases, which were less important to him (Rohde, 1972; Rathjen, 1974, cited by Baum, 1997, p. 111).

Support has been found for Murphy's expectation that opinion writing assignments would be given disproportionately to justices who are either pivotal or marginal (Brenner & Spaeth, 1988; Davis, 1990; Maltzman & Wahlbeck, 1996a; McLauchlan, 1972; reviewed by Baum, 1997, p. 111).

INDIVIDUAL DIFFERENCES

One way to look at the influence process is to examine individual differences between judges. Chapter 4 observed that even among chief justices, effectiveness varied with regard to the ability to influence. David O'Brien concluded that "chief justices vary in their skills, style, and ideological orientations" (1993, p. 240). As we have seen, these differences may manifest themselves with regard to the motivations for assigning draft opinions.

Associate justices also differ, both in their efforts to change the opinions of others and in the skillfulness of these efforts. John Marshall Harlan, a conservative on the liberal Warren Court, was nonetheless influential, because he possessed exceptional skill at crafting law (Baum, 1992). Justice Douglas claimed that he did not try to influence his compatriots, and he decried those who did as "evangelists" and "active proselytizers" (Douglas, 1980), but Chapter 3 described how he even used threats to blackmail the chief justice. He also flattered Harry Blackmun in an effort to solidify Blackmun's commitment to a strong ideological opinion.

As in all endeavors, the personality of the judge affects his or her ability to influence. One person who gets along with colleagues, who is likable and skilled in interpersonal relations (as Chief Justice Rehnquist is) gains influence (Baum, 1992). Laudatory biographies of Justice Brennan attest to his use of social skills to advance his policy goals (Clark, 1995; Eisler, 1993). In contrast, Justice James McReynolds (who served from 1914 to 1941) alienated colleagues with his unpleasantness, especially with his habit of noting on their opinion drafts, "This statement makes me sick" (Pusey, 1951). In this respect, Felix Frankfurter is an especially poignant example (Lash, 1975; Urofsky, 1991). As noted by Baum (1992):

> Frankfurter came to the court in 1939 expecting to play a major leadership role, and he made great efforts to influence his colleagues. He gave special energy to courting new colleagues. But these efforts suffered for his arrogance and his tendency to lecture his colleagues. His messages to other justices during the decision-making process included an abundance of statements like the following: "And so, please, Mr. Jackson, do find time to read, if you have not already read, the chapter on Presumption in J. B. Thayer's Preliminary Treatise." "I would like to ask you to read or reread in cold blood the following cases." He also reacted sarcastically to opinions with which he disagreed. Frankfurter unintentionally alienated several colleagues with his behavior, and his influence within the court was fairly limited. (Baum, 1985, p. 148)

COALITION FORMATION

Being human, justices tend to associate with those similar to themselves. When it comes to deciding ideologically related issues, coalitions are likely to form; that is, certain justices are more likely to try to influence—and to be influenced by—certain other justices. These coalitions may evaporate as new issues surface, or they may take on a formal structure. When Taft was chief justice, he held occasional sessions with the other conservative justices on Sunday afternoons so that they could "present a unified front to the rest of the Court" (Murphy, 1964, p. 79). Chief Justice Warren would meet with Justice Brennan before judicial conferences to discuss important cases and to decide how to handle them (Cooper, 1995; Schwartz, 1983). After Warren's resignation, Brennan served as a rallier of the liberal forces on the Court when their numbers diminished during the 1970s and 1980s; the earlier example illustrated how he sought to bolster the confidence of Justice Blackmun. He was also a beacon to Justice Marshall when the latter despaired over the Court's actions.

WRITING THE DRAFT OPINION

GOALS

The most obvious goal of the judge chosen to draft the opinion is to "get the law right." But other goals may also be present: to be fair, to advance social values, to resolve conflict, or even to set policy (Baum, 1997). Most judges given this task probably seek to write an opinion that will maintain the majority; thus, a certain amount of vote counting is a part of the process. Justice Brennan used an informal communications network of law clerks to ascertain the views of the other justices (O'Brien, 1993).

PROCEDURES

In addition to vote counting, other activities take place, at least inside the head of the writer, as the task proceeds. How much should be included? How broad should the opinion be? Is it better to write an opinion with a limited application in order to gain support of more justices, or to write a more elaborate draft that may generate only a 5-to-4 majority? The opinion writer recognizes that though some alliances within the Court are stable, some may be specific to a particular issue or case. Other justices may assist in keeping an alliance of voters together. In a controversial abortion case in which his side held a slender majority, Justice Brennan wrote to Justice Marshall, urging him to join the opinion and asking for "as much support as possible" (quoted in B. Schwartz, 1996, p. 34).

AN EXAMPLE

Because the process of moving from judicial conference to announcement of the Court's final opinion is not public, an example is useful. Melvin I. Urofsky (1997) has carefully pieced together the process that took place in an affirmative action case, *Johnson v. Transportation Agency, Santa Clara County, California* (1987).

The facts of the case reflect the basic dilemma. Paul Johnson and Diane Joyce both sought the position of East Yard dispatcher with the highway department of Santa Clara County, California. In the spring of 1980, Johnson took the examination for the job and placed second among seven finalists. He had occasionally substituted for the dispatcher, he liked the job, and the supervisor could, under the county rules, choose any of the top seven. Diana Joyce was also eager to be dispatcher. Soon after she began to work as a clerk in the dispatcher's office, she realized that she had the skills for the job, but to qualify for the position, she would have to have experience on a road crew, a job no woman had held. After getting the road department to hire her, she worked on road crews for four years. She took the dispatcher's test at the same time Paul Johnson did. She ranked fourth.

Joyce began to hear rumors that the job had been unofficially awarded to Johnson. She contacted the county's affirmative action supervisor, who intervened, leading to the hiring of Diane Joyce as dispatcher in June 1980. Nine months later, Paul Johnson's attorney filed suit in federal court. At a trial in August 1982, the judge concluded that Santa Clara County's affirmative action procedure did not measure up to criteria established in Title VII and thus was discriminatory. In the spring of 1983, Johnson replaced Joyce and Joyce was reassigned to another dispatcher's position in a different yard.

An appeal by the county led the Ninth Circuit court to reverse the district court's opinion, just about the time that Paul Johnson retired from the job. Two years later, in July 1986, the Supreme Court agreed to review the circuit court's decision during its next term. In November 1986 oral arguments were held, and at the subsequent judicial conference, by a 6-to-3 vote, the justices tentatively decided to uphold the circuit court's reversal of the district court's decision. Voting in the majority to uphold the county's affirmative action plan were Brennan, Marshall, Blackmun, Powell, Stevens, and O'Connor. Voting to reject it were White, Scalia, and Rehnquist. Because the chief justice (Rehnquist) was in the minority, it fell upon the senior associate justice to assign the draft writing; Justice Brennan chose to do the draft himself.

The conference vote took place on November 14, 1986. Soon after, Justice Brennan met with one of his law clerks, Mitt Regan, Jr.; the justice went over his notes from the conference, focusing especially on how the justices in the majority differed in their views. It was Regan's job to do an initial draft, and he paid "special attention to what the clerks in Lewis Powell's office said to him" (Urofsky, 1997, p. 153). After two weeks, he gave a draft to Justice Brennan, who edited and distributed the 18-page document to the other justices on the morning of December 1. By that afternoon he had two responses. Thurgood Marshall wrote, "Dear Bill: Please join me," reflecting that he subscribed to the draft without alteration. The second response was less positive. Justice Brennan had hoped to recruit Byron White even though Justice White had voted in the minority; Justice White had in the past supported some affirmative action plans, and Brennan by emphasizing certain criteria in his draft opinion, had hoped to win White over. Justice White remained unconvinced and wrote Brennan that he wanted to wait and see what the dissent had to say.

The next day Justice Brennan received another assent (from Justice Stevens) plus an indication from Justice Scalia that he was preparing a dissent. Justice O'Connor's response was the most disturbing. Though she had voted in the majority, she was troubled by the contents of the draft opinion; she believed that it "did not address the question of what precise evidence would be necessary to justify an affirmative action plan" (quoted by Urofsky, 1997, p. 155). She wanted that spelled out more specifically. Two days later Justice Powell, another majority vote, wrote that he shared Justice O'Connor's concerns; he suggested a modification in the wording and the addition of a footnote. Brennan still had his majority, but a possibility existed that one justice, at least, would write a concurring opinion rather than fully signing on to Brennan's.

Justice Brennan incorporated Justice Powell's suggested changes into his second draft, circulated on December 9, but this draft, in the view of another majority voter, was even less satisfactory; in fact, Justice Stevens, who had previously joined, was now threatening to distribute a concurrence instead. After the Christmas break, Justice Brennan received a detailed response from Justice O'Connor; it now became clear that Stevens' and O'Connor's interpretations of the basics of the hiring plan were diametrically opposed. O'Connor's draft, in fact, specifically attacked Stevens's view as contradictory to the Court's earlier decisions. So on January 8, 1987, Brennan circulated a third draft, which responded to O'Connor's concerns (Brennan leaned more toward the view of Stevens than of O'Connor).

With that, he lost O'Connor from the majority, but Brennan could sacrifice a vote and still keep the five votes he needed. He saw no way to reconcile the positions of Stevens and O'Connor, but before circulating another draft he wanted to see what Justice Scalia's dissent would say. That did not arrive until February 24. It was a powerful indictment of affirmative action plans, and Brennan realized that his next draft had to acknowledge and refute at least some of Scalia's charges or he would lose his majority. Two days after receiving Scalia's dissent, Brennan circulated his fourth draft of the majority opinion, attempting to answer the most important points raised by Scalia. Only Justice Powell responded to this draft, suggesting that some justifications were too broad. Brennan himself believed in these justifications, but recognized that they went beyond the views of centrist members of the Court, whose votes he needed to keep, so he acquiesced to Powell's suggestions.

Meanwhile, Justice O'Connor was caught in the middle. She was "apparently stung by the bitterness of the Scalia dissent" (Urofsky, 1997, p. 165) but at the same time she disagreed with some of Brennan's rationale. After revising her draft two more times, she announced that she concurred in the result, and Brennan kept a firm majority of five. On March 25, 1987, Justice Brennan announced the Court's decision.

RECIPIENTS' RESPONSES TO A DRAFT OPINION

Typically, in the judicial conference each justice has indicated his or her vote; that is how the initial majority is ascertained. But such votes are not binding, as we have seen. Just how does an appellate justice respond when faced with a draft of the majority opinion? Both political science and psychology offer theoretical constructs and research findings that can be applied in answering this question.

INDIVIDUAL GOALS

Like all humans, judges have a variety of goals in their professional work. As Baum (1997, p. 16) notes, most scholars who study judicial behavior have focused on proximate goals, the ones most directly related to the judge's behavior on the bench, but to varying degrees, judges also seek popularity and respect in the legal community or in the community as a whole, power within the court, and improvement in their financial status. Although responses to influence may reflect the judge's desire to achieve an accurate interpretation of the law or to further the judge's policy goals, responses may also reflect more personal, even self-centered, concerns, such as maintaining good personal relationships with the other judges or limiting one's own work load.

Additionally, the judge's goals may reflect a desire to satisfy a portion of the public. We should remember that every federal judge is a political appointee, and many of these drew the attention of the president or of senators from the judge's home state because of their support of a political party. Even though federal judges do not have to stand for reelection, the political nature of their appointment (and confirmation) means that the goal of being sensitive to the community's needs is not far away from awareness.

Classifications of judges' goals reflect this mixture of personal and professional; for example, Eisenstein and Jacob (1977) described four kinds of goals sought by judges and their associates: rendering justice, maintaining cohesion, disposing of caseload, and reducing uncertainty. This variegated conception of a judge's motives seems to me more in keeping with the reality of human behavior than does the conception of a judge as driven by a single purpose. The emphasis on multiple purposes is a theme of Baum's sensible book, *The Puzzle of Judicial Behavior* (1997). In fact, Baum has offered as a limitation of the attitudinal model its image of justices as single-minded; he noted that proponents of the model in its purest form take the position that "justices act only on their interest in the content of legal policy they seek to achieve good policy rather than good law, and their votes on case outcomes are direct expressions of their preferences rather than deviating from those preferences for strategic reasons" (Baum, 1997, p. 25).

Judges' goals also interact with the nature of the specific case. Some issues draw out strong policy preferences; others do not. A recent decision on a conflict between New Jersey and New York about which "owned" Ellis Island probably did not strongly stir the policy concerns of any of the justices.

BARGAINING

Bargaining can occur at several stages of the decision making process, even at the initial conference devoted to *cert.*, petitions. As soon as the case conference is over, bargaining can be resumed, even before the draft opinions start to circulate; this is especially true when the conference has produced something short of a consensus (Epstein & Knight, 1998). A typical bargaining message is the one that Justice Brennan sent to Justice White in December 1976; part of it follows:

> I've mentioned to you that I favor your approach to this case and want if possible to join your opinion. If you find the following suggestions . . . acceptable, I can, as stated in the enclosed concurrence, join you. I'm not generally circulating the concurrence until you let me have your reaction. (quoted by Epstein and Knight, p. 69)

Bargaining can take different forms: privately contacting the opinion drafter with a bargaining statement as Justice Brennan did, or circulating a separate writing to the panel in hopes of having it incorporated in the final opinion. In an analysis of memoranda issued during the 1983 term of the Supreme Court, Epstein and Knight found that in only 16% of the cases were no memoranda circulated. The average case generated six memos; sometimes the proposed changes ran on for more than 10 pages. Of course, not all these memoranda conveyed an attempt at bargaining. Some reflected an intention of writing a separate opinion or dissent. But the magnitude—one case generated 35 such memoranda—clearly reveals that, as Epstein and Knight put it, "justices respond to one another's opinions" (1988, p. 72) and that "bargaining is a regular feature of the process by which the justices reach their decisions" (p. 74).

Justices are all aware of what is taking place and sometimes even use the *language* of bargaining in their memos, as the following memorandum from Justice Rehnquist to three others illustrates: "I have been negotiating with John Stevens for a considerable time in order to produce a fifth vote for my *Bildisco* opinion. I have agreed to make the following changes in the currently circulating draft, and he has agreed to join if I do" (quoted by Epstein and Knight, 1998, p. 74).

Important cases, as expected, generate more communication; Epstein and Knight concluded that "in more than two-thirds of the most important cases of the 1970s and 1980s, at least one justice attempted to bargain with the opinion writer—with a good deal of the negotiation done through private memos" (1998, p. 73).

The second procedure, the circulation of a separate writing, may also communicate to the opinion drafter that he or she cannot count on support unless changes are made. But Epstein and Knight noted two other possible goals for such separate writings: they may be a way to alert other groups to alternatives to the majority's policy, and they may be leaving a record for future decisions, reflecting a belief that the resolution of the issue is not complete.

CONFORMITY PRESSURE

Social psychologists make distinctions between two processes that occur when a person's response is consistent with the attempt to influence it: compliance and internalization (Kelman, 1958). Compliance is an overt, public acquiescence to achieve some instrumental gain, whereas internalization is an actual acceptance of the values or beliefs espoused in the influence attempt. Applied to decisions made after the assignment of an opinion writer, compliance would be reflected by a justice whose vote goes along with the majority because of some reason other than a deeply held belief, and internalization would be exemplified when a justice becomes internally convinced of the legitimacy of the draft writer's position. For example, Justice Brennan once told Justice Stewart, "I voted the other way at conference but you've convinced me" (quoted by Maltzman & Wahlbeck, 1996b, p. 581). Similarly, Justice Stevens once wrote to Justice Blackmun, "Although I voted the other way at Conference and was asked by Bill Brennan to prepare a dissent, your opinion sent me back to the brief and I am now persuaded that you have the better part of the argument. I therefore expect to join you" (quoted by B. Schwartz, 1996, p. 56). In the discussion on strategic voting later in this section, we will illustrate how compliance applies to individual votes on certain cases.

The Concept of Fluidity

Do conformity pressures exert any influence on the votes of Supreme Court justices? One approach to answering this question is to determine just how often justices change their vote from the conference's tentative vote to the final vote that is published when the opinion is announced. J. Woodford Howard, Jr. (1968), was apparently the first political scientist to advocate the study of vote shifts, or what has come to be called *fluidity*, on the Court. Based on his inspection of the available docket books and other records, he concluded that fluidity was "commonplace," and thus the study of judicial decision making should focus on the *shifts* in decisions rather than assuming that decisions, once made, remain stable. Howard's article can be considered a "call to arms" (Silvia, 1997) to study fluidity, but he did not provide empirical data of any systematic nature. Other political scientists, notably Saul Brenner and colleagues, have since generated convincing empirical support as well as a more refined analysis of fluidity. For example, three kinds of vote shifts were distinguished:

- *Conformity voting,* or voting with the minority at the original conference vote and with the majority at the final vote (this assumes that the outcome of the two votes is the same; i.e., to affirm on both votes or to reverse on both votes).
- *Counter-conformity voting,* defined as voting with the majority at the conference and with the minority at the final vote, when the Court favors the same outcome on both votes.
- *Shifting* when the Court is also shifting; this kind of switching could involve either minority–minority or majority–majority voting (Dorff & Brenner, 1992).

The most basic question is, how often does fluidity occur? An initial answer was, at least half the time. Brenner (1980) first analyzed the docket books of Justice Harold Burton, who served on the Court from 1945 to 1958, and found vote shifts in 61% of the cases. He then looked at the docket books of Justice Tom Clark, who served from 1956 to 1967; fluidity was found here in 55% of the cases. The importance of the case, however, has an effect on the likelihood of vote shifts; in the Burton dockets, fluidity was found in 52% of the major cases but in 6296 of the less important ones. In the Clark dockets, the percentages were 44% for major and 56% for minor cases (Brenner, 1982a).

These figures confirm our hypothesis that the actual votes reflect a person-situation interaction. As Silvia (1997) has observed, justices may feel more accountable when they know a decision will be scrutinized by the media and by legal scholars, so they may pay more attention to the briefs and the oral arguments, making their initial vote harder to dislodge. Furthermore, the salience of the case is probably related to what Silvia (1997) called its "ideological relevance." As noted by Justice Souter's only half-joking response in Chapter 4, few justices are passionate about taking on tax cases or patent controversies, and such cases are hence rarely salient. In contrast, cases involving affirmative action, abortion, or federalism issues are usually ideologically important to both the conservative justices and the liberal ones. Justices are more resistant to social influence in those cases that, for them, are ideologically relevant. Furthermore, it is not the decision itself, but the rationale for it, that is of concern; judges care about the legal rules articulated in opinion drafts and may shift their votes when these are not congruent with their goals. In other cases the judge's initial opinion may be uncertain, leaving the justice more susceptible to a vote shift and to persuasion by colleagues (Maltzman & Wahlbeck, 1996b). In fact, Howard's groundbreaking work on the topic of fluidity suggested uncertainty as a determining factor: "Shifting perspectives appear to have been a function of additional thought and homework, by a clerk or a justice, into issues that were only partially perceived at first because of inadequate argument, briefs, or time" (1968, p. 47). Not surprisingly, when justices describe how they reached viewpoints that were different from their original ones, they use terms like "mature reflection" or "research and labor" (p. 584).

Consistent with an "uncertainty" explanation of fluidity, Maltzman and Wahlbeck (1996), in analyzing shifts from conference votes to final votes during the 1969 to 1985 terms, found that "freshman" justices (defined as those during their first two years on the Court) shifted their votes significantly more often than did their seniors, a finding consistent with the analysis of votes from earlier terms done by Dorff and Brenner (1992).

In summary, Baum (1997) has stated: "Evidence gathered from justices' papers and other primary sources makes it clear that justices often change their positions in the process of moving toward a collective decision. In particular, it is standard practice to modify the language of opinions in an effort to win colleagues" (p. 106).

A recent study by Maltzman and Wahlbeck (1996b), relying on votes in all the cases from 1969 to 1985, emphasizes the situation-specific nature of fluidity. Vote shifts are strongly determined by the sets of opinions and coalitions that emerge during the case conference. Justices "who find themselves closer to the opposing coalition . . . are more likely to switch than those whose ideologies differ significantly" (p. 591).

The Direction of Shifts

Social psychologist Solomon Asch's classic 1958 work on conformity pressures has documented how a lone holdout will often succumb to the majority, even when the holdout's opinion is correct and the majority's is wrong. Research on the direction of shifts in Supreme Court justices' votes reflects the power of the majority to attract the minority, although not all of the effects parallel the findings of social-psychological research. Baum (1997) observed that the justices are "far more likely to abandon positions in the original minority than to leave the majority" (p. 109). During Justice Burton's service, 78% of the strong fluidity votes were moves toward the majority position, and in 86% of these shifts, the majority already had enough votes to win before the justice shifted (Brenner, 1980). In the analysis of Justice Clark's docket, the figures were similar: 84% of the shifts were toward the majority. In an analysis of more than 24,000 pairs of votes from the 1945 Supreme Court term through the 1975 term, Dorff and Brenner (1992, p. 764) found that 2.2% of the justices in the majority switched, while 26.9% of those in the minority did; that is, justices are 12 times more likely to shift from the minority to the majority than to reflect a counter-conformity shift. Analysis of conference and final votes over 15 terms by Maltzman and Wahlbeck (1996b) found that justices who initially voted with the majority switched only 4.6% of the time, whereas justices who initially dissented shifted 18.1% of the time. Dissenters face a tough task if they try to shift the majority to their thinking. The author of the majority opinion has little incentive to be responsive to the suggestions of a dissenter.

What is the explanation for such a pattern? Lawrence Baum suggested: "The most credible explanation is that justices want to be part of the majority (Brenner & Dorff, 1992). In turn, that interest could reflect a variety of motivations, from an interest in shaping the majority opinion to an interest in achieving maximum clarity in the law. It is very difficult to distinguish empirically among these motivations, and we have little sense of their relative importance" (Baum, 1997, p. 109).

One motivation may reflect awareness by justices of a norm against "minimum winning coalitions," or decisions that squeak through with a 5-to-4 vote. Murphy (1964) wrote: "In the judicial process a 5–4 decision emphasizes the strength of the losing side and may encourage resistance and evasion. The greater the majority, the greater the appearance of certainty and the more likely a decision will be accepted and followed in similar cases" (p. 66).

A minimum winning decision fuels the fires of discontent and can damage the Court's image of authority (Silvia, 1997). What Murphy wrote 35 years ago about the *Brown* decision would also apply to cases involving presidential executive privilege and controversial issues: "One hesitates to imagine how much more difficult implementation of the school desegregation decisions would be had there been a four or three or even two judge minority willing to claim in public that 'separate but equal' was a valid constitutional doctrine" (1964, p. 66). Narrow decisions also do not fulfill the Court's purpose of resolving lower court conflicts and establishing precedent; as Brenner, Hagle, and Spaeth (1990) have observed, a 5-to-4 decision "is likely to result in an unstable precedent for the Court, which might be overturned if membership changes or if one of the justices in the majority changes his mind" (p. 309).

In summary, the norm of seeking to achieve unanimity in highly visible

cases is a powerful one. A minimum winning coalition is seen as less definitive by the public and by those who have the task of implementing the decision; as Silvia (1997) put it, "The desire to appear authoritative is not mere
judicial vanity" (p. 9).

Thus we would expect that if the possibility of a 5-to-4 vote creates fluidity among the minority, there should be greater evidence of vote shifts toward
unanimity when the majority is tenuous. Brenner's (1980) analysis of Justice
Burton's records supports this. When all the instances of fluidity were tallied,
little in the way of shifts was found when the initial majority was seven or
eight. But conformity voting was substantially more frequent when the initial
majority was only five or six (Brenner, 1980, Table 3), but only to a point:
When the winning coalition is large enough to appear legitimate and authoritative, conformity voting tapers off.

Regardless of the motivations—and these are specific to the justice and to
the content of the case—the conclusion is that fluidity is not a random, unsys-
tematic phenomenon, but rather is reflective of group processes present in
any decision-making group.

A danger of the foregoing analysis is the impression it conveys that responses to influence within the Court are simply and always *passive* responses.
It must be remembered that policy-oriented justices have their votes available
as bargaining chips; they may side with the majority but want the opinion to
be written a certain way, as we saw earlier in Justice Douglas's position on *Roe
v. Wade*. They may even switch their votes to achieve decisions consistent with
their views and goals. An analysis of cases handled by the Burger Court (Wood,
1996) concluded that 85% of the requests to the opinion writer for a change in
language indicated that the requester's joining the opinion was contingent on
the change being made.

STRATEGIC VERSUS SINCERE VOTING

A recent book by Lee Epstein and Jack Knight, *The Choices Judges Make* (1998),
uses a rational model of judicial decision making and expands on the distinction, first introduced by Waiter Murphy in 1964, between *strategic voting* and
sincere voting.

Murphy's theory of judicial decision making capitalized on the *rational-
choice* model from political science and economics. He proposed that appellate judges often make their decisions—including which cases to hear and which
decisions to join—with policy considerations as predominant in their mind.
(By *policy* is meant proposed courses of action or general plans the Court should
advance.) Also, judges are social beings; they do not make their choices in
isolation. They must pay heed to the preferences of others. Thus, the decision
and the vote are not straightforwardly determined, and not necessarily "sin-

cere" in the sense of reflecting only what the judge prefers. Since Murphy's book appeared, other political scientists have had mixed reactions to his proposal that voting by justices is often strategic in character. *Elements of Judicial Strategy* is recognized and cited for its intuitions based on detailed analyses of specific case decisions (usually landmark cases), but in the early 1960s little in the way of rigorous empirical work had been done on the issue (and, of course, few judicial records were public).

Epstein and Knight (1998) have given a new life to Murphy's perspective by putting it in a modern, interdisciplinary context chat is congenial with the models from social cognition described in Chapter 2; perhaps more importantly, they have done extensive analyses of court dockets to support Murphy's claims. They urge their colleagues to view justices *not* ". . . as unconstrained decision makers who are free to behave in accord with their own ideological attitudes, [but] rather . . . [as] the sophisticated actors Murphy made them out to be" (p. xii). James Gibson has expressed this view succinctly: "Judges' decisions are a function of what they prefer to do, tempered by what they think they ought to do, but constrained by what they perceive is feasible to do" (1983, p. 9). Epstein and Knight reinforce this conclusion:

> Justices may be primarily seekers of legal policy, but they are not unsophisticated characters who make choices based merely on their own political preferences. Instead, justices are strategic actors who realize that their ability to achieve their goals depends on a consideration of the preferences of others, of the choices they expect others to make, and of the institutional context in which they act. In other words, the choices of justices can best be explained as strategic behavior, not solely as responses to either personal ideology or apolitical jurisprudence. (1998, p. xiii)

A key aspect of Epstein and Knight's use of strategic voting is its *interdependence*; individuals' actions are a function of their expectations about the actions of others. Sometimes these considerations lead judges to make choices that reflect their sincere preferences, but in other cases strategic calculations lead a judge to act in a way that does not accurately reflect his or her true preferences. They would rather support "a ruling that comes close to their preferences than to see their colleagues take positions that move policy well away from their ideal and see another political institution (Congress, for example) completely reverse [the Court's] decision" (1998, pp. 19–20).

If we accept the proposal that strategic voting does exist, those justices who are "swing votes" take on particular importance. Being a pivotal vote becomes an attractive option to some justices, possibly leading them to shift to the ideological center (Epstein & Knight, 1998, p. 128). Consider, for example, Justice O'Connor and her propensity to join the winning side of 5-to-4 majorities on the Court. Political scientist Nancy Maveety (Bradley & Maveety, 1992; Maveety, 1996) sees this as an example of strategic voting: "The tactical maneuver of going along with the majority offers the advantage of influence through bargaining" (Maveety, 1996, p. 4).

Political scientist Lawrence Baum, a longtime observer of the Court and author of several books about it, has concluded that judges employ sincere voting when they support the case outcome that they most prefer "without considering the impact of their votes on the collective result in their court" (1997, p. 90). Judges who vote strategically consider the effects of their choices on "collective results"; that is, their motivation is to achieve the most desirable results in their own court and in government as a whole (Baum, 1997). Two well-documented case decisions may reflect strategic voting on the part of some of the justices. In the 1954 *Brown* decision, several of the justices initially did not advocate outlawing segregated schools, but gradual shifts in position and especially their realization that it was in the best interests of the country eventually led to the unanimous vote sought by Chief Justice Warren (Gray, 1997; Kluger, 1975). And the final opinion in the *Roe v. Wade* (1973) case looked quite different from the original draft by Justice Blackmun, as noted earlier.

Baum limits the use of the term "strategic voting"; he does not include, for example, a judge who votes in a way opposite to his or her preferences in order to get reelected. In another example, a judge may be willing to abandon a minority position that reflects his or her preference so as to avoid the time and effort needed to write a dissenting opinion; Baum does not term this change "strategic," either.

Yet a number of tactics can fall under this label, "from arguments in an opinion aimed at winning a colleague's support to efforts at influence over appointments to other courts" (p. 92). Threats are not beyond the pale; justices may refrain from joining an opinion until their wishes are met. Even concerns about the relationship of the Supreme Court to the other federal courts can come into play. For example, one example of the distinction between strategic and sincere voting is the decision of whether to write a separate concurring opinion or to join the majority opinion. In a memo to Justice Powell, Chief Justice Burger urged his colleague not to publish a concurrence: "Would it not be better to try for a 'united front' instead of a cluster of concurring opinions-a practice of which I increasingly receive complaints from judges all over the country" (quoted by Epstein & Knight, 1998, p. 42).

DECISION TO DISSENT

Of course, on many occasions judges cannot accommodate their views to the majority. The decision to dissent is illustrative of the importance of the person-situation interaction. During his early terms on the Court, Justice Rehnquist was known as "the Great Dissenter" by his clerks because of the number of times he was in the minority, but with the ideological shift in the Court's membership, he no longer writes many dissents.

The decision to write a dissent, rather than simply signing on to someone else's dissent, may reflect a number of motives. Certainly, compared with a majority opinion, it reflects *sincere* voting. Deborah Gruenfeld's 1995 study of the levels of integrative complexity in opinions, described in detail in Chapter 2, concluded that minority opinions are more integratively simple than majority opinions, a finding consistent with the proposition that the motive for writing dissents is often a cathartic one.

Individual differences exist in not only the frequency with which judges dissent, but in their style of doing so. Justice Stevens is "an enigmatic independent jurist" (Smolla, 1995, p. 12) who feels the need to provide a separate opinion when he is in the minority, or even when he is in the majority. Justice Scalia's dissents often reflect attacks on the logic or conclusions of the majority opinion; as noted earlier, he rarely reflects a desire for compromise or conciliation. In an article he has made his satisfactions clear:

> To be able to write an opinion solely for oneself, without the need to accommodate, to any degree whatever, the more-or-less differing views of one's colleagues; to address precisely the points of law that one considers important and *no others*; to express precisely the degree of quibble, or foreboding, or disbelief, or indignation that one believes the majority's disposition should engender—that is indeed an unparalleled pleasure. (Scalia, 1994, p. 42, italics in original)

Reactions to consistently being on the losing side also reflect differences. In the last decade of their service on the Court, the triumvirate of Justices Brennan, Blackmun, and Marshall were increasingly in the minority with respect to cases involving conflicts between individual rights and state power. Justice Blackmun often wrote strong dissents, Justice Brennan kept trying to win majority support, and Justice Marshall seemed to become resigned to the unwanted outcome and shifted his influence attempts to the public. One former clerk described Marshall's reaction as follows: "Unable to exert much influence beyond casting his vote, Marshall reacted as many proud people would: instead of futilely trying to influence his colleagues inside the Court, he concentrated on making sure that his views reached the public through the pages of the *United States Reports*" (Tushnet, 1992, pp. 2109–2110).

CONCLUSIONS

The title of this book asks if psychology is relevant to judicial decision making, and the first half of the book has examined this question in light of the *process* of deciding. In answering this question, two points seem salient: First, traditional models have emphasized the *opinion-formation* phase and neglected the process of negotiation between judges after their initial opinions have been expressed. Second, the whole process of forming an opinion and then voting on it is more complicated than the simple models—legal *or* attitudinal—would lead us to believe. Although both of these may be considerations in a motivated reasoning process that leads to opinion formation, the eventual vote may reflect a strategy to achieve policy goals.

I am appreciative of the contributions of Paul Silvia and Aaron Hull to this chapter.

6

History of the Psychology–Law Relationship

Scientists do research for a variety of reasons. Some will tell you that it's simply their job; the extrinsic motivations of job security and financial success are sufficient. Recognition by peers and the public reflect other examples of external inducements. In contrast, some scientists seek understanding of a process-perhaps the mastery of an elusive phenomenon, whether physical or mental.

Probably most scientists believe that the products of their research endeavors can have-will have-some utility in the world, and they offer this as the major reason why they do research. Such research applications can take a variety of forms, from a vaccine that alleviates a dreaded disease to a microchip that facilitates computer analyses. Social scientists, including psychologists, generally seek to apply their research findings. Reducing prejudice, improving interracial understanding, facilitating learning in the classroom—the possibilities for the application of psychological knowledge are multitudinous.

The court system has of course, been one venue for this. Chapter 6 examines the history of psychology's attempts to influence court decisions, especially U.S. Supreme Court decisions. Judicial decisions have impact on a number of phenomena that are subject to a psychological analysis; school desegregation, sexual harassment, eyewitness identification, and the competence of a defendant to stand trial are but a few examples.

Several methods exist to influence judicial decisions. Experts may testify at a hearing or at a trial. When the field of psychology seeks to bring about a particular judicial ruling, it may, as a plaintiff, file a lawsuit and seek redress through the courts. In certain so-called guild, or professional, issues, the American Psychological Association has done this; for example, the APA filed suit when insurance companies denied coverage of insurance clients' psychotherapy bills. More often, however, psychologists have sought to educate or influence the court not as a contesting party, but rather through the submission of *amicus curiae* briefs that reflect organized psychology's position on the issue before the court.

The interaction between psychology and the law stretches back for a hundred years, but the relationship has been a checkered one, reflecting some successes and, in particular, one embarrassing failure that lead to a virtual freeze on interaction between psychology and the court system for the first 40 years of this century.

EARLY ASPECTS OF THE RELATIONSHIP

The case of *Muller v. Oregon*, which the Supreme Court resolved in 1908, is generally offered as the first Supreme Court case to benefit from a social science perspective. Certainly it is a landmark, because it contained a brief (prepared by Louis Brandeis, later to become a Supreme Court justice himself) reviewing what the experts believed about the topic at hand. This brief, however, was more a collection of opinions, often based on rather casual observation, than an objective review of empirical research. As such, it was not the kind of evidence that modern observers would consider as social science (Bersoff & Glass, 1995).

The case developed as follows: In 1905 Curt Muller, who owned the Grand Laundry in Portland, Oregon, was convicted of breaking a state law, passed two years earlier, that no woman could be employed in a factory, laundry, or similar establishment for more than 10 hours a day. Muller appealed his conviction to the U.S. Supreme Court, perhaps assuming that the Court would rule that the new Oregon law conflicted with the long-established "liberty of contract" principle of the employer—employee relationship.

At the request of the National Consumers' League, the state of Oregon was represented by Louis D. Brandeis, then a prominent Boston lawyer involved in social legislation; he served on a *pro bono* basis. The brief he prepared "was recognized immediately as an innovation in American advocacy"

(Rosen, 1972, p. 78). Brandeis was aware of the fact that "although judges had systematically struck down social legislation, they had done so because they had seen no relationship between the statutes and public health" (Strum, 1984, p. 120). Thus, only two of the 113 pages of his brief reflected a traditional type of legal argumentation. More than 110 extralegal sources were cited in much of the rest (95 pages), including statistics and reports by physicians, psychologists, economists, and social critics dealing with working conditions, and especially, their effect on female workers. This unique compilation of information represented "the first brief ever based upon authoritative extralegal data" (Mason, 1933, p. 107). Brandeis used these sources and data to substantiate propositions that were then part of the conventional social science and public health viewpoints:

- Women were physiologically different from men and more susceptible to injury resulting from unregulated working conditions.
- Excessive hours of labor generally endangered the health and safety of women.
- Shorter workdays fostered the health of workers and improved home life.
- Shorter workdays produced economic benefits because of increased efficiency and quality of the work.

The purpose of the brief was to demonstrate that the Oregon law was a reasonable one; Brandeis used the extralegal data to substantiate the argument that it was harmful for women to work more than 10 hours a day, but he had to convince the Court that his massive collection of information could serve as a basis for a judicial decision.

Brandeis also presented the oral argument. It was successful; the Court upheld the Oregon law and specifically credited Brandeis and his approach. Indeed, it is rare to mention an advocate by name in a Court decision (Strum, 1984), but Justice Brewer, writing the unanimous decision for the Court, stated:

> It may not be amiss, in the present case, before examining the constitutional question, to notice the course of legislation as well as expressions of opinion from other than judicial sources. In a brief filed by Mr. Louis D. Brandeis . . . is a very copious collection of all these matters . . .
>
> [The extralegal data] may not be, technically speaking, [legal] authorities, and in them is little or no discussion of the constitutional question presented to us for determination, yet they are significant of a widespread belief that a woman's physical structure, and the functions she performs in consequence thereof, justify special legislation restricting or qualifying the conditions under which she should be permitted to toil. (p. 419)

Though Justice Brewer denied that constitutional questions could be settled by "a consensus of present public opinion," he recognized that empirical data and matters of general knowledge were "worthy of consideration," and by praising Brandeis' presentation, the Court "declared publicly that it was ready to be persuaded by compilations of social facts" (Strum, 1984, p. 122). Hence, such briefs have come to be known as *Brandeis briefs*.

Yet although the *Muller* case is often cited as the starting point of the relationship, we need to ask if the social science perspective had an even earlier history in the Court's decision making. Tomkins and Oursland (1991) have argued that it did, concluding that "social scientific perspectives have *consistently* been a part of legal decision making in cases that address social issues" (p. 103, italics in original). Although those judicial opinions that came before *Muller v. Oregon* did not cite social facts or perspectives as the *authority*, the impact of those facts and perspectives can be detected.

Tomkins and Oursland chose two cases as examples of their claim; both were race-related, a fortunate choice, as the determinants of judicial decisions about the proper role of race in our society serve as one of the themes of this chapter. The Dred Scott case (*Dred Scott v. Sandford*) in 1857 brought into focus the question of whether—given the legality of slavery in many states at that time—Black persons were citizens of the United States and hence had the right to sue in federal court. The case, which began more that a decade earlier, reflected the petitions filed by Dred Scott and his wife, Harriet Scott, who sought freedom from their owner, Irene Emerson.

The majority opinion of the Supreme Court, in a 7-to-2 vote, was delivered by Chief Justice Roger Taney, a Southerner, four years before the onset of the Civil War. The massive, 241-page opinion noted that "for more than a century [the black race has] been regarded as beings of an inferior order, and altogether unfit to associate with the white race, either in social or political relations" (*Dred Scott v. Sandford*, 1857, p. 407). Relevant to our present emphasis was the Chief Justice's opinion that the above-quoted view was the dominant "social scientific" view of the time (Hovenkamp, 1985), or as Chief Justice Taney expressed it, a belief "regarded as an axiom in morals as well as politics" (p. 407).

This predominant view did not change during the last half of the nineteenth century, even though the focus shifted from slavery to interracial association. The *Plessy v. Ferguson* decision in 1896 is of note for social scientists interested in racial desegregation, because it was the Supreme Court case that was overturned by the *Brown v. Board of Education* decision in 1954. It is instructive to examine the rationale used by the Court in 1896 in its 7-to-1 *Plessy* vote.

Homer Plessy, classified a Black person in Louisiana because one of his great grandparents was Black, protested the constitutionality of an 1890 Louisiana law that required "equal but separate accommodations for the white and colored races" on all passenger trains (*Plessy v. Ferguson*, 1896, p. 540). Not only did the Court uphold this law, it did so because the measure was consistent with the "established usages, customs, and traditions of the people" (p. 550). Even while claiming that the law did not imply invidious distinctions between the races, Justice Henry Brown's majority opinion concluded that the Louisiana law "could not have been intended to abolish distinctions based upon color, or to enforce social, as distinguished from political equality, or a commingling of the two races upon terms unsatisfactory to either" (p. 544).

Hovenkamp (1985) has concluded that the *Plessy* decision reflected the then-commonplace assumption that racial "mixing" was harmful. Tomkins and Oursland noted that a belief about the inferiority of Blacks "was basic to most white Americans (including scientists) and the prospect of miscegenation was particularly horrifying to many whites who feared that sexual intermingling with the black race would toll the death knell for the white race" (1991, p. 112). In fact, the *Plessy* decision apparently evoked little comment at the time, reflecting how congruent were its values with those of the educated and scientific communities (Lofgren, 1987).

Thus it has been argued that in the broadest sense, the courts have acted in ways consistent with the thinking of social scientists (Tucker, 1994), but such a conclusion seems more fitting for earlier times than for today. To anticipate a conclusion that emerges in subsequent chapters, the Court today chooses to agree with the empirical findings of psychology only when the latter are in agreement with the values of the justices. Why this shift? Did psychology try to force its values and beliefs too strongly on the courts? The example of Hugo Munsterberg causes us to conclude that the answer is, unfortunately, yes.

THE ROLE OF HUGO MUNSTERBERG

Consider the following quotation from a book by a prominent psychology-and-law researcher regarding his building facilities: "Visiting friends [would find], with surprise, twenty-seven rooms overspun with electric wires and filled with [equipment], and a mechanic busy at work" (p. 3). Five pages later, this psychologist wrote that "experimental psychology has reached a stage at which it seems natural and sound to give attention to its possible service for the practical needs of life" (p. 8).

A contemporary statement? No, that was from *On the Witness Stand*, written by Hugo Munsterberg almost a century ago (Munsterberg, 1908). Three months before the founding of the American Psychological Association, Munsterberg in September of 1892 arrived in the United States to establish—at William James' invitation—the psychological laboratory at Harvard University. At the APA's first annual meeting in December, a dozen papers were presented. Munsterberg's was the final one; in it he criticized his colleagues' work as being "rich in decimals but poor in ideas" (Cattell, 1894). Thus he set the tone for his attempts to apply psychological laboratory-based knowledge to the real world.

Munsterberg was to spend less than 25 years in the United States—he died prematurely in 1916 at the age of 53—but he was a prolific writer on topics ranging from child development to industrial psychology to crime. Among his Ph.D. students were Edward Tolman and Mary Caulkins; Gordon Allport took his first psychology class from Munsterberg

Despite the fact that psyche-legal issues captured only a small portion of his professional time, his impact on the field was such that he may be considered "the father of psychology-and-law." His choices of what to do and say are still somewhat reflected in the things that psychologists contemplate when they consider the court system. For example, the following are covered in Munsterberg's 1908 book: memory distortions, eyewitness accuracy, confessions, suggestibility, hypnosis, crime detection, and crime prevention—all still topics for contemporary forensic psychology.

The above does not mean that Munsterberg was the sole instigator of a movement. In some ways he was a less-than-ideal symbol; he was pugnacious and self-deceptive, and he often sought the sensational as the focus of his work. More important, there were other pioneers. Even before the publication of Munsterberg's book, Hermann Ebbinghaus (1885), using himself as the subject, had demonstrated the rapid rate of early memory loss. Yarmey (1984) has noted that Alfred Binet as early as 1904 was seeking to understand just how competent children were as eyewitnesses. Binet (1900) argued for "the advantage that would accrue from the creation of a practical science of testimony" (quoted by Wells & Loftus, 1984, p. 4). In Germany, Louis William Stern had begun publishing eyewitness research by 1902; the next year he was admitted to German courts of law to testify as an expert on eyewitness identification, and he established a periodical dealing with the psychology of testimony (Stern, 1903). True, much of the early work was classificatory (for example, six types of questions that might be asked of an eyewitness), but other contributions were empirical; for example, Stern compared the memory abilities of children and adults. Wells and Loftus observed that "not surprisingly, the early empirical work was not of the quality and precision that exists in psychology today" (1984, p. 5). Yet the foundation was set; a central goal was the *application* of research findings in order to influence courtroom procedures.

Guy Montrose Whipple (1909, 1910, 1911, 1912), in a series of *Psychological Bulletin* articles, brought the *Aussage* (or eyewitness testimony) tradition into English terminology, introducing American audiences to classic experiments that related testimony and evidence to perception and memory. Prior to World War I, "law was acknowledged as a fit concern for psychology and vice versa" (Tapp, 1976, pp. 360–361). Especially with regard to the accuracy of eyewitness identification, the persistent interest of recent times can be directly traced to Munsterberg's work. Some of the studies done by Munsterberg prior to 1908 that are reflected in contemporary research include these:

- Undergraduates heard two loud clicks separated by 10 seconds. Their estimates of the actual time interval ranged from 0.5 seconds to 60 seconds; the average was approximately 45 seconds.
- Subjects were shown printed words that were briefly illuminated; immediately before this, the experimenter spoke a sentence to the subjects. Hearing the sentence caused the subjects to misperceive the illuminated word; they reported seeing "college" rather than "courage" and "Philippines" rather than "Philistines.
- At a meeting of scholars, the doors suddenly burst open and a clown in a highly colored costume and a Black man with a revolver entered. They shouted at each other, a shot was fired, and one briefly fell to the floor; then they suddenly left the room. Everything happened in less than 20 seconds. Each of the scholars was asked to write a complete account of what happened; more than a third omitted more than half of the actions, and 32 of 40 reports contained false statements.

MUNSTERBERG'S GOALS

In the first decade of the twentieth century, Munsterberg's frequent articles in the highly popular *McLean's Magazine* made him probably the most widely recognized psychologist in the United States, other than William James. His goal was clear: Munsterberg's mission was to raise the position of the psychological profession to one of importance in public life (Kargon, 1986), and he saw the legal system as a vehicle for doing so. Loftus wrote in 1979: "At the beginning of the century, Munsterberg was arguing for more interaction between the two fields, perhaps at times in a way that was insulting to the legal profession" (p. 194). For instance, Munsterberg wrote: "It seems astonishing that the work of justice is carried out in the courts without ever consulting the psychologist and asking him for all the aid which the modern study of suggestion can offer" (1908, p. 194). At the beginning of the 20th century, chemists and physicists were routinely called as expert witnesses; why not psychologists? Munsterberg saw no difference between the physical sciences and his own science.

MUNSTERBERG'S VALUES

It is important to understand Munsterberg's pessimistic view of the court system, because it helps us to understand his actions, actions that in retrospect were self-defeating. His view conflicted with the legal system's beliefs about human capabilities. The jury system rests on a positive assumption about human nature: that collections of reasonable people are able to judge the world about them reasonably accurately. As Kalven and Zeisel put it, the justice system

> recruits a group of twelve lay [people], chosen at random from the widest population; it convenes them for the purpose of a particular trial; it entrusts them with great official powers of decision; it permits them to carry out deliberations in secret and report out their final judgment without giving reasons for it; and, after their momentary service to the state has been completed, it orders them to disband and return to private life. (1966, p. 3)

Munsterberg took a very different view of juror capabilities and the role of the psychologist as expert. "The central premise of his legal psychology . . . was that the individual could not accurately judge the real world that existed outside him, or for that matter the nature and processes of his own mind" (Hale, 1980, p.121). Thus, everything from police investigations to jury instructions required the assistance of a psychologist.

Munsterberg was a rationalist; he sought to "expunge all irrationality and unpredictability from the world" (Hale, 1980, p. 7). He and William James engaged in a delightful exchange in 1906 that illustrated the values underlying their contrasting positions. "I am satisfied with a free wild Nature," James wrote; "you seem to me to cherish and pursue an Italian Garden, where all things are kept in separate compartments, and one must follow straight-ruled walks." Munsterberg's reply was that the world of immediate experience comprised for him also "a wild nature without ways and flower beds and with plenty of weeds" but that "Our life's duty makes us gardeners, makes us to unweed the weeds of sin and error and ugliness and when we finally come to think over what flowers were left as valuable, and we bring together those which were similar-then we finally have indeed such an Italian garden as the world which we are seeking, as the world which has to be acknowledged as ultimate" Games letter to Munsterberg, June 28, 1906; Munsterberg's reply, July 1, 1906; quoted in Hale, 1980, p. 7).

MUNSTERBERG'S ACTIVITIES

Munsterberg reflected his desire to bring psychology into the courtroom main ways:

- He demonstrated the fallibility of memory.
- He produced *On the Witness Stand* (1908), a compilation of his magazine articles, to show that "experimental psychology had reached a stage at which it seems natural and sound to give attention . . . to its possible service for the practical needs of life" (p. 8).

- He offered testimony as an expert witness in highly publicized trials. It was here that his values and his arrogant manner created the greatest problems.

Perhaps most controversial was his intrusion into a highly publicized 1907 trial of labor leader "Big Bill" Haywood (Hale, 1980; Holbrook, 1957; Lukas, 1997). The International Workers of the World (IWW) leader was charged with conspiracy to murder Frank Steunenberg, a former governor of Idaho and a well-known opponent of organized labor. On December 30, 1905, in Caldwell, Idaho, Steunenberg opened the gate to his home and was blown apart by a bomb. The murder trial transformed Haywood into an international symbol of labor protest. Clarence Darrow offered his services as defense attorney, and prominent people such as Eugene Debs and Maxim Corky rallied support.

The case against Haywood rested on the testimony of Harry Orchard, a onetime IWW organizer who—after a four-day interrogation—confessed to committing the bombing (as well as many other crimes) at the behest of an "inner circle" of radicals, including Haywood. Munsterberg examined Orchard in his cell *during* the trial and conducted 100 tests on him over a period of 7 hours; in Munsterberg's mind, the most important of these was the word association test. Upon returning to Cambridge, Munsterberg was interviewed by the *Boston Herald* (July 3, 1907), which quoted him as saying, "Orchard's confession is every word of it true" (Hale, 1980, p. 117). This disclosure, coming before a verdict had been delivered, threatened the impartiality of the trial process. Still, the jury found Haywood not guilty because the state did not produce any significant evidence corroborating Orchard's confession, as Idaho required. Two weeks later, Munsterberg slightly amended his position by introducing the concept of "subjective truthfulness." His free association tests, he now concluded, revealed that Orchard *believed* he was telling the truth, but they couldn't discern the actual facts of the matter.

Despite the adverse publicity, Munsterberg maintained his inflated claims. In a letter to a newspaper he wrote: "To deny that the experimental psychologist has indeed possibilities of determining the 'truth-telling' process is just as absurd as to deny that the chemical expert can find out whether there is arsenic in a stomach or whether blood spots are human or animal origin" (quoted by Hale, 1980, p. 118). He began to use exaggerated metaphors; he could "pierce into the mind" and bring to light its deepest secrets.

Two observations are of note: First, Munsterberg did not limit his advocacy to one side in criminal trials. In a case where he felt that the defendant's confession was the result of a hypnotic induction and hence false, Munsterberg offered to testify for the defense. In the Idaho case his conclusions supported the prosecution. Second, Munsterberg, like many true believers of innovative theories, may have exaggerated his claims to get attention and to convince himself of their merits. Hale, his biographer, makes a strong case that Munsterberg "deceived himself with alarming frequency, and his distortions in certain cases bordered on outright falsification" (1980, p. 119). Ironically, a colleague to whom *On the Witness Stand* was dedicated, Edwin B. Holt, later called Munsterberg as "one of the most unconscious liars who ever existed" (Holt, 1915, p. 38, quoted by Hale, 1980).

Reactions by the Legal Community

Not surprisingly, Munsterberg's advocacy generated withering abuse from law-yers and law professors. In one attack, titled "Yellow Psychology," Charles Moore concluded that the laboratory had little to lend to the courtroom and he doubted that Munsterberg had discovered a "Northwest Passage to the truth" (quoted in Hale, 1980, p. 115).

The most damaging criticism was an article by John Henry Wigmore (1909), an esteemed law professor and leading expert on evidence. His article, cast in the form of a trial against Munsterberg and including cross-examina-tion of him for inflated assertions, has been described as "mercilessly satiric" (Loh, 1981, p. 316). It suggested that experimental psychology did not have enough knowledge to be practical. Furthermore, proposed Wigmore, the jury system distrusted those outside interferences, such as Munsterberg's, that in-truded upon their common-sense judgments. These themes—the resistance to input from other disciplines and a reliance on logic and common sense—have recurred throughout the years as reactions of the judicial system to psychology's input.

Despite his criticisms, Wigmore made a telling point at the end of this article. Before the jurors were excused, the judge took a few moments to ex-press his personal views. He said, basically, this: "In no other country in the civilized world had the legal profession taken so little interest in finding out what psychology and other sciences had to offer that might contribute to the nation's judicial system" (Loftus, 1979, p. 203; Wigmore, 1909, p. 433). Some have even speculated that Wigmore was sympathetic but disappointed at the extremity of Munsterberg's comments (Tomkins & Penrod, 1996). Perhaps so. In retrospect, we can say that Munsterberg's own actions prevented the ac-commodation he sought.

MUNSTERBERG'S IMPACT

Perhaps for these reasons—exaggeration by Munsterberg and avoidance by legal authorities—the research and scholarship of scientific psychology that was applicable to the courts languished from the first World War until the latter half of the 1970s. There were contributions in the 1930s through the 1960s, but these were infrequent. In fact, the piece of scientific research that had the greatest impact on the courts during this period, Clark and Clark's 1952 doll study, did not originate specifically from a desire to change the legal system. Historical treatments of the psychology-and-law field (e.g., J. H. Davis, 1989; Foley 1993; Kolasa, 1972) noted that few works examined the legal system from the psychological perspective. Those that did included books such as Burtt's *Legal Psychology* (1931), Robinson's *Law and the Lawyers* (1935), and some speculative reviews in law journals (Hutchins & Slesinger, 1928a, 1928b; Louisell, 1955). During this period, more work on the legal field was done by anthropologists, sociologists, and psychiatrists (Tapp, 1977).

The relationship between eyewitness confidence and accuracy is an example of the gap in research activity. Munsterberg did one of the first empirical tests of this relationship; he had children examine pictures for 15 seconds and then write a report of everything they could remember. Subsequently they were required to underline the parts of their report for which they had absolutely certainty. Munsterberg reported that there were almost as many mistakes in the underlined sentences as in the rest. Other studies in the first years of this century, by Stern and by Borst, were reported by Whipple (1909). Paradoxically, no more empirical interest surfaced until nearly 65 years later (Wells & Murray, 1984).

Sporer's 1981 explanation for the "dead period" (cited by Wells & Loftus, 1984, p. 6) was "zealous overgeneralizations drawn from experimental studies that did not meet adequately the demands of complex courtroom reality. Another reason was offered by Wells and Loftus: "Psychological research during that time was oriented primarily toward theoretical issues with little focus on practical problems" (1984, p. 6).

THE 1970S: RENEWED INTEREST

A resurgence of interest by experimental and social psychologists occurred in the 1970s. With regard to one topic, eyewitness identification, as an example, Wells and Loftus (1984) estimated that more than 85% of the entire published literature surfaced between 1978 and the publication of their book in 1984.

Why the sudden rise of interest? A renewed emphasis on the necessity to make observations in natural contexts in order to understand social behavior and memory was one reason, according to Wells and Loftus (1984). More generally, social psychology in the 1970s responded to criticisms of its irrelevance by extending its concepts to real-world topics, including law (J. H. Davis, 1989). Social psychologists acknowledged the failure of their discipline to advance social policy. Davis described the approach as follows:

It is tempting to draw a general parallel between the temporal sequence of the past: Munsterberg's proposals; reaction and critique of other scholars, disenchantment among social psychologists; and finally, abandonment of efforts at application of psychology to law. But something different happened "the next time around." The general disenchantment that was characteristic of the latter "crisis" period was not followed by an "abandonment phase." Rather, we have seen a continuous evolution and strengthening of some new developments during the succeeding years—a period in which applied research in social *psychology came to be recognized in its own right* (p. 201, italics in original)

THE PRESENT

Where do we stand now? Psychologists are researching a number of topics relevant to the legal system; beyond the extensive work on jury decision making, psychologists have studied such diverse phenomena as sentencing decisions, the impact of the various insanity definitions and the battered-woman defense, and children's abilities as eyewitnesses. Yet much of this work has been done in laboratories, with limitations on its application to real-world decisions.

At the same time, judges, trial attorneys, police, and other representatives of the legal system are making such real-world decisions-about the rights of criminals, about the definition of sexual harassment, about the confidentiality of conversations during psychotherapy—every day. This book's credo is that psychologists must now move beyond their laboratories and ask how their perspective can improve judicial decisions. The remaining chapters of this book examine just how successful organized attempts to have an impact have been.

PSYCHOLOGY'S ROLE IN *BROWN V. BOARD OF EDUCATION*

Even though experimental psychologists stuck to their laboratories during the period surrounding the two world wars, things were different for a group of social scientists concerned using psychological knowledge to improve human welfare. They played a role—albeit a controversial one—in the momentous decision by the Supreme Court to desegregate the public schools in 1954. As a case study of the influence of social science knowledge, the *Brown* case is instructive. How did social scientists get involved? Did they act as advocates or as objective scientists? What data supported their conclusions? Most important, what impact did they have?

THE NAACP'S RECRUITMENT OF SOCIAL SCIENTISTS

The NAACP's Legal Defense Fund spearheaded the challenges to racial segregation of the schools. These court tests began in the early 1950s in South Carolina, Virginia, and other Southern states, as well as in Kansas, the home of the first-named respondent in the landmark case decided by the Supreme Court in 1954. In developing the appeals, Thurgood Marshall—who was then with the NAACP—learned of the work of Kenneth and Mamie Clark, psychologists who had been studying reactions of Black children to segregation. Marshall recruited Dr. Kenneth Clark, who then testified in several of the hearings and trials that led to the *Brown* appeal to the Supreme Court.

THE CLARK AND CLARK DOLL STUDY

Kenneth and Mamie Clark (1952) had compared the responses of Black children living in segregated conditions with those of Black children residing in a desegregated part of the country. They concluded that the differences in reaction should be interpreted as indicating that segregation was harmful to the emotional development of Black children.

In one of their studies, the Clarks showed a set of dolls, some Black and some White, to 134 Black children (ages 6 to 9) in the segregated schools of Pine Bluff, Arkansas, and to 119 Black children in the unsegregated schools of Springfield, Massachusetts. They asked the children to do certain things, such

- Give me the doll you like best.
- Give me the doll that looks like you.
- Give me the doll that looks bad.

It was expected that the segregated children would prefer the White doll and say that the Black doll "looked bad." Instead, the segregated children, the Clarks discovered, were "less pronounced in their preference for the White doll"; when asked to hand their questioner "the doll that looks like you," 39% of the unsegregated Massachusetts children picked the White doll, compared with only 29% in the segregated Arkansas children. When asked for the "nice" doll, 68% of the Massachusetts children chose the White one; only 52% of the Arkansas children did. Which doll "looked bad?" More than 70% of the unsegregated children chose the Black doll, whereas only 49% of the segregated children did. (Table 6-1 is a reprint from the Clarks' article, reflecting these responses and others.)

What are we to make of these findings? Do they, as the Clarks concluded, show invidious effects from segregation? The straightforward interpretation, for the critics of the Clarks's conclusions (cf. Van den Haag, 1960), was that if the tests demonstrated psychological damage to Black children at all, they demonstrated that the damage was greater in an *unsegregated* environment.

Kenneth and Mamie Clark's interpretation of the results, however, was just the opposite. Essentially, the Clarks concluded that "black children of the

TABLE 6-1. RESULTS OF CLARK AND CLARK'S DOLL STUDY:
CHOICES OF SUBJECTS IN NORTHERN (MIXED SCHOOLS) AND
SOUTHERN (SEGREGATED SCHOOLS)

	Groups (Requests 1 through 4)*	
Choice	North, percent	South, percent
Request 1 (play with)		
Colored doll	28	37
White doll	72	62
Request 2 (nice doll)		
Colored doll	30	46
White doll	68	52
Request 3 (looks bad)		
Colored doll	71	49
White doll	17	16
Request 4 (nice color)		
Colored doll	37	40
White doll	63	57

* Individuals failing to make either choice not included, hence some percentages
add to less than 100.
(*Source*: Clark & Clark, 1952, Table 8, p. 559)

South were more adjusted to the feeling that they were not as good as white,
and because they felt defeated at an early age, did not bother using the device
of denial" (quoted by Kluger, 1976, p. 356). This explanation may, to some,
seem circuitous at best, but Kenneth Clark was convinced of its validity. He
was even quoted to the effect that he had to argue with lawyers "for the integrity of social science; not that they wanted me to pervert it, but some of them
wanted me to make statements that 1 did not believe the evidence would support" (quoted in Evans, 1980, p. 67).

Surely the Clarks' interpretation is not the simplest one. Did they predict
this finding before the data were collected? The research report does not say
so. The Clarks stated that some children, when asked which doll they resembled, broke down and cried; such behavior, they reported, "was more preva-
lent in the North than in the South" (1952, p. 560). Research results that are
subject to conflicting interpretations—especially when they are not consistent
with a desired explanation—demand that the researchers begin with a theory
that produces testable hypotheses.

THE SOCIAL SCIENCE STATEMENT

The Society for the Psychological Study of Social Issues (SPSSI) is an organization of social psychologists and others concerned with using psychological
research to alleviate social problems. About 1950, a SPSSI committee collected

and analyzed available theory and data on the psychological, social, and economic effects of racial segregation (Kimmel, 1994). According to Kenneth Clark (a member of this committee) as the court cases developed and the NAACP attorneys requested assistance, committee members, especially Stuart W. Cook, circulated a summary of the committee's findings to their colleagues. Cook, Clark, and Isidor Chein reworked it into a 24-page brief, which was signed by 32 prominent social scientists. The brief appeared as the *Appendix to the Appellants' Briefs in Brown v. Board of Education* and was reprinted in the *Minnesota Law Review* (Allport *et al.*, 1953).

The statement, accompanied by 35 footnotes, was low-key and authoritative. Its conclusions were the same as those exemplified in Dr. Clark's testimony: that segregation created feelings of inferiority and humiliation in Black youth, and that their self-esteem was replaced with self-hatred, rejection, and frustration. Furthermore, it concluded that minority children, learning of the inferior status to which they were assigned, might react with aggression and hostility toward their own group. The institutionalization of segregation by the school system was seen as more powerful than the expression of prejudice by individuals, as the school system reflected the full authority of the state.

The *Brown* Decision and the Impact of Psychology

The *Brown* decision referred to the contributions of the social scientists in Footnote 11. It is uncertain how much the justices, in overturning school segregation, were influenced by the social scientists' statement (Cook, 1984). Certainly some of the wording in the Court's opinion reflected the social scientists' position—statements such as "the policy of separating the races is usually interpreted as denoting the inferiority of the Negro group," or "A sense of inferiority affects the motivation of a child to learn." Stuart Cook, one of the original signers, still felt 30 years later that the brief had produced a positive effect; he wrote in the mid-1980s that

> there are grounds for believing that the Court made use of . . . the Appendix in formulating its decision to ban state laws requiring or permitting school desegregation. Because this decision has been widely regarded as the critical final step in abandoning legal and judicial support for racial discrimination in the U.S., the statement has occupied a prominent spot in the history of psychology. (1984, p. 830)

If the data from the doll study were so subject to a multitude of interpretations, why did the Supreme Court not simply note that school desegregation, on the face of it, induced an assumption of inferiority leading to a response of humiliation? It may have been "precisely because the Court knew it was [overturning] a firm precedent and entering a heated debate that it wished to garner *all* the supporting evidence that was available. Without data, there was a danger that the arguments on both sides might merely have become so much moral posturing and empty assertions" (Perkins, 1988, p. 471). As Thurgood Marshall noted in 1952, the earlier separate-but-equal doctrine "had become so ingrained that overwhelming proof was sorely needed to demonstrate that equal educational opportunities for Negroes could not be provided in a segregated system" (quoted by Rosen, 1972, p. 130). This is confirmed by a later comment by Otto Klineber& one of the signers, who spoke with Chief Justice Warren a few years later:

> He told me that the members of the Court would probably have come to the same conclusion in any case, but they (and he in particular) felt their position was strengthened by the clear support of the present generation of psychologists (1986, p. 54) . . . We were all proud that the psychological research findings were included in . . . the legal brief . . . to which Chief Justice Warren made approving reference. (1986, p. 53)

Regardless, decades later social scientists still differ about the desirability of the social science statement. Stuart Cook (1979) concluded that the information in the statement was sound, but Harold Gerard (1983) felt that the statement was based on "well-meaning rhetoric rather than solid research" (p. 869). The statement can legitimately be viewed as a series of generalizations based on less-than-rigorous research studies (Eshleman, 1997); for example, many of the studies cited did not even compare segregated and desegregated children, and comparison groups that controlled for other influences were absent.

LATER INTERACTIONS WITH THE SUPREME COURT

Before describing the active involvement of the American Psychological Association in the preparation of amicus briefs for the courts, we will examine the efforts by psychologists and other social scientists to influence the decision in two other Supreme Court cases.

BALLEW v. GEORGIA 1978

Claude Ballew managed an adult theater in Atlanta in the mid-1970s. He was convicted by a five-person jury of showing an obscene film (*Behind the Green Door*). The use of only five persons to determine a defendant's fate was a recent development, reflecting a trend in many states to move away from the more costly 12-person juries, and Ballew decided to challenge the Georgia law that permitted this jury size, claiming that his constitutional right to a jury trial had been restricted. The Georgia courts, to his displeasure, upheld the state law, so he sought redress through the U.S. Supreme Court.

Tanke and Tanke Offer Their Services

When Elizabeth Decker Tanke and Tony J. Tanke (a social scientist and a law-yer, respectively) learned that the Supreme Court had agreed to rule on Ballew's appeal, they offered their assistance to each side. Ballew's attorney never re-sponded, apparently because of an address change, but the attorney repre-senting the State of Georgia did, and so the Tankes provided him with ex-cerpts from Michael Saks' 1977 book on jury size and decision rules, and also with materials from their bibliography on jury research (Tanke & Tanke, 1977); both dealt with studies on the effect of the jury size.

One Side's Use of the Social Science Research

The counsel for the state of Georgia cited the studies during the oral argu-ments, and later the Court's library obtained a copy of the bibliography from the Tankes. It is important to note that the direct availability of these materials was probably why they were cited in the Court's majority opinion in *Ballew*.

The American Psychological Association did not file an *amicus* brief in the *Ballew* case; the only one submitted was done by the Citizens for Decency through Law, an organization that sought to uphold Ballew's obscenity con-viction. It would have been to the Court's benefit to have had "a true *amicus* brief—a presentation by concerned social scientists who, without seeking to advance a special interest in the merits of the case, offered guidance to the court in a discussion of their work" (Tanke & Tanke, 1979, p. 1137).

Justice Blackmun's Reliance on Empirical Research and Statistical Logic

It is especially fortunate that Justice Harry Blackmun, who wrote the decision in Ballew, had access to social science research, because previous decisions by the Court on matters of jury size and decision rule were devoid of any aware-ness of quality in relevant empirical work. The issues had surfaced a decade earlier. In *Williams v. Florida* (1970), the Supreme Court upheld a robbery con-viction by a Florida jury of six persons, thereby rejecting the claim that the defendant was constitutionally entitled to twelve-person jury under the Sixth and 14th Amendments.

The Court saw the issue of size as related to the jury's function; it ac-knowledged the need for "the number [of jurors to] be large enough to pro-mote group deliberation, free from outside attempts at intimidation, and to provide a fair possibility for obtaining a representative cross-section of the community," but ruled that a jury of six persons fulfilled such requirements (*Williams v. Florida*, 1970, p. 100).

Do 6- and 12-person juries render different verdicts? Is a smaller jury

prejudicial to a criminal defendant? The absence of an *amicus* brief from organized psychology in the *Williams* case was most disturbing, because the Court's
opinion noted that the available research findings—using trials of civil cases—
found "no discernible difference" in the decisions of 6- and 12-person juries.
But these so-called jury experiments were mostly expressions of opinion based
on "uncontrolled observations that might be likened to clinical case studies"
(Saks, 1977, p. 9).

As Saks' thorough review notes, none of the studies was published in a
refereed social science journal. One simply asserted its conclusion without
any evidence; three were anecdotal observations, one reported only that a
smaller jury was used, and the last focused on the money saved by using smaller
juries. None of these would qualify as well-designed empirical research. Subsequent work by psychologists, it must be noted, did not find large differences
in the verdicts of juries of different sizes, but certainly group-process differences were present. Saks described these as follows:

> Large juries, compared to small juries, spend more time deliberating, engage in
> more communication per unit time, manifest better recall of testimony, induce
> less disparity between minority and majority factions in their rating of perceived
> jury performance and in sociometric ratings, and less disparity between convict-
> ing and acquitting juries in number of arguments generated, facilitate markedly
> better community representation, and though not achieving statistical significance,
> more consistent verdicts. (1977, p. 105)

In a follow up 20 years later, using meta-analysis to examine the effects of
17 studies that included more than 2000 juries of 6 persons or 12 people, Saks
and Marti (1997) found that the early conclusions were verified by more recent studies: larger juries were more likely to be racially heterogeneous, they
deliberated longer, they were more likely not to reach unanimity, and—to some
extent-they recalled the testimony more accurately.

So certainly there is room to question, on the basis of rigorous empirical
work, whether 6-person and 12-person juries function equivalently. Recall,
however, that Ballew's jury was composed of only 5 jurors.

As noted, the majority opinion in the *Ballew* case was written by Justice
Blackmun, using empirical research; for example, it contained "a 10-page, well-
documented discussion of legal and social scientific literature on group size
and jury size" (Tanke & Tanke, 1979, p. 1132). Apparently for the first time,
discussion of social science research was elevated from a footnote to the text
of a Supreme Court opinion. Justice Blackmun noted that:

- Smaller juries are less likely to encourage dissent, to overcome biases
  of individual jurors, or to aid the jurors in recalling significant evidence.
- Smaller juries produce less-consistent and less reliable verdicts, and
  increase the likelihood of a conviction.

- Smaller juries are less apt to be hung juries.
- Smaller juries, by that very fact, are less representative of minority populations.

But Justice Blackmun chose to focus his distinction between juries of six persons (which had previously been approved by the Supreme Court) and Ballew's five-person jury. His majority opinion concluded that although it could not "discern a clear line between six members and five," it had substantial doubt about "the reliability and appropriate representation of panels smaller than six" (*Ballew v. Georgia*, 1978, p. 239). Thus, it ruled that five was too small.

No research was (or is) available comparing juries of five and six persons, so it is ironic that Justice Blackmun used social science and statistical findings "to support his belief that juries of five are too small, but he was not willing to use the same body of research, almost all of which compared 6- and 12-person juries, to refute the Court's approval of the six-person jury" (Tanke & Tanke, 1979, p. 1133). Judges are reluctant to overturn past decisions, and in this case the research came too late.

Other Justices' Opinions

The *Ballew* decision was by no means a complete victory for psychology and empirical research. Even though the Court unanimously voted to overturn Ballew's obscenity conviction, only one other justice, Stevens, endorsed Justice Blackmun's reasons. Justice White voted against the rule of five jurors because "a jury of fewer than six persons would fail to represent the sense of community" (p. 245). Most disturbing was the opinion of Justice Powell (with which Chief Justice Burger and Justice Rehnquist concurred). Though noting that "a line must be drawn somewhere," Powell added:

> I have reservations as to the wisdom—as well as the necessity—of Mr. Justice Blackmun's heavy reliance on numerology derived from statistical studies. Moreover, neither the validity nor the methodology employed by the studies cited was subjected to the traditional testing mechanisms of the adversary process. The studies relied on merely represent unexamined findings of persons interested in the jury system. (p. 246)

Conclusions

The decision in the *Ballew* case was a bittersweet triumph for social science. As Tanke and Tanke observed, "For the first time, inferences drawn from such research became the central justification for the Court's decision rather than merely a pedagogically interesting sideshow" (1979, p. 1133). The opinions of the other justices, however, reflected the legal system's heavy reliance on the precedent of past rulings and on use of the adversary process (especially crossexamination) to evaluate the claims of science.

McCLESKY V. KEMP 1987

Warren McCleskey was a Black man who participated in the armed robbery of an Atlanta furniture store in the late 1970s. He was convicted of killing a White police officer who responded to the alarm of a robbery in progress. McCleskey was sentenced to death, but he challenged the constitutionality of this sentence on the grounds that the state of Georgia administered its death sentences in a racially discriminatory manner.

What was the basis for McCleskey's claim? What was the basis for the Court's rejection of this claim? McCleskey's appeal used statistical analysis, a fundamental method of the field of psychology. A law professor at the University of Iowa, David Baldus, and his associates (Baldus, Woodworth, & Pulaski, 1990) carried out two studies of Georgia's use of the death penalty. The larger of these consisted of the 2,484 homicide cases in Georgia between 1973 and 1979 that led to a conviction for murder or voluntary manslaughter. Of these, 65% included facts that made the defendant eligible for a death sentence under Georgia law. Of these, 8.7%, actually received a death sentence.

Analysis of the data found that defendants whose victims were White had a substantially higher likelihood of receiving a death sentence than those with Black victims. When the victim was White, 11% of homicide defendants were sentenced to death; with Black victims, only 1% of defendants received a death sentence. When the four possible combinations of race of the defendant and race of the victim were compared, the combination that led to a death sentence most often (in 21% of the cases) was White victim/Black defendant. The other combinations had the following percentages: White defendant/White victim, 8%; White defendant/Black victim, 3%; Black defendant/Black victim, 1%.

The Georgia figures are consistent with nationwide statistics. As a result of this survey, the Congress commissioned the General Accounting Office to do a study in 1990; the subsequent report concluded: "The race of the victim was found to influence the likelihood of being charged with capital murder or receiving the death penalty, i.e., those who murdered whites were found more likely to be sentenced to death than those who murdered blacks" (quoted by Coyle, 1994, p. A6). The mild tone of this conclusion does not fully convey certain important facts; for instance, since 1977 (through mid-1994), 63 Blacks have been executed for murdering Whites, whereas only one White has been executed for murdering a Black (Smolowe, 1994).

Can we then conclude, based only on such results, that the race of the participants (especially the victim) is the determining factor influencing the choice of a death sentence rather than a lesser punishment? Attorneys for the state of Georgia, in responding to McCleskey's appeal, argued that the homicides involving White victims were more violent and brutal than those involving Black victims (Russell, 1994). Baldus and his associates recognized that the characteristics of some cases made them more susceptible to severe sentences; for example, if the victim was also raped or tortured, or if the defendant also killed others. It is possible that the victims in these most heinous of homicides were more often White than Black, thus contributing to the results in the initial analysis. By evaluating the role of these factors, Baldus and his colleagues were able to clarify and pinpoint the racial discrimination. For example, when the crime involved extremely aggravating factors, such as multiple stab wounds, armed robbery, a child victim, or a prior record, the race of the victim had little effect on the sentence given, but with respect to homicides with only moderately aggravating factors, the race of the victim is quite influential, leading to a ratio of 3 to 1 (38% death-sentencing rate for murderers with White victims versus 13% death-sentencing rate for murderers with Black victims).

Interestingly, in the case of Warren McCleskey the aggravating factors fell into the midrange, where the race-of-victim effects were strongest (Baldus, Woodworth, & Pulaski, 1992, p. 262).

McCleskey's attorneys advanced two claims: The first was that "the persistent race-of-victim disparities, which [Baldus's] studies identified after adjusting for all plausible legitimate aggravating and mitigating circumstances, provided a sufficient basis for invalidating McCleskey's death sentence under the equal-protection clause of the Fourteenth Amendment" (Baldus *et al.*, 1992, p. 262). The second claim derived from the cruel and unusual punishments clause of the Eighth Amendment.

Neither of these claims was endorsed by the Supreme Court. In its majority opinion, Justice Lewis Powell chose to focus on *intent* to discriminate; he wrote that no equal-protection violation occurred, because McCleskey's attorneys did not prove "that the decision-makers in *his* case acted with discriminatory purpose," and that no evidence was presented "specific to his own case that would support an inference that racial considerations played a part in his sentence" (*McCleskey v. Kemp*, 1987, pp. 292–293). He even went on to write that statistical evidence of purposeful discrimination was not even relevant to equal protection claims of racial discrimination in death sentencing cases (*McClesky v. Kemp*, 1987, pp. 296–297). Furthermore, the Court held that any suggestion of discrimination in McCleskey's case was overcome by the presence of two factors that by statute were cited as aggravating—the previously mentioned armed robbery and the victim's being a police officer. For the Court, each of these provided a sufficient basis for imposing a death penalty.

As an aside, it should be noted that the courts, including the U.S. Supreme Court, have regularly used statistical evidence to infer intent to discriminate. They have also endorsed jury decisions and employment discrimination rulings brought under Title VII of the 1964 Civil Rights Act that rely on such data. Here, paradoxically, the Court imposed a more severe burden of proof on the appellant. (As Justice Blackmun noted on pages 347–348 of his dissenting opinion, one would have expected the Court to impose a less stringent burden of proof, because in death sentence cases society's ultimate sanction is involved.)

Additionally, Justice Powell's majority opinion suggested that the proper way to redress any claimed racial discrimination in sentencing was for legislatures to pass appropriate laws, rather than falling back on the courts for solutions. "McCleskey's arguments are best presented to legislative bodies," he wrote. When the Clinton administration proposed enacting a comprehensive crime control bill in 1994, the 38-member Congressional Black Caucus offered a provision–called the Racial Justice Act–that would have protected death row inmates from racial discrimination. Specifically, the proposal would let defendants who had been convicted in capital murder cases use statistical evidence of racial bias in past executions as a way of proving that their own death sentences were motivated by discrimination. The provision would have allowed inmates to establish a presumption that their sentences had been influenced by racial bias if they could show statistically significant patterns of bias in similar cases tried in the same courts; the burden of proving that the defendant's sentence was not due to discrimination would then fall on the prosecution. The Court would have to be satisfied that race was *not* the cause of apparent bias (Wines, 1994).

The proposed legislation would have applied only to capital cases tried in the federal courts; 99 out of every 100 homicides are state cases rather than federal. The federal death penalty was reenergized by the 1988 "drug kingpin" law that allowed it for certain drug-related murders. No inmate has been executed under federal law since 1963, but since passage of the new law, federal prosecutors have asked for death sentences in 37 drug-related cases. Almost 90 per cent of the defendants were minorities (29 Blacks and 4 Hispanics), even though the majority of drug kingpin defendants are thought to be White (Berkman, 1994; Marshall, 1994). For example, of those convicted of participating in a drug enterprise under the general provisions of the new law, 75% were White.

Furthermore, early evaluations of the revised sentencing guidelines for federal crimes, instituted in 1987, showed a racial bias in sentencing. The U.S. Sentencing Commission found that from October 1, 1989, through September 30, 1990, about half (54%) of the Whites facing mandatory minimum sentences actually received them, whereas nearly two-thirds (68%) of the Blacks did.

Critics of the proposed Racial Justice Act responded in various ways. Some said the act's real purpose was eliminating the death penalty entirely; some claimed it would force the courts to reevaluate every capital murder trial since 1976 (Snow, 1994). Others argued that the figures on executions showed that the law was unnecessary. For example, here is the FBI's Uniform Crime Reports homicide data for 1992:

> For white victims, 4490 cases with White of fenders and 794 cases with Black offenders.
>> For Black victims, 291 cases with White offenders and 5164 cases with Black offenders.

Despite the fact that Blacks committed more overall homicides (5958 to 4790), Blacks comprised 39% of those executed, as compared with 54% for Whites.

The Racial Justice Act passed the U.S. House of Representatives but was defeated in the Senate. When the Clinton administration's anticrime bill was adopted by both houses in August 1994, the Racial Justice Act was not part of it. Thus the statistical analyses and related psychological research had no impact on either the Court or the Congress.

CONCLUSIONS

The century-long interaction between experimental psychology and the law began with a leading spokesperson for psychology making inflated promises about the impact of his field. The reaction by the legal profession was defensiveness followed by neglect. It was not until the middle of the century that psychology again attempted to have an influence on the courts, and the impact of its findings and testimony remains controversial. At the very least, however, the Supreme Court showed that it was willing to pay attention to psychology's conclusions if they provided support for a decision favored by the justices. The last quarter of the century has seen a more organized attempt by the field of psychology to have an impact; specific approaches are described in Chapters 8 and 9, after the general use of *amicus* briefs by the American Psychological Association is described in Chapter 7.

7

The American Psychological Association's Organized *Amicus* Activity

HISTORY AND FUNCTION OF *AMICUS* BRIEFS

Historically, *amicus curiae* briefs were offered by bystanders or others who had no interest in the outcome, but had knowledge relevant to a point of law or evidence in the case. The inclusion of such briefs has been traced back to an appearance by Henry Clay before the Supreme Court in 1821 (Krislov, 1963), although more than a hundred years would pass before anything about *amicus* briefs was incorporated into the Supreme Court's rules of procedure (Menez, 1984). The designation *amicus curiae* (friend of the court) is now something of a misnomer in most examples, as the organization submitting the brief is typically aligned with one party to the dispute.

Why submit an *amicus* brief? Probably the most frequent reason is to persuade the Court to render a favorable ruling. Scientific organizations such as the American Psychological Association, however, can play a "knowledge broker" role through their briefs; that is, they can inform the courts of relevant research evidence and its implications without necessarily pushing for one outcome, as is discussed in detail later in this chapter.

One reason for organizations to submit briefs is as a response to membership pressure to try to influence public policy; an organization lacking much in financial resources or legal staff may find an *amicus* brief a much less expensive way of participating in a case than initiating a court action on its own (Wasby, 1992). Organizations on one side of a controversial, highly publicized issue may also submit briefs to counteract the sheer number of briefs submitted by organizations on the other side.

Not just anyone can submit an *amicus* brief. For Supreme Court cases, an organization wanting to submit a brief must either obtain permission from each party or petition the Supreme Court for permission (Tremper, 1987). The most frequent participants are corporations and business groups, citizen organizations, and states (Caldeira & Wright, 1990); *amicus* briefs by individuals are rare. Briefs may be submitted prior to the *cert.* decision—perhaps to alert the Court of the case's importance—as well as after the case has been accepted for review.

Generally nongovernmental organizations seeking to submit *amicus* briefs are allowed to do so. Between 1969 and 1981, only 11% of such requests were denied (O'Connor & Epstein, 1983). The solicitor general may submit a brief on behalf of the United States without the consent of the parties involved; so too may federal agencies or states. Sometimes the Court will invite the solicitor general to submit an *amicus* brief reflecting the federal government's position. Whatever the sponsor, *amicus* briefs must not duplicate the content of briefs from the contesting parties (Supreme Court Rule 40).

At the point when judges were deciding whether to grant *certiorari*, the submission of a large number of *amicus* briefs advocating review increased the likelihood that *cert.* would be granted (Caldeira & Wright, 1988, 1994), but if *amicus* briefs were submitted arguing that the case should *not* be heard, the result was also to improve the chances that it would be. Baum (1997) saw this latter result as reflecting the Court's concern with achieving legal accuracy and clarity.

Attorneys who submit *amicus* briefs on behalf of interested organizations are not allowed to participate—as such representatives—in the oral arguments before the Court except "in the most extraordinary circumstances" (Supreme Court Rule 38.7). But they may participate by representing one of the interested parties in the case. For example, in the case of *Brown v. Board of Education* (1954), the petitioner, Linda Brown, was represented by Thurgood Marshall, who was then chief counsel of the NAACP's Legal Defense Fund. So for public interest lawyers who represent organizations such as the American Civil Liberties Union (ACLU) or the National Association for the Advancement of Colored People (NAACP), submission to the Supreme Court has two goals: to promote the cause that the group advocates, and to win the case (Gasper, 1972).

Unlike private organizations that submit *amicus* briefs, the solicitor general is often permitted some time at the oral arguments to present the government's position. If the government is not the initiating party, the solicitor general's remarks cannot usually exceed 5 to 10 minutes.

When the solicitor general submits a brief requesting the Supreme Court to grant *cert.*, the petition is much more likely to gain approval for review (Caldeira & Wright, 1988). For example, in the 1995 term, *cert.* was granted 78% of the time when the government requested it; only 1% of other petitions were granted *cert.* (Baum, 1997). Similarly, when a case is decided by the Court, litigants are much more likely to win if the solicitor general's office has joined their side (George & Epstein, 1992; Segal & Reedy, 191)8). As noted by Baum (1997), scholars have offered a variety of explanations for the solicitor general's success:

- The expertise of the solicitor general's office in litigation (Provine, 1980)
- The office's *perceived* expertise, which gives greater weight to its viewpoints (Scigliano, 1971)
- The justices' gratitude to the executive branch for its self-restraint in petitioning for *cert.* (Scigliano, 1971)
- The Court's dependence on the executive branch to give implementation and legitimacy to its decisions (Pure, 1981; Salokar, 1992)
- An unusually strong set of petitions via the solicitor general's careful case screening (O'Connor, 1983)
- Overlap in perspective between the current president's appointments to the Court and the solicitor general's office (Scigliano, 1971)

According to Baum's 1997 review, the most systematic research on possible reasons is that of McGuire (1996), who analyzed *decisions on the merits* during the 1977–82 terms. McGuire concluded that "the expertise of lawyers in the Solicitor General's Office based on their experience before the Court accounted for at least the preponderance of their high rate of success" (Baum, 1997, p. 33).

USE OF *AMICUS* BRIEFS BY OTHER ORGANIZATIONS

Professional organizations and interest groups have not been reluctant to submit *amicus* briefs to the courts. In fact, some observers consider the increased use of *amicus* briefs as taking on "the appearance of group combat" (Menez, 1984, p. 111). Even back in 1950, approximately 40 organizations filed briefs in the appeal of "The Hollywood Ten." In that matter the Communist-sponsored *Daily Worker* urged individuals to file "personal briefs" by writing letters to the Supreme Court justices (Menez, 1984). In the following paragraphs, three prominent cases are described, with emphasis on the frequency and impact of *amicus* briefs submitted in support of one side or the other.

REGENTS OF THE UNIVERSITY OF CALIFORNIA V. BAKKE 1978

Allan Bakke was one of 2,664 applicants for admission to the medical school at the University of California at Davis in 1973. Only 100 applicants were admitted; 84 places were filled through the regular admissions procedures and 16 by minority applicants who were "disadvantaged." The regular and special admissions programs were not just separate, they were screened by an entirely different student-faculty committee using different criteria. In 1973 the 16 applicants admitted under the special program had undergraduate grade point averages of 2.88, as compared with 3.49 for the 84 students admitted through the regular admissions process (Schwartz, 1988). The "disadvantaged" students' scores on the medical school aptitude test were also lower.

Allan Bakke's application was denied, even though his credentials were stronger than those of the 16 minority students who were admitted. (His scores fell just short of being admitted through the regular admissions process.) Bakke filed a lawsuit claiming that preferential treatment of minorities was a form of racial discrimination and that the university's procedure of reserving positions for minorities denied him equal protection of the law under the 14th Amendment. Both the state trial court and the California Supreme Court had ruled that racially exclusionary preferences constituted a quota and that such quotas were a denial of equal protection, unless there was evidence of prior discrimination. Thus, the Regents of the University of California appealed to the U.S. Supreme Court.

The *Bakke* case aroused great interest across the country. Some 63 *amicus* briefs were filed with the Court; of these, probably the most important was that of the federal government. It considered the key question to be whether a state university's admissions program may take race into account. The brief answered its own question by saying: "Insofar as the judgment of the Supreme Court of California declares that the Medical School may not consider the race of applicants for the purpose of operating a properly administered affirmative action admissions program, the judgment should be reversed" (quoted by B. Schwartz, 1988, p. 45).

Did the government's brief have an influence on the Court in the *Bakke* case? We cannot say for sure; the Supreme Court's ruling was more complex than the thrust of the brief. By a narrow vote of 5 to 4, the Court held that a university may consider racial criteria as part of the admission process as long as "fixed quotas" were not used. The justices were not of one mind, however; six different opinions were submitted. Justice Powell, writing for the majority, authorized the permissibility of racial considerations in admissions but also ordered that Allan Bakke be admitted, because the process used in the Davis program had "totally foreclosed" (p. 305) him from competing for the 16 special positions; thus, he had been denied equal protection.

Allan Bakke, upon hearing the decision, announced that he would enter the medical school the following September. At age 38, he would be a decade or more older than most of his classmates.

WEBSTER V. REPRODUCTIVE HEALTH SERVICES 1989

In 1989 the Supreme Court faced another case concerning abortion—this one dealing with the legality of a Missouri law's restrictions, which included barring state hospitals from being the site of abortions, and requiring physicians to determine the viability of the fetus in cases in which conception, in the judgment of the physician, had occurred 20 or more weeks earlier. (Since there is a 4-week error in judging gestational age, a "20-week" fetus might be 24 weeks, or into the third trimester. Under *Roe v. Wade,* states can regulate third-trimester abortions to protect viable fetuses.)

Again organizations on both sides of the argument took positions; a total of 78 *amicus* briefs were filed, more than in the *Bakke* case. Both sides went even further. They sought to influence public opinion through the media, they marched and protested, and they held vigils outside the Supreme Court building (Epstein, 1991).

BOWEN V. KENDRICK 1988

The case of *Bowen v. Kendrick* (1988) was another one involving abortion restrictions. It derived from the passage of the Adolescent Family Life Act, a law that gave federal grants to organizations providing services and research on adolescent sexual relations and pregnancy. Of relevance here is not just the number of *amicus* briefs filed, but also the number of organizations signing onto a brief. For example, an organization called the National Coalition for Public Education and Religious Liberty prepared a brief arguing that the law should be struck down; almost 30 other groups joined, including the National Congress of Parents and Teachers and the Society for the Scientific Study of Sex. The National Organization for Women (NOW) was also opposed; almost 20 other organizations signed on to the brief submitted by NOW's Legal Defense and Education Fund.

PSYCHOLOGY'S USE OF *AMICUS* BRIEFS

The submission of *amicus* briefs that have the endorsement of the American Psychological Association is largely a phenomenon of the last 25 years. Although the first APA-sponsored brief was submitted in 1962 (the case of *Jenkins v. United States,* involving the right of psychologists as expert witnesses to state professional opinions), the next was not submitted until 1971. This section describes how the process evolved.

INVOLVEMENT BY PSYCHOLOGISTS AS INDIVIDUALS

Psychologists as individuals have shown interest in submitting briefs, as Chapter 6 demonstrated. Although the statement submitted in the Brown case reflected an organized effort by more than 30 psychologists and other social scientists, on other occasions, individuals, such as the Tankes or Professor Baldus, have offered a relevant social science perspective to the Court. Organized psychology has been active in this regard only since the mid-1970s.

ORGANIZED PSYCHOLOGY'S RELUCTANCE TO GET INVOLVED

The APA's membership of more than 100,000 psychologists reflects a wide range of values. One reason that psychology as an organization has been slow to move may be the varying opinions within the field about the acceptability of applying knowledge to real-world issues. Even among those who believe in the applying such knowledge, a second disagreement exists, a disagreement about the nature of *amicus* briefs. Should they objectively report scientific findings, or should they reflect an advocate's stance? Both of these questions are considered after a brief history of APA's *amicus* involvement.

FORMATION OF COLI AND THE OFFICE OF GENERAL COUNSEL

The year that the *Ballew* case was decided—1979—the American Psychological Association established the Office of General Counsel and the Committee on Legal Issues (COLI); their presence gave greater impetus to the submission of APA briefs.

One of the functions of the two organizations is to decide whether the psychological data, conclusions, and recommendations are relevant to the cases being appealed. If so, then the APA submits an *amicus curiae* brief. In fact, almost 100 such briefs have been prepared, about one third for Supreme Court cases and two thirds for other appellate courts (Foote, 1998).

The procedure is as follows:

1. Any member of the APA or an organization within the APA can submit a request to the Office of General Counsel that the APA file a brief for an upcoming case.
2. The office then develops relevant case materials and a written analysis of the case.
3. These are submitted for review to the appropriate APA directorates,

which consult with their constituencies, such as APA divisions and state associations. It must be established that there is broad-based support within the APA's membership (Foote, 1998).

4. The chair of COLI appoints a panel to examine the materials and responses from the directorates.
5. The panel then decides whether to recommend to the APA board of directors whether the brief should be filed.
6. If the recommendation is favorable, the board of directors votes on whether to approve it or not. (In the past 5 years, the board has accepted every recommendation from COLI.)
7. If approved, the Office of General Counsel prepares the brief, with consultation from COLI members and perhaps other APA members.

Throughout this process certain questions serve as determinants (Foote, 1998):

- Is participation consistent with the objectives and polices of the American Psychological Association?
- Is the issue significant to the field of psychology?
- Can the APA make a significant contribution?
- Is there sufficient research to address the issue?
- If so, does it present a strong position on the case?
- What are the anticipated policy implications?

Not all requests survive the review process; sometimes there is no body of research or accepted viewpoint on the topic (McHugh, 1998). An example is physician-assisted suicide. An APA member, James L. Werth (19911), proposed that the APA submit a brief because mental health professionals had much to contribute to an understanding of the topic. With his colleague Judith Gordon, he prepared a set of materials that was submitted to the APA for review. But when the Office of General Counsel sought responses, the feedback noted that the APA had never taken a position on the controversial issue of physician-assisted suicide (McHugh, 1998). The timing was also very tight on this request.

CLASSIFYING APA BRIEFS

The APA's *amicus* briefs have covered a variety of topics, from the right to execute mentally retarded offenders to the rights of homosexual persons to the uses of psychological tests in personnel selection. Abortion cases generated 9 briefs; confidentiality issues generated 8. Often, the brief's purpose is to offer psychological expertise on challenging legal issues, such as the death penalty (4 cases), insanity (4 cases), battered woman syndrome (2 cases) and children as court witnesses (2 cases). As noted, a number have dealt with professional or guild issues, such as access to patients (10 cases) and advocacy for mentally ill people in their interaction with the legal and treatment systems (17 cases).

Several classifications of these briefs have been proposed. Roesch, Golding, Hans, and Reppucci (1991) suggested organizing them along a continuum. At one end would be the *science-translation brief,* intended to be "an objective summary of research" (p. 6); at the other end would be the *advocacy brief,* which "takes a position on some legal or public policy issue" (p. 6). But often this distinction is blurred, because all briefs must evaluate and interpret research, and inevitably the values of the brief writers will be reflected. For example, in the case of *Price Waterhouse v. Hopkins* (1989)—to be examined in detail later in this chapter—psychologist Susan Fiske testified as an expert witness for Ann Hopkins when she first brought suit against Price Waterhouse for sex stereotyping and discrimination. Professor Fiske was later one of the co-authors of the APA's brief when Price Waterhouse appealed the trial decision to the Supreme Court. Concluding that the brief Fiske helped to write "sought to vouch for the general acceptance of what she had earlier testified to," Michael Saks (1993) noted that "this is somewhat like signing one's own letter of recommendation" (p. 238).

Where do we draw the line between a science-translation brief and an advocacy brief? Saks (1993), commenting on APA briefs, observes:

> In least three cases I know of (*Hopkins* not among them), some members of the brief-writing group came away with the distinct impression that the brief was being written in order to advance the interests of one of the parties to the litigation, or to produce a particular outcome, rather than to share knowledge with the Court for the Court's benefit. (p. 243)

This comment reflects the necessity for brief writers to clarify their goals before they begin the task.

Another way to classify APA briefs is to distinguish between those that, as above, seek to translate scientific knowledge into relevant applications and those concerned with issues central to the *profession* of psychology. The latter, called *guild-interest briefs*, seek to protect the psychology profession's integrity, and they implicitly assume that what is good for psychology is good for society. Most of the briefs reviewed in this book are not guild-issue briefs, but one example of such a brief is included here as an illustration.

In the case of *Oregon v. Miller* (19115), the APA and the Oregon Psychological Association filed an *amicus* brief in support of a criminal defendant's contention that Oregon's therapist–patient privilege of confidentiality should apply to his having called a mental hospital and told both a receptionist and a psychiatrist that he had just killed a man. The Oregon Supreme Court adopted the APA's interpretation of what constituted a privileged communication.

The APA's Goals for Science-Translation Briefs

Psychologists disagree as to how much advocacy is appropriate in APA briefs. These disagreements also influence the stated goals when the APA has submitted science-translation briefs.

One goal is to inform the Court. Perhaps the best way to express this goal is to state that the APA has knowledge the Court doesn't have. Saks (1993), emphasizing the objective goal of such briefs, sees the APA as a knowledge broker, "a neutral, honest provider of information, unconcerned with which party is helped or harmed by the data and the brief" (p. 243). Implicit here is the expectation that the brief reports any differences in psychologists' conclusions and the distribution of opinions (Saks, p. 243). It seems to follow that if the court pays attention to the psychological input and reflects awareness of it in its decisions, the goal of submitting the brief has been met.

A related goal is to show to the Court where the appropriate research can be found; that is, to educate the Court in distinguishing between good research and bad research. Such briefs "may reduce the likelihood that judicial use of spurious, unsubstantiated opinions about human behavior will establish precedent for future cases" (Grisso & Saks, 1991, p. 207). Chapter 6 described the reliance on nonempirical "studies" in the *Williams v. Florida* case concerning jury size. We now have empirical studies that are relevant. Again, recognition by the courts that some research is better than other research would suffice for achieving this goal.

A general question remains: How much do we have to know to submit a brief? How much do psychologists have to agree? Saks (1993) has noted that we have no clear-cut standards to guide us. This may be true, but we have concepts that can help us to understand why psychologists' opinions differ. Kassin and Wrightsman (1983) proposed that jurors contemplating evidence in a criminal trial possess varying degrees of either pro-prosecution or prodefense biases, derived from their positions on two dimensions: their standard for reasonable doubt and their estimate of the probability that the defendant committed the crime. A juror's verdict could be predicted from his or her position on these two dimensions. This analysis can be extended to differences in psychologists' reactions to involvement with the court system. First, instead of a standard of reasonable doubt, an analogous standard of reliability may exist. How consistent should a phenomenon be to declare it reliable? And how is consistency measured: a box score of different studies' results, the percentage of variance accounted for, a meta-analysis? Monahan and Walker (1988) proposed the same standard for going public as for peer evaluation.

Rogers Elliott (1991) has sought a higher standard. Psychologists, he believes, should reflect "organized skepticism." Self-labels to describe those who insist on an exceedingly high standard include "cautious" and "prudent." It would seem that for these psychologists, the state of knowledge must reach certainty. Does this mean that no situation exists in which they would endorse involvement with the courts? Elliott's response: "The claim made here is not that scientific organizations should not or may not (or should or may) take moral positions. Rather, it is that, if they do so, they should not affect to base them on scientific foundations when such foundations are insufficient to bear the argument constructed on them" (p. 74).

In a critique of his peers testifying on eyewitness accuracy, Elliott (1993) referred to one of the findings of a survey of 63 psychologist experts by Kassin, Ellsworth, and Smith (1989). They had asked these experts if the empirical evidence supported the statement that "the use of one-person showups instead of full lineups increases the risk of misidentification" (p. 1091); 83% indicated that it was reliable enough to justify testifying to that effect, even though the authors point out that no studies have compared lineups with showups, so the experts are extrapolating from related research and theory. Elliott argued that in such cases, psychologists should say nothing at all. "Scientists will always know more about their issues than nonscientists, but up to some point that we are far from attaining, the temptations of our new knowledge will lead us to promise more than we can deliver" (1993, p. 425).

In contrast, those psychologists who support submitting *amicus* briefs and testifying as expert witnesses, although demanding a generally consistent pattern of research findings, do not share Dr. Elliott's standards regarding reliability. The "best available evidence" argument proposes that it is appropriate for psychologists to testify even if their conclusions are tentative (McCloskey, Egeth, & McKenna, 1986). Yarmey (1986) argued that an expert's statements should conform to the criterion of scientific respectability, but that absolute certainty is not required. He suggested the following criterion: Is the evidence clear, convincing, reliable, and valid, or is it so ambiguous that experts could find support for whatever position they wished to defend? Similarly, in support of the "clear and convincing" standard of proof, Ellsworth wrote, "To keep silent until our understanding is perfect is to keep silent forever. . . . I think we should file briefs when we believe that we have something to say that would improve the quality of the court's decision making" (1991, p. 89). Donald Bersoff (1987) has asked what state of data would ever be strong enough to persuade critics and skeptics to testify? And Elizabeth Loftus (1986) noted that "we do not have the luxury of waiting until researchers get around to completing all the studies that would be desirable" (p. 249).

The second dimension developed by Kassin and Wrightsman, (1983) *probability of commission,* may also be used to understand differences among psychologists, because psychologists, like jurors, differ in the perception and weighing of the facts. Bermant (1986) proposed that these assessments of the strength of available evidence are major factors in the propriety of psychologists' involvement. Part of the difference in evidence interpretations results from the degree to which psychologists show sympathy for the defendant and display a concern about erroneous convictions. This, of course, operates on a case-by-case basis, even though individual differences in general predispositions are also present.

As Ring (1971) observed more than two decades ago, most social psychologists are politically liberal, but not all are. Social scientists who sympathize with the defendant are often skeptical that the defendant truly committed the crime, or that the eyewitnesses were truly accurate, or that the confession was truly voluntary. A major concern of politically liberal psychologists is that some defendants will be wrongly convicted, imprisoned, and executed. Their critics do not share this view. McCloskey and Egeth (1983) argued that wrongful convictions from mistaken eyewitness testimony reflect only a "small fraction of the 1% of the cases in which defendants were convicted in least in part on the basis of eyewitness testimony" (p. 552). Konecni and Ebbesen approvingly quote the above, and conclude from it "that in the state of California one person is wrongfully convicted approximately every three years because of mistaken eyewitness testimony" (1986, p. 119).

Thus, the second dimension: How many errors of *omission* are we willing to make to avoid making one error of *commission*? Konecni and Ebbesen went on to say:

> One wrongful conviction every three years because of mistaken identification in a state the size of California (if the estimates given above are correct) may be one wrongful conviction too many, but most reasonable people would probably regard it as well within the domain of "acceptable risk'—acceptable because no workable system of justice is perfect. (1986, p. 119)

But for politically liberal psychologists, one wrongful conviction really is too many. In that regard, they seek a standard of perfection in some ways similar to the standard of perfect research consistency sought by their critics. Both seek "zero defects."

AN APA *AMICUS* BRIEF: *PRICE WATERHOUSE V. HOPKINS* 1989

Psychology's involvement in the court action that reached the Supreme Court as *Price Waterhouse v. Hopkins* (1989) reflects both the benefits and the temptations of organized psychology's attempt to give direction to the courts. The APA felt that it had "special knowledge" to impart to the Court in this case; specifically, it believed it could assist the justices in their understanding of the role that gender stereotyping sometimes played in employment decisions, hence a committee of APA members drafted an *amicus* brief that received APA authorization (Fiske, Bersoff, Borgida, Deaux, & Heilman, 2991). The brief sought to present research findings relevant to the question of whether Ms. Hopkins was treated differently from male candidates for promotion. It is true that the Court's decision acknowledged the presence of sex discrimination under Title VII of the 1964 Civil Rights Act after reviewing testimony by a psychologist and an APA *amicus* brief on the psychology of stereotyping, but neither the process nor the outcome were free of criticism.

Ann Hopkins in 1982 was a very successful salesperson and a senior manager at Price Waterhouse, one of the nation's leading accounting firms. She had brought in business worth $25,000,000. Her clients raved about her, and she had more billable hours than any other person proposed for partner that year. According to company policy, partners were to submit written comments and recommendations with respect to each partnership candidate. The company's policy board made the final decision. Some of the written commentaries about Ms. Hopkins were positive, some were negative. Several comments emphasized the impressive and central role she played in securing a contract worth millions of dollars for the company (in fact, she was the only one of the 88 candidates that year to have secured a major contract for Price Waterhouse). They also praised her character and described her as "an outstanding professional" who had a "deft touch" and "a strong character, independence, and integrity" (*Price Waterhouse v. Hopkins*, 1989, p. 233). But other comments reflected some partners' dislike of her personality, portraying her as "macho," as "a lady [who] us[ed] profanity," and as a "masculine hard-nosed manager" who "overcompensated for being a woman" (p. 235).

The result was that she was not made a partner—that year or the next. The powers that be at Price Waterhouse ostensibly rejected her because of "interpersonal skills problems"; she was even described as needing "a course at charm school." A colleague reportedly advised her that she would improve her chances if she would "walk more femininely, talk more femininely, dress more feminine, wear make-up, have her hair styled, and wear jewelry" (*Hopkins v. Price Waterhouse*, 1985, p. 117).

After the second straight year of rejection, Ann Hopkins took her employer to court for sex discrimination and a violation of Title VII of the 1964 Civil Rights Act. The above information, while disturbing, was not enough to win the case; she had to demonstrate that the stereotypical remarks amounted to discrimination in the decision not to make her a partner. Thus social psychologist Susan Fiske of the University of Massachusetts at Amherst was asked to testify as an expert witness. She agreed to do so because she felt the case fit with the scientific literature on gender stereotyping to a striking degree.

Dr. Fiske's testimony included general information and also applications to the specific situation; such testimony has come to be called "social framework" testimony (Monahan & Walker, 1988) because it may assist the factfinder in determining the facts in the case at hand (Monahan & Walker, 1991).

In recent years trial courts have been more willing to admit such testimony (Goodman & Croyle, 1989; Goodman, 1993).

An account by Fiske and her colleagues describes the nature of her testimony in the trial (called *Hopkins v. Price Waterhouse*):

> [It] drew on both laboratory and field research to describe antecedent conditions that encourage stereotyping, indicators that reveal stereotyping, consequences of stereotyping for out-groups, and feasible remedies to prevent the intrusion of stereotyping into decision making. Specifically, [Fiske] testified that stereotyping is most likely to intrude when the target is an isolated, one-of-a-kind or few-of-a-kind individual in an otherwise homogeneous environment. The person's solo or near-solo status makes the unusual category more likely to be a salient factor in decision making. (Fiske *et al.*, 1991, p. 1050)

Of 88 candidates proposed for partner in 1982, Ann Hopkins was the only woman; of 662 partners, only seven were women.

Among many relevant matters, Fiske also testified that subjective judgments of interpersonal skills and collegiality—apparently central to the partnership decision—are quite vulnerable to stereotypic biases, and that decision makers should be alert to the possibility of stereotyping when they employ subjective criteria.

In the decisions by Price Waterhouse about new partners, the opinions of persons with limited hearsay information were apparently given the same weight as the opinions of those who had more extensive and relevant contact with Ann Hopkins (Fiske et al., 1991). Furthermore, Price Waterhouse had no policy prohibiting sex discrimination. As Fiske and her colleagues observed, "Consistent with this failure to establish organizational norms emphasizing fairness, overt expressions of prejudice were not discouraged" (p. 1051). In her testimony, Fiske noted that many of Price Waterhouse's practices could be remedied with the firm application of psychological concepts and findings.

At the trial the presiding judge, Gerhard Gesell, after evaluating all the testimony, ruled that an "employer that treats [a] woman with [an] assertive personality in a different manner than if she had been a man is guilty of sex discrimination" (*Hopkins v. Price Waterhouse*, 1985, p. 1119). He concluded that Price Waterhouse had legitimately used interpersonal skills as one of the factors in the partnership decision but that the decision had also relied on comments that resulted from gender stereotyping. He imposed liability on the employer, partly because Price Waterhouse took no steps to prevent or eliminate sexism in promotion decisions.

Price Waterhouse—not surprisingly—appealed Judge Gesell's decision, and in doing so argued that the social psychologist's testimony was "sheer speculation" of "no evidentiary value" (*Price Waterhouse v. Hopkins*, 1987, p. 467). The majority of the three-person appeals court panel disagreed with this portrayal, ruling that "partners at Price Waterhouse often evaluated female candidates in terms of their sex. . . . The partnership selection process at Price Waterhouse was impermissibly infected by stereotypical attitudes toward female candidates" (*Price Waterhouse v. Hopkins*, 1987, p. 468).

But not all the appellate judges had a positive reaction to the testimony of the social psychologist. The dissenting judge described Dr. Fiske as someone "purporting" to be an expert and he sarcastically concluded that: "To an expert of Dr. Fiske's qualifications, it seems plain that no woman could be overbearing, arrogant, or abrasive: any observation to that effect would necessarily be discounted as the product of stereotyping" (*Price Waterhouse v. Hopkins*, 1987, p. 477). This circuit-court judge implied that the intensity of the negative reaction was, for Dr. Fiske, sufficient to detect the presence of gender stereotyping.

After Judge Gesell's decision was upheld by this three-judge circuit court panel, Price Waterhouse asked the Supreme Court to review the case, and because various appellate court decisions in the *Hopkins* case and in other similar cases had been in conflict, the Court accepted the case for review. The American Psychological Association submitted an *amicus* brief, drafted by Dr. Fiske, Donald Bersoff, Eugene Borgida, Kay Deaux, and Madeline E. Heilman (summary is reprinted in the 1991 *American Psychologist*, 46, pp. 1061–1070).

On May 1, 1989, the Supreme Court handed down its decision, voting 6 to 3 to uphold a significant portion of Judge Gesell's decision. (The majority opinion was written by Justice Brennan; others in the majority were Justices Blackmun, Marshall, Stevens, White, and O'Connor; the minority included Justices Kennedy, Rehnquist, and Scalia.) Specifically, the majority ruled that in such cases as these "it is not permissible for employers to use discriminatory criteria, and they (not the plaintiff) must bear the burden of persuading the trier of fact that their decision would have been the same if no impermissible discrimination had taken place" (quoted by Fiske *et al.*, 1991, p. 1054). However, the Court also ruled that Judge Cesell had held Price Waterhouse to too high a standard of proof (i.e., clear and convincing evidence) and that he should review the facts in light of a less stringent standard (preponderance of the evidence) to see if Price Waterhouse was still liable. Specifically, he was to determine whether Price Waterhouse met the preponderance of evidence standard in asserting that it had a legitimate reason for denying Ms. Hopkins a partnership. If it could prove by this standard that it would have made the same decision even if it had not taken the plaintiff's gender into account, then Price Waterhouse could avoid liability.

It appeared that the testimony of a research psychologist and the subsequent APA brief had a significant impact on the judge's decision in a landmark case—a case for which a major aspect of the ruling was upheld by the Supreme Court. The Court agreed with the trial judge that:

> The reactions of at least some of the partners were reactions to her as a woman manager. Where an evaluation is based on a subjective assessment of a person's strengths and weaknesses, it is simply not true that each evaluator will focus on. or even mention, the same weaknesses. Thus, even if we knew that Hopkins had 'personality problems,' this would not tell us that the partners who base their evaluations of Hopkins in sex-based terms would have criticized her as sharply (or criticized her at all) if she had been a man. It is not our job to review the evidence and decide that negative reactions to Hopkins were based on reality; our perception of Hopkins' character is irrelevant. We sit not to determine whether Ms. Hopkins is nice, but to decide whether the partners reacted negatively to her personality because she is a woman. (*Price Waterhouse v. Hopkins*, 1989, pp. 1794–1795)

Justice Brennan's majority decision went on to state:

> In the specific context of sex stereotyping, an employer who acts on the basis of a belief that a woman cannot be aggressive, or that she must not be, has acted on the basis of gender. . . . We are beyond the day when an employer could evaluate employees by assuming or insisting that they matched the stereotype associated with their group. . . . An employer who objects to aggressiveness in women but whose positions require this trait places women in an intolerable Catch 22: out of a job if they behave aggressively and out of a job if they don't. Title VII lifts women out of this bind. (pp. 1790–1791)

But the decision disregarded the *amicus* brief and downplayed the impact of the expert witness's testimony; in fact, the majority opinion stated:

> Indeed, we are tempted to say that Dr. Fiske's expert testimony was merely icing on Hopkins' cake. It takes no special training to discern sex stereotyping in a description of an aggressive female employee as requiring "a course at charm school." Nor . . . does it require expertise in psychology to know that, if an employee's flawed "interpersonal skills' can be corrected by a soft-hued suit or a new shade of lipstick, perhaps it is the employee's sex and not her interpersonal skills that has drawn criticism. (*Price Watehouse v. Hopkins*, 1989, p. 1793)

In their article describing this case, Susan Fiske and her colleagues made the following response to this part of the decision: "One can interpret this comment in various ways; as dismissive, saying that the social science testimony was all common sense; as merely taking the social psychological expertise for granted; or as suggesting that one does not necessarily require expert witnesses to identify stereotyping when the evidence is egregious" (1991, p. 1054).

Though any one of these is a possibility, none is congruent with the claim that social science evidence really made a difference. In fact, the decision may be read as a subtle putdown of psychology "invading the turf" of another discipline.

Furthermore, not all psychologists have endorsed Fiske's conclusions. Gerald V. Barrett and Scott B. Morris (1991) have criticized her testimony and also criticized the APA *amicus* brief, claiming that the latter accepted Hopkins' version of the facts, selected only those psychological theories that supported their position, and incompletely represented the empirical literature. Fiske and colleagues (Fiske, Bersoff, Borgida, Deaux, & Heilman, 1993) marshaled a detailed reply, which included a review of several meta-analyses that confirmed the original conclusion about conditions under which stereotyping of female employees is most likely to occur.

The APA's behavior in this case reflects one of the obstacles it faces when interacting with the courts. The brief had noted that the APA wished to inform the Court "of scientific thought regarding stereotyping, particularly as it affects judgments of women in work settings" and that it would leave it to the parties "to argue the merits of the question presented" (p. 10). But the drafters clearly had their preferences about the Supreme Court's decision, and as we have noted, not all psychologists support their conclusions.

In fact, another goal of the APA *amicus* brief was to refute the attacks on Dr. Fiske's testimony that were part of Price Waterhouse's brief in its appeal to the Supreme Court. It noted that the attack made by Price Waterhouse against Dr. Fiske "exposes a lack of sophistication and knowledge about the nature of scientific research in general and sex stereotyping in particular" (APA brief, p. 11). The body of social science research on sex stereotyping was extensively covered in the brief, specifically, sex stereotyping in the workplace was covered, and the methods by which discriminatory stereotyping could be prevented were reviewed. The brief noted that Price Waterhouse failed to use any of these methods, and concluded that gender stereotyping was present at Price Waterhouse, that it was "transformed into discriminatory behavior," and that it played a significant role in denying Ms. Hopkins a partnership.

Was this a science translation brief or an advocacy brief? The part that focused on educating the Court about the scientific studies regarding gender stereotyping was consistent with the APA's science-translation goal of applying research findings to legal questions. The brief's recognition that the indices of gender stereotyping were present at Price Waterhouse-based on the evidence presented by Ms. Hopkins-may also be consistent with the science-translation goal, although it more clearly borders on advocacy. The connection here between the laboratory research and the workplace may be seen as assisting the Court to recognize the application of the research to this particular case. Still, Jane Goodman, in reviewing the brief, said: "There is little question that the APA's brief has more features in common with an appellate brief submitted by advocates for one party or another than it does with a traditional nonpartisan *Brandeis brief*" (1993, p. 252).

But when the APA brief concluded that gender stereotyping was "transformed into discriminatory behavior" (APA brief, p. 12), it was clearly stepping outside of its educator role and into the role of advocate. Was it not presumptuous of the APA to offer a *legal* argument? What qualifies as "dis-

criminatory behavior" to the courts is a legal question, determined by refer-
ring to statutes, precedents, and burden of proof. The APA, as a presenter of
social science data, has no expertise with regard to legal arguments. When it
starts calling the shots on legal issues, the APA jeopardizes its science-translation role's credibility.

THE EFFECTIVENESS OF *AMICUS* BRIEFS

One purpose of this book is to examine how psychological concepts, methods,
and findings, are applied to judicial decision making. Central to this purpose
is the question: How effective are psychologists in these applications? Do APA
amicus briefs achieve their goals?

MEASURING EFFECTIVENESS

The simplest way to measure effectiveness would be to determine whether the
Court's opinion was consistent with the thrust of the APA brief. This assumes
that the direction or recommendation of the APA brief can be clearly determined; this is more easily done in regard to advocacy briefs. With science-
translation briefs, other criteria must be applied. The success rate or "hit rate"
for advocacy briefs can be determined by the outcome. Even if the brief and
the majority opinion are congruent, however, it is still difficult to know whether
the effect is attributable to the brief, because there are many possible determinants of every Supreme Court decision.

A second approach to assessing effectiveness is to determine if a specific
amicus brief is cited or quoted in the Court's decision. Roesch *et al.* (1991)
noted that "impact studies rely primarily on citation counts for the indication
of whether the courts have used such research in their opinions" (p. 3). Yet
even when a brief is cited, we don't know *why* is was cited. Was it because of
perceived relevance, or was the citation just post hoc justification, mere win-
dow-dressing? Recall the controversy over Footnote 11 in the *Brown v. Board of
Education* decision.

If a brief is cited, is that better than having it ignored? Several psychologists (including some who have drafted APA briefs) apparently consider it
noteworthy any time a brief receives attention from the justices or the media
even if the attention is negative. Regarding the *Lockhart v. McCree* (1986) decision—described in Chapter 9—Tremper (1987) wrote: "The majority regarded
the research as sufficiently important to warrant devoting several pages of its
opinion to critiquing the studies' methodologies" (p. 499). Regarding two cases
(*McCleskey v. Kemp* and *Bowers v. Hardwick*), Grisso and Saks (1991) concluded
that the Court took psychological evidence seriously enough to discuss it. With

respect to *Bowers v. Hardwick*, introduced in Chapter 1 and described in Chapter 9, Bersoff and Ogden (1991) wrote: "Although the [APA] brief did not persuade the majority to modify its pinched interpretation of the right to privacy, its position was prominently and positively represented in the media" (p. 953).

General Effectiveness

As noted earlier, a number of professional and civic organizations have used *amicus* briefs to try to shape public policy. (Reviews of such efforts may be found in articles by Kobylka, 1987, and by Songer and Sheehan, 1993.) Can we make a general statement about the effect of such *interest groups* on the courts? In *Mapp v. Ohio*, 367 U.S. 643 (1961), the Supreme Court relied upon an ACLU *amicus* brief in converting what had been a local obscenity case to one in which the Court extended the exclusionary search and seizure rule from federal to *Terry v. Ohio*, 391 U.S. 1 (1968), the *amicus* brief by Americans for Effective Law Enforcement may have convinced the Court that danger to police could be lessened by use of the stop-and-frisk measures (Wasby, 1992). Reviewing the professional literature, Segal and Spaeth (1993) made a distinction between effectiveness in getting cases on the Supreme Court's agenda and a brief's actual influence on the Court. They noted that political science journals are awash with "evidence" that interest groups are effective appellate litigators, but most of these reports are case studies of particular organizations that are visible because of their success. In contrast, Epstein and Rowland (1991), in what Segal and Spaeth call the best systematic study of such influences, found no evidence that interest group briefs make a difference in federal district court decisions. The Epstein and Rowland study used precision matching to compare cases sponsored by interest groups with similar cases that had no interest-group involvement. Segal and Spaeth continued: "we have virtually no evidence to date that interest groups have an independent impact on Supreme Court decisions on the merits" (1993, p. 241). But the Epstein and Rowland study used cases before federal district judges, whose functions include being the *triers of fact*. This is not a function of appellate courts, including the Supreme Court. It is possible that briefs are more effective when facts are not in dispute.

The APA's Effectiveness

When the APA submits a brief, several possible outcomes may result:

- The Court's decision may be consistent with the APA's position, and the rationale of the Court for its opinion may clearly reflect the APA's perspective and concepts. In extremely clear examples of this type, the opinion may use language drawn directly from the APA brief.

- The Court's decision may be consistent with the psychological perspective, but the written opinion may not reflect any detectable APA influence. In some cases, the psychological rationale may have been reviewed and ignored, even though the Court's decision is congruent with the APA's values.
- The Court's decision may be contrary to that explicitly endorsed by the APA in an advocacy brief, and the grounds on which the decision is based different from those that psychology had advanced.
- The Court's decision may be not only contrary to the APA's position, but the opinion may include a critique of the psychological perspective and an indication of its limitations or inadequacies.

Chapters 8 and 9 offer a number of cases for which the APA submitted an *amicus* brief. Cases that fit one of the above categories are evaluated in detail.

SUMMARY

Amicus briefs are submitted by organizations that have an interest in the outcome of a case or a desire to provide information that is relevant to the court's decision. Certain cases that come before the Supreme Court may generate numerous *amicus* briefs on both sides.

The first brief sponsored by the American Psychological Association was submitted in 1962, with most of its nearly 100 briefs having been submitted in the last 25 years. The Office of General Counsel and COLI follow a standard procedure in deciding whether to recommend to the APA board of directors the endorsing of a brief. Yet controversy remains regarding the proper role for such briefs. Some propose that they should be *science-translation briefs*, that is, organized summaries of the appropriate research findings. Others believe that the APA has a place in the submission of *advocacy briefs*, which take a position on the issue at hand.

Are *amicus* briefs effective? The next two chapters illustrate specific cases in which effectiveness can be directly demonstrated (in that portions of the brief are quoted in the opinion) and also cases in which the majority opinion directly refuted the conclusions of an APA brief. Often, however, the influence or effectiveness is more subtle.

8

The APA's *Amicus* Attempts
to Influence the Supreme Court

About half the time the American Psychological Association submits an *amicus* brief to the Supreme Court, the Court's eventual decision is consistent—or at least partly consistent—with the APA's position. This chapter examines in detail some cases that reflect, for want of a better term, "success" on the APA's part. That is not to say that in all of these cases the APA's position was directly reflected in the wording of the decision; the brief may have achieved some success by causing the Court to think about new issues, even if the process is not clearly discernible in the eventual published opinion. The examples that follow reflect such qualifications.

HARRIS V. FORKLIFT SYSTEMS, INC. 1993

The Supreme Court's decision in *Harris v. Forklift Systems, Inc.* is an example of a Court decision that was extremely congruent with parts of the APA's *amicus* brief. Not only was the Court's reaction to the basic matter of dispute consistent with the APA's—by a unanimous vote!—but on the fundamental issues, the Court also ruled in a way that reflected APA's position.

The Facts

Teresa Harris made $40,000 a year as a rental manager at Forklift Systems in Nashville, Tennessee. Her boss, Charles Hardy—who was also the company's president—made a number of insulting and embarrassing comments to her, such as:

"Let's go to the Holiday Inn and negotiate your raise."

"I have a quarter way down there; would you get it out of my [front] pocket?"

"You're just a dumb ass woman."

Ms. Harris said that she found his comments demeaning, humiliating, and infuriating. At first, she tried to ignore them, but they persisted; she then tried to confront him, but that didn't work either. Hardy promised to stop, but a month later, in public, he asked her whether she had promised to "bugger" a customer to get his account. This especially personal comment was the last straw for Teresa Harris. After working for Forklift Systems for two and one-half years, she quit. She also sought relief from the Equal Employment Opportunity Commission (EEOC), claiming that her boss's behavior had created a "sexually hostile" workplace, and she asked for back wages. Harris confided that the disgusting behavior had driven her to drink, but she did not claim that her job performance had noticeably suffered.

The EEOC referred her claim to a U.S. magistrate judge who, in a bench trial, ruled that the employer's behavior was not offensive enough to qualify as sexual harassment. The judge labeled Mr. Hardy "a vulgar man who demeans the female employees at his workplace" and he found Ms. Harris to be "the object of a continuing pattern of sex-based derogatory conduct from Hardy," but he also wrote, "This is a close case, but Charles Hardy's comments cannot be classified as much more than annoying and insensitive" (quoted by Plevan, 1993, p. 20). The judge noted that other female employees were not offended by Mr. Hardy's jokes; in fact, they claimed surprise that Ms. Harris was. Testimony was also presented that Ms. Harris and her husband had socialized with Mr. Hardy and his wife.

At the trial Mr. Hardy's lawyer said that Ms. Harris had tried to be "one of the boys" in weekly bull sessions and that she "at times utilized language herself that sank below the generally accepted norm" (quoted by Greenhouse, 1993, p. A1). His brief asserted that Ms. Harris began to complain only after a business relationship between her husband and Mr. Hardy deteriorated.

The judge concluded that Ms. Harris's ability to function in the Forklift Systems workplace was proof that the environment wasn't severely hostile; no "serious psychological injury" had been shown—a criterion earlier employed by several courts as necessary to prove sexual harassment. The United States District Court for the Middle District of Tennessee accepted the magistrate's recommendation. Although it acknowledged that Mr. Hardy's behavior was vulgar and crude and that such actions were offensive not only to Ms. Harris but to a "reasonable woman," it also decided that Ms. Harris hadn't proved that she suffered serious psychological damage. The court's opinion stated that Mr. Hardy's comments were not "so severe as to be expected to seriously affect [Ms. Harris's] psychological well-being. . . . his conduct would not have risen to the level of interfering with that person's work performance" (quoted in *Harris v. Forklift Systems, Inc.,* 1993, p. 370).

The U.S. Circuit Court of Appeals for the Sixth District affirmed the Tennessee district court's opinion. Teresa Harris appealed to the Supreme Court. She claimed that the conduct of Forklift's president toward her constituted "abusive work environment" harassment because of her gender, in violation of Title VII of the 1964 Civil Rights Act. Harris noted in her brief that decisions in several federal circuit courts had been inconsistent. In considering whether sexual harassment was present, some courts had adopted a subjective approach, focusing on the impact of the alleged harassment on the plaintiff; other courts took an objective approach, asking whether a "reasonable person" would find the environment abusive. The subjective approach makes a distinction between conduct that interferes with a complainant's work performance and conduct that causes psychological injury; thus some courts had required proof of psychological damage, whereas others had only required plaintiffs to meet variations of a "reasonable person" standard, meaning that a reasonable person would find the harassing behavior extremely offensive in a way that affected conditions of employment. So the question became: Does a work environment have to seriously affect an employee's psychological well-being to qualify as sexual harassment?

Also relevant was the fact that the EEOC had rejected a psychological injury requirement for hostile work environment claims in its 1990 guidelines, noting that it was enough for plaintiffs to show that the harassment was unwelcome and that for a reasonable person, it substantially affected the work environment.

The Supreme Court agreed to hear Teresa Harris's appeal in order to reconcile inconsistent decisions at the circuit court level. Prior to this, the Court had established that sexual harassment could be included as an aspect of a "hostile work environment" under Title VII (*Meritor Savings Bank v. Vinson,* 1986), but that the harassment had to be "sufficiently severe or persuasive to alter the conditions of [the victim's] employment and create an abusive working environment."

THE BRIEF

The American Psychological Association was one of 12 organizations to file amicus briefs in this case. The APA brief took to task a requirement that "psychological injury" must be present. "Scientific research suggests that a psychological injury requirement is not an adequate or even useful measure of what the courts of appeals use it to measure: sexual harassment sufficiently severe or persistent to alter conditions of employment," read the brief (1993, p. 5). Having to prove psychological injury places the burden on the victim and his or her "ability to withstand harassment" instead of placing the onus on the conduct of the alleged harasser (DeAngellis, 1993). For those reasons, the APA urged the Court to rule that "psychological injury" is *not* an element of a hostile work environment claim. Furthermore, the brief asked the Court to hold that harassing conduct is actionable "if it is severe and/or pervasive enough to provide different conditions and privileges of work to members of a protected class than to other employees" (p. 6). This portion of the APA brief appears to be more of an advocacy brief that a science-translation brief.

The brief's second contribution was a review of empirical studies on the differences in women's and men's perceptions of sexual harassment. The studies consistently found that men are more tolerant of sexual harassment than are women, and women are more likely than men to label sexually aggressive behavior as harassment. Other studies cited in the brief found that men are much more likely to attribute the causes of harassing behavior to qualities of the victim, whereas women are more likely to attribute them to qualities of the perpetrator. These and other research findings were offered "as a factor the Court may find helpful in fashioning an objective test for determining whether a work environment is actionable under Title VII" (APA brief, p. 6). Thus the brief partially reflected a traditional science-translation brief, focusing on an empirical argument, but it also attempted to clarify the courts' various definitions of harassment.

THE DECISION

The unanimous decision, written by Justice O'Connor, ruled in favor of Ms. Harris. It was announced only 27 days after the oral arguments and was just six pages long; apparently the opinion was freer of negotiated revisions and controversy within the Court than any other decision considered in this book. Its ruling mandated the return of the case to the lower court, which was expected to examine the ruling and decide how much back pay, if any, Harris deserved. In early 1995 a settlement between Ms. Harris and Forklift Systems was completed; the dollar amount of damages was not announced.

The Supreme Court decision listed a menu of factors that reflect illegal harassment, including frequency and severity of statements or actions, physically threatening or humiliating behavior, and conduct that "unreasonably interferes with an employee's work performance" (p. 370). Specifically, the Court ruled that "Title VII comes into play before the harassing conduct leads to a nervous breakdown" (p. 370). In the Court's view, an abusive work environment can reflect sexual harassment even if it does not seriously affect the employee's psychological well-being, and Title VII simply requires that the "environment would reasonably be perceived, and is perceived, as hostile or abusive" (p. 371). This wording from Justice O'Connor's opinion is completely in agreement with portions of the APA's brief, but she did not cite any of the psychological research reviewed in the brief, nor did she discuss the strong gender differences in determinations of what is and is not harassment.

THE "REASONABLE PERSON" STANDARD

Noteworthy in O'Connor's opinion was her use of the "reasonable person" standard, replacing the "reasonable man" standard while avoiding the other extreme of a "reasonable woman" criterion.

In commenting on this decision, Rosen (1993a) observed:

> Feminists are divided . . . about whether sexual harassment should be viewed from the perspective of the "reasonable woman" or the "reasonable person." The special treatment camp argues that a sexless "reasonable person' standard ignores the different perspectives of women. The equal treatment camp counters that for centuries stereotypes about "reasonable women" have been used to enshrine the idea that women are unable to cope with ordinary job pressures. (p. 13)

The "reasonable woman" standard was apparently first used in 1991 in a Ninth Circuit case, *Ellison v. Brady*. In this case Kerry Ellison, an IRS agent, was pressured for dates by Stanley Gray, a co-worker whom she hardly knew. He wrote her a series of love letters; the first stated: "I cried over you last night and I'm totally drained today. I have never been in such constant term oil [sic] . . . I could not stand to feel your hatred for another day." Soon she received another letter: "1 know you are worth knowing with or without sex. . . . Watching you, experiencing you . . . so far away. Admiring your style and elan. . . . " (quoted by McCandless & Sullivan, 1991, p. 18).

The Ninth Circuit decided to focus on the perspective of the victim; thus it used a subjective definition. The court's explanation was that "if it examined only whether a "reasonable person would find the conduct harassing, it would run the risk of reinforcing the prevailing level of discrimination" (McCandless & Sullivan, 1991, p. 18). In changing the focus, the court accepted the position that men and women may differ, with men more likely to see sexual harassment as "comparatively harmless amusement."

With regard to the letters sent to Ms. Ellison, the court concluded that a "reasonable woman" could have had the same reaction that she had—fright and shock. Thus the court ruled that the letters and conduct may have been unlawful. It overruled the lower court's summary judgment against Ms. Ellison and sent the case back to the district court for a decision.

CRITICISMS OF THE COURT'S OPINION

A Supreme Court decision that is unanimous, prompt, and brief would seem to be a cause for joy. Not so, say critics of this decision; John Leo even twisted the above qualities into "indicators that the Court was determined to duck the prickly issues involved" (1993, p. 20). Among these indicators, Leo claimed, is the issue of what a "hostile environment" is. Some have concluded that Justice O'Connor's opinion "lacks clarity" (Plevan, 1993, p. 20); she locates a hostile environment beyond isolated jokes and comments—a "mere offensive utterance Is not enough—and relies on "totality of the circumstances." But how far? O'Connor said only "before the harassing conduct leads to a nervous breakdown."

Leo cites some outcomes that, in his opinion, stretch the standard:

> At a TV network, a female employee reportedly noticed a postcard from Paris in the mailroom, sent by one employee to another. Since the postcard featured a nude photo of the Folies-Bergere, a source said the woman turned in the sender of the postcard, and he was suspended.
>
> In *Robinson v. Jacksonville Shipyards* (1991), male workers clearly and consistently harassed Lois Robinson, a shipyard welder. But the judge's decision went way too far, banning not only the pornographic and cheesecake calendars posted at the shipyard but also all the pictures of men and women not in business attire that served to call attention to parts of the human body. As a result a male employee can't have a photo of his wife in a swimsuit on his desk. (1993, p. 20)

Leo proposed that "what we need from the courts is a definition of 'hostile environment' that focuses sharply on harassment and harm and veers away from equating harassment with 'offensiveness'." One suggestion, from the Feminists for Free Expression: "A pattern of conduct or expression that is directed at a specific employee; which a reasonable person would experience as harassment; and which has substantively hindered the employee's job performance" (quoted in Rosen, 1993a, p. 21). But should a decrement in job performance be a requirement? Isn't it enough that reasonable people would agree that the behavior is hostile and demeaning?

Jeffrey Rosen (1993a, b), lawyer and writer for *The New Republic*, was also disturbed about the very brief decision (1,473 words total), which simply reaffirms the standard of "sufficiently severe or pervasive" conduct that creates a "hostile or abusive work environment," with no elaboration. Rosen also emphasized the free speech issue, concluding that this "hostile environment" test represents "a radical exception to the First Amendment axiom that speech cannot be punished merely because it is offensive" (1993a, p. 12). He mentioned an article in the *UCLA Law Review* by Eugene Volokh (1992), a law clerk for Justice O'Connor, that collected potentially actionable examples–gender-based job titles (like "draftsman" or "foreman") or any "sexually suggestive" material, defined broadly enough to include reproductions of classic nude paintings.

CONCLUSIONS

The *Harris* decision leaves some ambiguity about what is unacceptable behavior. Another reason for some of the criticism of the decision, however, is that it is a victory for feminists and for those who sought Court recognition that a hostile work environment was, in and of itself, sufficient to characterize harassment. As the APA was among these advocates, the case decision was clearly consistent with the APA's goals. Though pragmatists might disagree, 1 wonder if the APA overstepped its role by advising the Court on standards for defining a hostile work environment.

MARYLAND V. CRAIG 1990

An *amicus* brief prepared by a committee of the American Psychology-Law Society on behalf of the American Psychological Association was submitted in the case of Maryland v. Craig; portions of the brief are reprinted in an article by its drafters (Goodman, Levine, Melton, & Ogden, 1991).

The case reflected a clash between the right of defendants to confront their accusers and the right of sexually abused children to be protected from further psychological harm. Sandra Ann Craig owned a day-care facility; she was accused of sexually abusing several children under her care. At her trial the judge let four children, ages four to seven, testify over closed-circuit television. The child witnesses, the prosecuting attorney, and the defense attorney were in another room with a TV camera; the children could not see the defendant, who remained in the courtroom, as did the jury. The children watched the direct examination and cross-examination on a television monitor.

Ms. Craig was convicted. She appealed, claiming that the judge's procedure had violated her right to confront her accusers as part of the Constitution's Sixth Amendment rights. The Supreme Court agreed to review the case to determine whether the Constitution categorically prohibits a child witness from testifying outside the physical presence of the defendant.

The APA's brief argued that some, but not all, children may be sufficiently traumatized by the trial procedure to warrant limitation of the defendant's right to confront them. The Court, by a 5-to-4 vote, concluded that "the Confrontation Clause of the Constitution does not guarantee criminal defendants an *absolute* right to a face-to-face meeting with the witnesses against them at trial" (p. 3159, italics in original). The Court remanded the case to Maryland for a new trial, instructing the judge to determine beforehand whether the children would suffer emotional distress when testifying.

In reflecting concern for the welfare of a child who must testify, the majority opinion, written by Justice O'Connor, referred to large sections of the APA's brief. For example, the brief stated: "Requiring child witnesses to undergo face-to-face confrontation, therefore, may in some cases actually disserve the truth-seeking rationale that underlies the confrontation clause" (quoted by Goodman *et al.*, 1991, P. 14). Justice O'Connor wrote: "Indeed, where face-to-face confrontation causes significant emotional distress in a child witness, there is evidence that such confrontation would in fact *disserve* the Confrontation Clause's truth-seeking goal" (p. 3169, italics in original).

The recognition by the Court of the possible trauma of testifying is congruent with the APA's goal in its brief, and in this sense the case's outcome reflects a success for organized psychology. Of course, this was not the first time that the Court had faced the task of evaluating interventions that tried to reduce child witnesses' trauma; in *Coy v. Iowa* (1988) the Court established some guidelines that it used in the *Craig* case.

Not all psychologists supported the APA's position in *Maryland v. Craig*, or the majority opinion of the Court that the child's trauma center on the presence of the defendant and not the nature of the courtroom as a whole, and that the distress must be more than minor. Underwager and Wakefield (1992) believe that this creates an impossible situation:

> This ruling appears to demand that there will be an evidentiary hearing, prior to the trial, at which there will be testimony, most likely by experts, about the effect on the specific child of testifying in the presence of the person accused. This puts psychologists in an extremely difficult position. No professional can respond to this requirement with anything other than subjective opinion. There is no research that separates out the single factor of the defendant's presence from all other factors in assessing the effects of courtroom testimony on a child. Nobody knows how to determine whether the single factor of the presence of the defendant, by itself, causes serious emotional distress. However, the Supreme Court's ruling may require an expert to predict that the presence of a defendant alone will cause serious emotional harm. (pp. 239–240)

In a rejoinder to Underwager and Wakefield, the psychologists who drafted the APA's brief (Goodman, Levine, & Melton, 1992) disputed the claim that there are no studies focusing specifically on the psychological effects of testifying in front of the defendant. Five studies were cited in the APA brief; clinical literature also supported the viability of the conclusion. A recent comprehensive review concluded that "when children are required to give evidence from the courtroom, seeing the accused and fear of retribution from him are major causes of distress" (Spencer & Flin, 1990, p. 293).

AKE V. OKLAHOMA 1985

The decision in *Ake v. Oklahoma* is an example of a ruling that was in line with the APA's recommendation but showed no pervasive influence from its *amicus* brief. *Ake v. Oklahoma* can help to clarify my position on what the goals of APA briefs should be.

THE FACTS

Chapter 2 described the facts of this case when comparing the different emphases and interpretations of Justices Marshall and Rehnquist. After being charged with a double murder, Glen Ake's behavior apparently became so irrational that he was sent to a state hospital prior to trial. After being there for several months, he was declared competent to stand trial. When he claimed the insanity defense, the judge refused to appoint a state-paid psychiatrist to assist in that defense. After his conviction, his appeal was rejected by the Oklahoma Court of Criminal Appeals. The U.S. Supreme Court agreed to hear Ake's appeal.

THE BRIEF

One purpose of the *amicus* brief submitted by the APA (in conjunction with the Oklahoma Psychological Association, or OPA) was to reverse the Oklahoma appeals court decision and have the case remanded for a new trial. The APA and the OPA also wished to inform the Court about the nature of psychological evaluations and the need for expert testimony in proceedings involving insanity defense.

Yet most of the arguments in the brief were of a constitutional nature. For in its "Summary of argument" (p. 3), the brief noted:

> The Court has long recognized the special nature of capital cases and has interpreted the Constitution to require adherence to the highest standards of procedural fairness to minimize the possibility in such cases of erroneous determinations of criminal responsibility and excessive punishments. In this case, there is no doubt that the defendant committed the heinous offenses with which he is charged. However, there is serious question whether the defendant had sufficient understanding of the wrongfulness of his offenses to he criminally responsible for them under the laws of Oklahoma. *Amici* submit that fundamental fairness requires the state to provide defendant Ake an adequate opportunity to establish his insanity defense. (1984, p. 3)

Later the brief states: "*Amici* believe that to deny defendant an adequate opportunity to support his plea of insanity, solely because of his indigency, was to arbitrarily and effectively deprive defendant of the benefit of the insanity defense in violation of due process of law and other constitutional guarantees" (p. 5).

The brief also relied on logical argument, as follows: "In this case, the possibility for error in determining defendant Ake's criminal responsibility for the admitted homicides increased when the trial court refused to provide the defendant with a psychological evaluation of his state of mind at the time he committed the offense" (p. 7).

In furthering this argument, the APA noted that in Oklahoma, the insanity defense is an affirmative defense that requires the defendant to show evidence that generates a reasonable doubt about his sanity at the time of the crime, which, without a psychological evaluation, the defendant was unable to do. This was especially important given that less than 6 months after the crime, Ake had been determined by psychiatrists and by the presiding judge to be mentally ill and incompetent to stand trial. The APA argued that unless Ake was provided with a psychological evaluation, there was an unacceptably high risk for an erroneous determination of sanity at the time of the crime.

The emphasis on a logical approach to persuading the Court is reflected in this excerpt from the brief:

> It is difficult to imagine a more compelling case for the right to a court-appointed psychological expert. The defendant had confessed to a horrible offense committed immediately after losing his girlfriend and termination of his employment. He had taken a large amount of dregs and alcohol at the time of the offense and had acted irrationally immediately after the crime in using a credit card issued in the name of the woman he had just murdered to finance his escape. Furthermore, witnesses had testified that the defendant had had a troubled childhood and a father who physically abused him. (p. 13)

This and other evidence "supports an inference"—to quote the APA brief's emphasis—that Ake may have been psychotic at the time of the crime.

In keeping with its second purpose of informing the court, the APA brief proposed that "the detection and diagnosis of mental disorders and assessment of facts relevant to mental processes is recognized to be well beyond the competence of most lay people" (p. 4) and that psychological evaluations performed by qualified mental health professionals "to support their only defense to the charges against them is a small price to pay to maintain the integrity of our criminal process" (p. 5). The brief also noted that in other contexts expert psychological assessments of mental conditions have been viewed by the courts as being of considerable probative value and sometimes as being indispensable.

Only in its later arguments does the brief rely on psychological or empirical sources; the emphasis here is on the questionable ability to predict dangerousness in the future. The brief states: "In the present case, the state relied on the testimony of two state psychiatrists that defendant is likely to be dangerous in the future to support its request for the death penalty. But the state denied defendant the means to effectively cross-examine or rebut such testimony" (p. 5).

THE DECISION

The Court's decision in the *Ake* case was 8 to 1; only Justice Rehnquist dissented. The majority opinion, written by Justice Thurgood Marshall, stated that Ake should have been allowed a psychiatric evaluation to determine his state of mind at the time of the crime; thus he was denied due process of law.

Because his only defense was that he was insane at that time, he should have been granted court-appointed assistance. The decision stated:

> This Court has long recognized that when a State brings its judicial power to bear on an indigent defendant in a criminal proceeding, it must take steps to assume that the defendant has a fair opportunity to present his defense. This elementary principle, grounded in significant part on the Fourteenth Amendment's due process guarantee of fundamental fairness, derives from the belief that justice cannot be equal where, simply as a result of his poverty, a defendant is denied the opportunity to participate meaningfully in a judicial proceeding in which his liberty is at stake. (*Ake v. Oklahoma*, 1985, p. 1092)

The Court further noted that 40 states, as well as the federal government, already make psychiatric assistance available to indigent defendants, and they have not found the financial burden to be a great one.

The opinion did not cite the APA brief directly, but almost all of the issues the brief presented to the Court were mentioned. Examples are the fairness of procedures and the need for professional evaluation; in one paragraph, for instance, the Court described the psychiatric function, as follows:

> The assistance of a psychiatrist may well be crucial to the defendant's ability to marshal his defense. In this role, psychiatrists gather facts, through professional examination, interviews, and elsewhere, that they will share with the judge or jury; they analyze the information gathered and from it draw plausible conclusions about the defendant's mental condition, and about the effects of any disorder on behavior; and they offer opinions about how the defendant's mental condition might have affected his behavior at the time in question. They know the probative questions to ask of the opposing party's psychiatrists and how to interpret their answers. Unlike lay witnesses, who can merely describe symptoms they believe might be relevant to the defendant's mental state, psychiatrists can identify the "elusive and often deceptive" symptoms of insanity . . . and tell the jury why their observations are relevant. (p. 1095)

This section of the Court's decision generally resembled the contents of pp. 15–16 of the APA brief. The opinion next noted that psychiatry is not an exact science, and because psychiatrists may disagree as to a proper diagnosis, the jury remains the primary fact finder. The Court observed, "We neither approve or disapprove of the widespread reliance on psychiatrists" (p. 1096); rather, the evolving practice requires representation for each side.

The majority opinion had nothing to say about the difficulty of predicting future dangerousness, other than briefly recognizing that the consequences of an error are "so great" (p. 1097). Emphasis was on due process considerations.

THE DISSENT

If there is a dissenting opinion by the Court, such an opinion—though having no precedential impact—can be instructive for understanding the determinants of judges' opinions and the effectiveness of *amicus* briefs and other attempts to persuade. In the *Ake* decision, the minority opinion by Justice Rehnquist is especially useful for the reasons: It reflects a vastly different conception of the facts of the case, and the values of the opinion writer are made clear.

The Dissenting Opinion's Presentation of the Facts

Justice Rehnquist's opinion gives a much more extensive description of the case facts than do most dissenting opinions. His recounting of the events (summarized in Chapter 2) suggests that at various times Ake showed planned behavior: He looked for a place to burglarize, he bound his victims, and afterward he traveled widely. In these actions, says Justice Rehnquist, no question of insanity was raised. Only after he was arrested did the "psychotic" behavior surface.

Values Expressed by the Dissenting Opinion

Not only did Justice Rehnquist see the facts differently, but he also required a higher standard for proving a violation of due process, writing:

> I do not think due process is violated merely because an indigent lacks sufficient funds to pursue a state-law defense as thoroughly as he would like. . . . I do not believe the Due Process Clause superimposes a federal standard for determining how and when sanity can legitimately be placed in issue, and I would find no violation of due process under the circumstances. (*Ake v. Oklahoma*, 1985, p. 1100)

Rehnquist found no support for a decision permitting a psychiatrist for the defense. First, he saw no reason why the prosecution (i.e., the state) should be required to produce psychiatric witnesses for the benefit of the defendant. Even more disturbing to him was the majority opinion that granted Ake "access to a competent psychiatrist who will conduct an appropriate examination and assist in evaluation, preparation, and presentation of the defense" (p. 1097). He expresses his underlying values clearly:

> A psychiatrist is not an attorney, whose job it is to advocate. His opinion is sought on a question that the State of Oklahoma treats as a question of *fact*. Since any "unfairness" in these cases would arise from the fact that the only competent witnesses on the question are being paid by the State, all the defendants should be entitled to is one competent opinion—whatever the witness' conclusion—from a psychiatrist who acts independently of the prosecutor's office. Although the independent psychiatrist should be available to answer defense counsel's questions prior to trial, and to testify if called, I see no reason why the defendant should be entitled to an opposing view, or to a "defense" advocate. (p. 1101)

That is, justice Rehnquist saw a justification for the provision of an expert *witness* "independent of the prosecutor's office" on the grounds of fairness—but not for an *advocate*. Thus Justice Rehnquist had a very different conception than did the APA of the defendant's nature and motives. He did not mention Ake's loss of his girlfriend nor drugs and alcohol use. Whereas the APA brief mentions Ake's termination from his job, Justice Rehnquist says that Ake and Hatch "quit their jobs." Unlike the justice, the APA brief, in mentioning Ake's troubled childhood and his recent disappointments, seems almost to encourage the "abuse excuse."

IMPACT OF THE APA'S *AMICUS* BRIEF

What can we conclude about the impact of the APA–OPA brief upon the majority decision in the *Ake* case? The opinion does not cite, quote from, or refer to the brief, although it generally covers the same issues. The Court was already familiar with what psychiatry could provide when insanity was offered as a defense, and certainly matters of due process and procedural fairness, discussed in the APA brief, were already salient for the justices.

So in one sense, we can conclude that the contents of the APA brief made no difference in the majority opinion. Yet it was essential for the APA to express an opinion in the case. If professional organizations fail to justify their status in such a case, the Court might note a lack of confidence in their professional procedures. The submission of a brief was a necessity, even if the likelihood of specific demonstrable evidence is small. We find it surprising, however, that the brief chose to relegate issues of psychiatric competence in assessing insanity to its back pages.

FORD V. WAINWRIGHT 1986

The decision and procedures in the case of *Ford v. Wainwright* closely resemble those for *Ake v. Oklahoma,* decided the year before. Both cases dealt with the issue of the mental competence of the defendant. In both, the APA submitted an amicus brief focusing more on constitutional issues than on empirical ones. The majority opinion was again consistent with the APA's position, although it did not directly cite the APA's brief. Both decisions were assigned to Justice Marshall. Both had a strong minority opinion by Justice Rehnquist.

THE FACTS

In 1974 Alvin Bernard Ford was convicted of murder and sentenced to death by the state of Florida. Although there had been no indication that he was incompetent to stand trial, early in 1982 (eight years later) gradual changes began to appear in his behavior; at first just "an occasional peculiar idea or a confused perception" (p. 2597), but the changes grew more severe over time. For example, he became obsessed with the Ku Klux Klan and was seemingly convinced that he was "the target of a complex conspiracy, involving the Klan and assorted others, designed to force him to commit suicide" (p. 2598). His delusions also involved the prison guards as part of the conspiracy, his female relatives as torture victims, and his friends as hostages of the prison officials. He began to refer to himself as "Pope John Paul III" and claimed to have appointed nine new justices to the Florida Supreme Court.

His attorney asked a psychiatrist who had previously examined Ford to continue seeing him and to recommend treatment. After an evaluation lasting over a year, the psychiatrist concluded in 1983 that Ford suffered from "a severe, uncontrollable, mental disease which closely resembles 'Paranoid Schizophrenia with Suicide Potential' . . . a major mental disorder . . . severe enough to substantially affect Mr. Ford's present ability to assist in the defense of his life" (p. 2598).

About that time Ford refused to see this psychiatrist again, having concluded that he was a part of the conspiracy, but in November 1983, another psychiatrist elicited from Ford the statement that "I know there is some sort of death penalty, but I'm free to go wherever I want to because it would be illegal [to execute me] and the executioner would be executed" (p. 2598). Furthermore, Ford replied to a question by saying: "I can't be executed because of the landmark case. I won. *Ford v. State* will prevent executions all over" (p. 2598). This psychiatrist concluded that Ford sincerely did not understand why he was to be executed and in fact believed he could not be executed because he owned the prisons and could control the governor through "mind waves"; in addition, the examining psychiatrist found "no reasonable possibility that Mr. Ford was dissembling, malingering, or otherwise putting on a performance" (p. 2598). Shortly thereafter, Ford regressed into nearly complete incomprehensibility and spoke only in a code characterized by the intermittent use of the word "one."

At this point, about the beginning of 1984, Ford's attorney invoked procedures that the state of Florida used to determine the competence of an inmate condemned to die. The procedures required the governor of Florida to appoint a panel of three psychiatrists to evaluate whether Ford had the mental capacity to understand the nature of the death penalty and the reasons why it had been imposed on him.

The quality of this evaluation would seem to suggest a focus for the APA's brief, because the procedure was for the psychiatrists together to interview Ford for approximately 30 minutes. This questioning would be done in the presence of eight other people, including Ford's attorney, attorneys for the state, and state prison officials. Each of the psychiatrists would then file separate two- or three-page reports with the governor. The three psychiatrists agreed that Ford met the criterion of sanity as defined by the state law, but each provided a different set of diagnostic impressions. One concluded that Ford suffered from "psychosis with paranoia" but had "enough cognitive functioning to understand the nature and the effects of the death penalty, and why it is to be imposed on him"; a second stated that although Ford was "psychotic," he fully knew "what could happen to him"; a third diagnosed him as having a "severe adaptational disorder" but said Ford did "comprehend his total situation including being sentenced to death, and all the implications of that penalty" (p. 2599). This last psychiatrist speculated about malingering, noting that Ford's disorder, "although severe, seemed contrived and recently learned" (p. 2599).

The Florida governor's decision was announced on April 30, 1984; he signed the death warrant without an explanatory statement. Ford's attorneys brought suit against Louie L. Wainwright, the secretary of the Florida Department of Corrections.

THE BRIEF

The purpose of the brief submitted by the APA in conjunction with the Florida Psychological Association was to propose that the state did not provide an adequate assessment for Alvin Ford with regard to his understanding of what "sentenced to death" means. Page one of the introduction to the *amicus* brief states:

> This case raises two related issues regarding the extent to which the Eighth and Fourteenth Amendments prohibit the execution of condemned prisoners who are presently mentally incompetent, and, assuming such a prohibition, the minimum procedural safeguards that must be observed in determining such individuals' competency to be executed.

The brief proposed that:

- Condemned prisoners of questionable mental competence may not be executed without first having their competence determined through an accurate and reliable fact finding proceeding (p. 5).
- The procedures followed by the state of Florida in evaluating a convict's competence to be executed failed to provide an accurate and reliable determination of the issues (p. 18).

Four reasons were offered by the APA for its conclusion that the Florida procedure was unsatisfactory:

- A single, brief examination fails to reflect the changing and complex nature of psychological states.

- Proper evaluation requires the establishment of a trusting relationship with the examiner.
- A physical examination and the administration of a battery of tests should be included.
- The commission psychiatrists, in their report to the governor, made no reference to the grandiose delusions apparently expressed by Ford, nor of the more extensive earlier evaluations of two other psychiatrists that were contrary to the commission's findings.

The arguments in the APA brief were a mixture of constitutional, logical, and empirical ones. The authors of the brief explicitly state the problems associated with the constitutionality of the governor's decision to sign the death warrant after hearing only minimal evidence derived from a 30-minute evaluation. It also notes the APA's "expertise in the various methodologies for cognitive assessment that are integral components of all competency evaluations" (p. 2) and argues that due process requires "the effective assistance of mental health professionals, and the appointment of such professionals in the case of indigents, to conduct appropriate examinations of condemned prisoners and to assist them and their attorneys in evaluating and preparing all issues relevant to the accurate determination of their present competency to be executed" (pp. 4–5).

Many previous court cases (including *Ake v. Oklahoma*) were reviewed, but no specific research was cited in the brief.

THE DECISION

The Supreme Court's majority opinion was written by Justice Marshall and joined by Justices Blackmun and Brennan and (in part) by Justice Stevens. Concurring opinions were written by Justice Powell and by Justice O'Connor, who partially concurred and partially dissented. Her opinion was joined by Justice White. A dissent was offered by Justice Rehnquist, joined by Chief Justice Burger. The majority decision reversed and remanded the decision to execute Alvin Ford, based on the conclusion that his 8th and 14th Amendment rights had been violated. It ruled that the appellant was entitled to a *de novo* evidentiary hearing on the question of his competence to be executed.

In essence, the majority opinion concluded that it was basically cruel and unusual punishment to sentence to death someone who did not understand the meaning of that sentence. It wrote:

> The Eighth Amendment prohibits the State from inflicting the penalty of death upon prisoner who is insane. Petitioner's allegation of insanity in his *habeas corpus* petition, if proved, therefore would bar his execution. The question before us is whether the District Court was under the obligation to hold an evidentiary hearing on the question of Ford's sanity. In answering that question, we bear in

mind that, while the underlying social values encompassed by the Eighth Amendment are rooted in historical traditions, the manner in which our judicial system
protects these values is purely a matter of contemporary law. (p. 2602).

The decision said that the state of Florida had failed to provide an adequate psychological assessment of Alvin Ford with respect to his competence
to be sentenced to death, and that the governor signed a death warrant without having the information necessary to provide such an assessment. Though
not directly citing the APA brief, the Court's opinion included many of the
brief's arguments regarding the 8th and 14th Amendments. For example, the
fact that Florida's procedure failed to include the prisoner in the truth-seeking
process was noted (p. 2063). In a narrow sense the majority opinion was not
"psychology-based," but in broad sense, it is a psychologically oriented opinion. It states that without a psychological evaluation and the contributions of
mental health professionals, the mental state of an individual cannot be assessed. Furthermore, it states that a proper examination includes the opportunity to question the state's experts, reflecting the APA's recognition that psychological and psychiatric experts can disagree in their evaluations.

THE DISSENT

The dissent by Justice Rehnquist conceded that "no State sanctions execution
of the insane" (p. 2615), but he found it unnecessary to "constitutionalize" this
view and was very critical of the decision's claim that it was basically "keeping
faith with our common-law heritage" (p. 2613). Justice Rehnquist stated that
"the Court places great weight on the 'impressive credentials' of the common-
law bar against executing a prisoner who has lost his sanity" (p. 2613) but in
Rehnquist's view, the Court was going *against* the common-law heritage by
allowing someone other than the executive branch to determine the sanity of
a prisoner (p. 2613). What Justice Rehnquist was noting was the fact that the
majority opinion had been critical of Florida's procedure of leaving it to the
governor to determine an execution. The majority opinion had stated:

> Perhaps the most striking defect in the procedures [of Florida] is the State's place-
> ment of the decision wholly within the executive branch. Under this procedure,
> the person who appoints the experts and ultimately decides whether the State
> will be able to carry out the sentence that it has long sought is the Governor,
> whose subordinates have been responsible for initiating every stage of the pros-
> ecution of the condemned from arrest through sentencing. The commander of
> the State's corps of prosecutors cannot be said to have the neutrality that is neces-
> sary for reliability in the fact finding proceeding. (p. 2605)

Justice Rehnquist observed that assigning the ultimate responsibility to
the governor is fully consistent with the "common-law heritage"; it is an "unchallenged fact that it was thee *executive* who passed upon the sanity of the
condemned" (p. 2613, italics in original). Justice Rehnquist also stated that

one trial on the issue of guilt and one on the determination of a penalty are enough; a third trial was unnecessary. He wrote, "A third adjudication offers an invitation to those who have nothing to lose by accepting it to advance entirely spurious claims of insanity" (p. 2615). He was concerned about delays and invalid conclusions resulting from further evaluations:

> A claim of insanity may be made at any time before sentence and, once rejected, may be raised again; a prisoner found sane two days before execution might claim to have lost his sanity the next day, thus necessitating another judicial determination of his sanity and presumably another stay of his execution. (p. 2615)

WHAT TO ARGUE: *PENRY V. LYNAUGH* 1989

The issue in the appeal of Johnny Paul Penry was the right of the state to execute a person who is mentally retarded. Because this condition is defined psychologically, it would seem a case wherein the Court would be responsive to the APA's position. But the APA (and the other professional organizations that co-sponsored the brief) focused on just one aspect of the appeal, and its claims may have been too extreme for the Court.

THE FACTS

One morning in October 1979, a young woman was raped, beaten, and stabbed in her home in Livingston, Texas. She died a few hours later, but was able to describe her assailant before her death. The description led sheriff's deputies to question Johnny Paul Penry, age 22, who had recently been released on parole after a conviction for rape. He confessed to the crime and was charged with murder.

Although Penry was found competent to stand trial, a psychologist testified that he was mildly to moderately retarded and had a mental age of 6½ years. His IQ was estimated at 50 to 63 points. During his trial, he claimed the insanity defense and presented testimony from psychiatrists that he suffered from a combination of organic brain damage and moderate retardation and thus he lacked impulse control and the ability to learn from experience. It was also introduced at trial that he had been abused as a child. For example, Penry's sister testified that their mother had frequently beaten Penry over the head with a belt when he was growing up. His mother testified that Penry was unable to learn in school and had never completed first grade.

The state, using the testimony of two psychiatrists, claimed at the trial that Penry had an antisocial personality (i.e., an inability to learn from experience and a tendency to be impulsive and to violate society's norms) but that he was legally sane. The jury found Penry guilty of capital murder and during the sentencing phase responded yes to the three questions used in Texas to determine the death penalty:

- Was the defendant's act committed deliberately with the reasonable expectation that death would result?
- Is there a probability that he is a continuing threat to society?
- Was the killing unreasonable in response to any provocation by the victim?

By answering yes to these questions, the jury permitted Penry to be sentenced to death. The Texas Court of Criminal Appeals upheld the death sentence, as did the Fifth Circuit Court of Appeals, but the latter found considerable merit in Penry's claim that the instructions given to the jury at the sentencing phase of the trial did not permit the jury to consider mitigating evidence, such as his retardation and past history.

THE BRIEF

The relevant brief in this case was submitted by 11 professional associations, including the APA. The first organization named was the American Association on Mental Retardation (AAMR). The goal of the brief was to define the limits that mental retardation places on an individual in all aspects of his or her life. The brief argued that when characteristics of the offender "do not match the high level of culpability required by the Constitution" (p. 4)—for example, if the offender is retarded—death is a disproportionate punishment. The brief identified the characteristics that play a role in lack of culpability as follows:

> Capital defendants who have mental retardation lack this constitutionally required level of blameworthiness. The effects of their disability in the areas of cognitive impairment, moral reasoning, control of impulsivity, and the ability to understand basic relationships between cause and effect make it impossible for them to possess that level of culpability essential in capital cases. (p. 4)

The brief also argued that the "execution of a person with mental retardation, such as John Paul Penry, cannot serve any valid penological purpose" (p. 4). Its argument was buttressed by both logical and constitutional justifications, with many references to the reduced level of functioning by a person with mental retardation. For example:

> People who have mental retardation have a reduced ability to cope with and function in the everyday world. This reduced ability is found in every dimension of the individual's functional; including his language, communication, memory, attention, ability to control impulsivity, moral development, self concept, self perception, suggestibility, knowledge of basic information, and general motivation. (p. 6)

The constitutional argument was introduced within the logical one: "A minimal level of cognitive ability and moral reasoning development are necessary for the level of culpability that will satisfy the requirements of the Eighth Amendment in capital cases" (p. 9). This statement emphasizes the claim that a person with mental retardation is not able to function in a "normal" manner and that when charged with a crime, this person will probably not realize what he or she has done wrong, why he or she has done it, or what the consequences will be. Thus culpability is a main issue for the APA; an accused person's 8th Amendment rights must be protected in these cases because such people cannot protect their own rights.

The APA brief did not propose that persons with mental retardation should not be held responsible for criminal acts; rather, it held that they should be given an appropriate punishment, which did not include the death penalty: "The nature of mental retardation is sufficiently severe that any person who has that disability and commits a capital offense lacks, by definition, that level of culpability that would allow the state to take his life" (p. 15).

The brief did not give specific research examples; it did refer to other cases relevant to the same issue.

THE DECISION

Justice O'Connor wrote the majority opinion. The earlier decision was affirmed in part, reversed in part, and remanded for resentencing. In essence the Court stated that execution of a mentally retarded murderer does not violate constitutional safeguards, but the jury (if involved in the sentencing) must be instructed that it has the right to consider mitigating evidence. Several points were made in this opinion:

- Texas juries must, upon request, be given an instruction that allows them to take into account ("give effect to") mitigating evidence in determining whether to impose the death penalty.

The opinion stated:

> Penry argues that his mitigating evidence of mental retardation and child abuse has relevance to his moral culpability beyond the scope of the special issues, and that the jury was unable to express its "reasoned moral response" to that evidence in determining whether death was the appropriate punishment. We agree. Thus, we reject the State's contrary argument that the jury was able to consider and give effect to all of Penry's mitigating evidence in answering the special issues without any jury instructions on mitigating evidence. (p. 2948)

- In this particular case, Penry was supported in his claim that evidence of his mental retardation and childhood abuse should have been presented.

- The absence of instructions in this case indicates that the jury was not provided with a way to express its "reasoned moral response" to mitigating evidence, as required by earlier Court decisions reflecting the 8th and 14th Amendments. "Those decisions are based on the principle that punishment must be directly related to the defendant's personal culpability, and that a defendant who commits a crime attributable to a disadvantaged background or emotional and mental problems may be less culpable than one who has no such excuse" (pp. 2938–2939).
- Despite the above, the 8th Amendment does not categorically prohibit the execution of mentally retarded capital murderers with the level of reasoning ability displayed by Penry.

In making this last distinction, the Court noted that Penry was found competent to stand trial, and that he "was found to have the ability to consult with his lawyer with a reasonable degree of rational understanding and was found to have a rational as well as factual understanding of the proceedings against him" (pp. 2954–2955).

Evolving Standards for "Cruel and Unusual Punishment"

The Court also evaluated the standards for "cruel and unusual punishment" and emphasized an "evolving standard of decency" (p. 2953). To define the national consensus, Penry's appeal used the results of public opinion polls noting that several such polls indicated strong opposition to executing persons who are mentally retarded. For example, a survey taken in Texas found that although 86% of respondents supported the death penalty, 73% opposed it for persons with mental retardation (quoted on p. 2955). The Court, however, considered polls to be "insufficient evidence of a national consensus" (p. 2955).

Rather, the standard for the Court comes from the legislative branch: "the dearest and most reliable objective evidence of contemporary values is the legislation enacted by the country's legislatures" (p. 2953). Judgments of juries are also considered to be objective evidence that society's standard accepts administering the death penalty to a person with mental retardation.

In its majority opinion, the Court made a distinction between cases like Penry's, with mild mental retardation, and cases of profound or severe retardation wherein the defendants are "wholly lacking in the capacity to appreciate the wrongfulness of their actions" (p. 2939). The Court concluded that people in the latter category are "not likely to be convicted or face the prospect of punishment today, since the modern insanity defense generally includes 'mental defect' as part of the legal definition of insanity, and since *Ford v. Wainwright* . . . prohibits the execution of persons who are unaware of their punishment and why they must suffer it" (pp. 2939–2940).

THE MAJORITY OPINION AND THE APA'S *AMICUS* BRIEF

The AAMR–APA brief was frequently cited in the *Penry v. Lynaugh* decision (see pp. 2955, 2957, 2950, 2961, and 2963). Not only was it referred to in the majority decision, but also in the concurring and dissenting opinions. The majority opinion displays a psychological orientation in basing its decision on the defendant's mental state at the time of the crime.

However, the majority opinion does not go as far as the APA would wish. The Court differentiated between levels of mental retardation:

> On the present record it cannot be said that all mentally retarded people—by virtue of their mental retardation alone, and apart from any individualized consideration of their personal responsibility—inevitably lack the cognitive, volitional, and moral capacity to act with the degree of culpability associated with the death penalty. (p. 2940)

Furthermore, the Court's opinion expressed a vastly different evaluation of the concept of mental age than did the APA's brief: "The concept of 'mental age' is an insufficient basis for a categorical Eighth Amendment rule, since it is imprecise, dues not adequately account for individuals' varying experiences and abilities, ceases to change after a person reaches the chronological age of 15 or 16, and could have a disempowering effect if applied to retired persons in other areas of the law, such as the opportunity to enter contracts or to marry" (p. 2940).

Did the *amicus* brief influence the Court? Probably not. The brief hoped for a ruling that the execution of persons with retardation is unequivocally unconstitutional because they cannot evaluate their own culpability. No such blanket ruling emerged.

The other decision in this complex opinion—that jurors must be told that mitigating circumstances can be considered—was in keeping with the APA's goals, but not emphasized in its brief. The brief stated: "*Amici* agree with Petitioner that he is entitled to reversal on the first question on which certiorari was granted, because the Texas system does not allow jurors to give adequate consideration to mental retardation as a mitigating factor, but *amici* will limit this brief to an analysis of whether the execution of a person with mental retardation is invariably a violation of the Eighth Amendment" (p. 4).

CONCURRING AND DISSENTING OPINIONS

Justice Brennan filed an opinion concurring in part and dissenting in part, in which Justice Marshall joined. Justice Stevens filed an opinion concurring in part and dissenting in part, in which Justice Blackmun joined. Justice Scalia filed an opinion concurring in part and dissenting in part, in which Chief Justice Rehnquist and Justices White and Kennedy joined. Justice Brennan concurred with the position that "jury instructions given at the sentencing in this case deprived Petitioner of his constitutional right to have a jury consider all mitigating evidence that he presented them before sentencing him to die" (p. 2958). Brennan dissented regarding the question whether the Eighth Amendment prohibits the execution of mentally retarded offenders who lack the full responsibility for their crimes. Similarly, Justice Stevens (who mentioned the APA brief in his dissenting opinion) concluded that the execution of a mentally retarded person is unconstitutional.

CONCLUSIONS

The American Psychological Association can legitimately take credit for having provided influential *amicus* briefs in a few selected Supreme Court decisions. In other cases facing the Court, the influence from organized psychology was subtle and hard to document. Even when the outcome was consistent with the APA's advocacy, not all of the organization's conclusions or suggestions were reflected in the Court's decision, and in some of these cases, it seems that the APA overstepped its jurisdiction by basing its brief on constitutional rather than empirical or professional considerations.

9

Unsuccessful Attempts to Influence the Court

OVERVIEW

By no means have all attempts by the American Psychological Association led to court decisions consistent with the APA's orientation. In fact, attempts that had no discernible impact may tell us more about the bases of judicial decision making than do the successful ones. This chapter describes several recent cases for which the APA submitted an *amicus* brief only to have its contents ignored in the majority decision, or worse, to have the majority opinion disparage its efforts. A goal of this and the concluding chapter is to understand why the briefs had little influence.

BOWERS V. HARDWICK 1986

THE FACTS

On July 5, 1982, at about 10:30 a.m., Michael Hardwick left the Cove, a gay nightclub in Atlanta. He had worked there all night and he was tired and thirsty. As be left, he grabbed a beer, took a few swigs, and tossed it aside. A patrolman, Keith Torrick, fed up with big city litter, spotted him and charged him with drinking in public. He wrote out a ticket for Hardwick with a court date scheduled for eight days later. He told Hardwick: "I'm counting on you to show up. If you don't, I'll take it that you're laughing in my face. And I'll come find you. And I will lock you up" (quoted by Harris, 1986, p. C4).

When Hardwick did not appear in court, Officer Torrick went after him with an arrest warrant. Hardwick wasn't at home, but when told by a friend that he'd missed his court date, he raced downtown, paid his $50 fine, got a receipt, and forgot about it. (He said that he missed the court date because the ticket was confusing.)

The paperwork never caught up with Officer Torrick; on a hot August afternoon three weeks later, he was back. At his knock, a houseguest answered the door. "Is Michael Hardwick at home?" "I don't know, but you can look around." Torrick went down the hall; a bedroom door was ajar, the room lit by a candle. Inside, he saw two men engaged in oral sex. He also spied a small bowl of marijuana. When he said, "You're under arrest," Hardwick protested that he had paid his fine. The arrest, however, was for sodomy and drug possession, with a possible sentence of 1 to 20 years in prison (Harris, 1986).

Hardwick paid his bail and was considering a plea bargain, but the American Civil Liberties Union had been waiting to challenge Georgia's sodomy law on behalf of homosexual persons as a violation of the privacy rights granted by the Constitution. The ACLU approached Hardwick and urged him to plead innocent and go to trial. Hardwick gave the matter some thought. If he went to trial, there would be headlines and he might be fired from his other job as a hotel trainee. Ultimately, he agreed to go to trial.

The case took an unexpected turn. The Fulton County district attorney decided not to prosecute. "I don't think a jury would have convicted him, from a privacy angle," he said. The ACLU's balloon was temporarily deflated; there was no conviction to appeal. Thus, on February 14, 1983, Hardwick's lawyers filed in federal district court to have Georgia's sodomy law declared unconstitutional for violating Hardwick's right to privacy. In May 1985 a three-judge panel of the U.S. Court of Appeals for the 11th Circuit ruled 2 to 1 that the Georgia law infringed on Hardwick's right to privacy (Harris, 1986).

The state appealed, and the Supreme Court agreed to hear the case. The American Psychological Association submitted an *amicus* brief.

The Brief

The APA brief made two basic arguments:

1. Same-gender sexual orientation is not pathological, nor is oral–genital sex.

The American Psychiatric Association had long since stopped classifying homosexuality as a mental disorder. Oral–genital sex is not only common between sexual partners regardless of orientation, but it is also a part of private sexual expression. In summary, sexual orientation does not affect a person's ability to contribute to society.

2. Criminal punishment has harmful psychological consequences for people who engage in the proscribed conduct. Fear and threat of criminal prosecution hurts the development of mental health among gay people by fostering detrimental labeling, by themselves and by society. Lesbians and gay men become stigmatized as "deviants" and are viewed as possessing undesirable stereotypes.

THE DECISION

On June 30, 1986, by a 5-to-4 vote, the Supreme Court ruled that the Constitution does not protect homosexual relations between consenting adults, even in the privacy of their own homes. Georgia's statute outlawing sodomy was upheld. In the majority were Justices White, Burger, Rehnquist, O'Connor, and Powell; dissenting were Justices Blackmun, Brennan, Marshall, and Stevens. Justice White's decision stressed the "ancient roots" in English common law of statutes criminalizing homosexual relations. He wrote: "The Court is most vulnerable and comes nearest to illegitimacy when it deals with judge-made constitutional law having little or no cognizable roots in the language or design of the Constitution" (p. 2846).

With regard to previous rulings, White wrote that various "fundamental rights" not specified in the Constitution could not be deprived without "due process of law"—fundamental rights being limited to those "deeply rooted in this nation's history or tradition" or "implicit in the concept of ordered liberty" (quoted by Taylor, 1986, p. A19).

Apparently homosexuality was such an anathema to Chief Justice Burger that he wrote a concurring opinion that didn't add anything other than to reaffirm that the restriction of same-gender sexual conduct was "firmly rooted in Judeo-Christian moral and ethical standards" (p. 2847).

THE DISSENT

Whereas the majority opinion ignored the APA brief and clearly rejected its points in the decision, relying instead on "historical views" of homosexuality, the minority opinion by Justice Blackmun did endorse the APA's views, at least in a footnote. (Gary Melton, 1989, p. 933, concluded that Blackmun was "relying heavily" on the APA's brief.) Blackmun wrote that "despite historical views of homosexuality, it is no longer viewed by mental health professionals as a 'disease' or disorder. See Brief for American Psychological Association and American Public Health Association as *Amicus Curiae* 8-11. But obviously, neither is it simply a matter of deliberate personal election. Homosexual orientation may well form part of the very fiber of an individual's personality" (p. 2850).

<h2 align="center">EVALUATION</h2>

The close decision was certainly a disappointment to the APA brief writers, who felt that what they offered was of relevance to the decision making of the Court, and when it was revealed several years later that Justice Powell, one of the majority, now differed from the majority, the feeling of disappointment was compounded.

But sometimes a brief's influence is subtle and slow-acting. As noted in Chapter 1, a decade after the *Hardwick* decision, the Court again considered the issue of the rights of persons with a homosexual orientation. The decision in *Romer v. Evans* (1996) not only was inconsistent with the earlier decision, it did not even cite it. The specific issues in the two cases were not similar, and the membership of the Court had changed over the decade—only Justices Rehnquist, O'Connor, and Stevens remained. Perhaps the APA brief for the earlier case—and the publicity resulting from it—had some effect in shifting public opinion regarding the acceptability of homosexuality and thus had an indirect impact on the *Romer v. Evans* decision.

ADOLESCENT ABORTION RIGHTS CASES

If, as Bersoff (1987) has indicated, one goal of submitting APA *amicus* briefs is for psychological research to not be ignored, the decisions in adolescents' abortion rights cases must be considered defeats. Certainly they reflect clashes in values between most psychologists and most of the justices. Two cases dealing with abortion rights illustrate this.

First, some background: 3 years after the famous Roe v. Wade (1973) decision, the Supreme Court confronted for the first time whether to extend constitutional protections to children when parental opposition to the child's decision was to be expected (Keiter, 1982). In *Planned Parenthood v. Danforth* (1976), the Court considered the constitutionality of a Missouri law requiring parental consent before an unmarried pregnant minor could obtain an abortion. The Court held that the state could not delegate to a third party the authority to decide whether a minor should abort her pregnancy, not even to her parents (1976, pp. 57–58). Justice Blackmun's opinion was explicit; minors could claim privacy rights similar to those available to adults under the due process clause when abortion was the issue (pp. 74–75). He wrote: "Any interest the parent may have in the termination of the minor daughter's pregnancy is no more weighty than the right of privacy of the competent minor mature enough to become pregnant" (p. 75).

The word "mature" in the above quotation is important, because the APA's amicus briefs in subsequent adolescent abortion cases emphasized the maturity of the adolescent. In the two decades after this 1976 decision by the Supreme Court, states began to restrict minors' rights to abortion, mostly by passing laws that required parental consent, or at least prior notification of the minor's parents. By the early 1990s, almost half the states had such laws (Ambuel & Rappaport, 1992).

The Minnesota law was typical; it required either notification of both parents 48 hours before an abortion, or else a "judicial bypass." In the latter procedure, a minor might avoid involving her parents by appearing before a judge and demonstrating that either she was sufficiently mature to make such a decision without her parents' participation, or that the desired abortion was in her best interests. This law and a similar law in Ohio were submitted to the Supreme Court for review; the APA prepared *amicus* briefs for each.

OHIO V. AKRON CENTER FOR REPRODUCTIVE HEALTH ET AL. 1990

Background

In 1985 the Ohio legislature passed a law making it a crime for a physician or other person to perform an abortion on an unmarried minor woman unless the physician provided timely notice (defined as 24 hours) to one of the minor's parents of the physician's intention to perform the abortion. However, an adolescent could avoid this notification if she filed a complaint in the juvenile court, stating:

- That she is pregnant
- That she is unmarried and less than 18 years of age
- That she desires to have an abortion without notifying one of her parents
- That she has sufficient maturity and information to intelligently decide whether to have an abortion without parental notification, *or* that one of her parents has engaged in a pattern of physical, sexual, or emotional abuse against her *or* that notice is not in her best interests

In such cases the juvenile court was required to hold a hearing no later than the fifth business day after the minor filed the complaint, and the court had to render its decision immediately after the hearing. If the minor had not retained her own counsel, the court had to appoint counsel to represent her. The minor was required to prove her claim of either maturity, pattern of abuse, or best interests by the clear and convincing evidence standard. The minor's anonymity was to be guaranteed.

As the law was about to go into effect in March 1986, it was challenged by a group that included the Akron Center for Reproductive Health (a facility providing abortions), a physician at the center, and "Rachel Roe" (a pseudonym for the unmarried minor who sought an abortion at the center). The District Court issued an injunction preventing the state of Ohio from enforcing the statute, and the Sixth Circuit Court of Appeals affirmed the decision, concluding that the Ohio legislation had a number of constitutional defects. Ohio challenged the appeals decision and asked for a U.S. Supreme Court review.

The Brief

The APA joined with the National Association of Social Workers and the American Jewish Committee to submit a brief. In addition to responding to the Ohio bill, the APA brief responded to another case before the Supreme Court, *Hodgson et al. v. Minnesota* (1990), which dealt with a recently passed Minnesota law. This statute was even more restrictive. It required the minor to notify both parents 48 hours before the scheduled abortion, whether or not the parents were currently living together or were ever married; furthermore, it did not provide for a bypass procedure unless it was judicially mandated.

The purpose of the brief was to present empirical research relevant to the requirement of parental notification. The brief argued that only minors who otherwise would not involve their parents in the abortion decision were directly affected by the laws, and that empirical research suggested that these adolescents typically had good reasons not to involve their parents in such decisions (APA brief, p. 2). The brief was also concerned about the welfare of young women who were making decisions about abortion. Pregnant minors in a state with a parental notification law might delay the decision, increasing the health risk of undergoing the procedure, or leading to de facto decisions to carry to term (p. 3). Furthermore, the parental notification statutes might place an unwarranted burden on an adolescent's right to choose.

The brief characterized the state of Ohio's view as seeing minors as "immature and unable to make competent choices concerning abortion" (p. 2). It challenged that assumption, and suggested that mandatory parental notification may actually undermine the goal of legislation, which sought to provide greater communication and understanding within the family.

The brief based its argument on both empirical research and constitutional considerations. The empirical research will be reviewed in detail; the constitutional issue centered on the adolescent's right to choose. The brief argued that the Ohio law requiring either parental notification or a bypass procedure confronted adolescents with an intolerable choice of either "foregoing their right to abortion and becoming adolescent parents, on one hand, or risking their physical and psychological health by complying with the notification statute, on the other" (p. 3).

Two studies were given detailed coverage in the APA brief because they · compared abortion decisions by adolescents and adults "at the time they received pregnancy tests in actual treatment settings" (p. 22). In the first study (Lewis, 1980), 16 unmarried adolescents aged 13 to 17, and 26 unmarried women aged 18 to 25 were asked to "consider their options for responding to their own pregnancies at the time of their pregnancy tests" (p. 22). No difference was found between the two groups in the decisions they made or in their knowledge of pregnancy-related laws. Minors "differed very little" (p. 23) from adults in the frequency with which they mentioned various considerations and consequences when asked to describe factors that could affect the choice of abortion or motherhood.

The second study, by Ambuel and Rappaport (1992), compared decision making in 15 adolescents aged 14–15, 19 adolescents aged 16–17, and 40 adults aged 18–21, when they sought a pregnancy test at a woman's health clinic. Individual interviews assessed decision-making competence through four measures: (1) consideration of risks and benefits, including immediate and future consequences; (2) quality and clarity of reasoning; (3) number and types of factors considered; and (4) volition; that is, making a decision without being coerced by or acquiescing to others. The minors who considered abortion as an option equaled the adults in all four measures.

In summary, the APA brief presented a view of adolescents as competent decision makers. Consider the following conclusions from the brief:

- "Developmental psychologists have built a rich body of research examining adolescents' capabilities for understanding, reasoning, solving problems, and making decisions, especially in comparison to the same capacities in adults. Research consistently supports the conclusion that there is a predictable development during late childhood and early adolescence of the capacity to think rationally about increasingly complex problems and decisions" (p. 18)
- "Research in social and personality development contradicts the stereotype of adolescence as a period when young people are paralyzed by a struggle for identity, social confusion and rebellion against parents. In fact, by middle adolescence (age 14–15) young people develop abilities similar to adults in reasoning about moral dilemmas, understanding social rules and laws, reasoning about interpersonal relationships

and interpersonal problems, and reasoning about custody preference during parental divorce" (pp. 19–20)
- "By middle adolescence most young people develop an adult-like identity and understanding of self" (p. 20)
- "The majority of adolescents do not repudiate parental values, but incorporate them, during their search for autonomy" (p. 20)
- "There is not as much information about the practical decision making competence of younger adolescents—those aged 11 to 13. Research has indicated that there is considerable variability in cognitive development and decision making competence among adolescents, and there are some 11-to-13-year-olds who possess adult-like capabilities in these areas" (p. 20)
- "The evidence does not support the assumption underlying notification laws that adolescents lack an adult's capacity to understand and reason about problems and decisions, including medical and psychological treatment alternatives, or the ability to comprehend and consider risks and benefits regarding treatment alternatives" (p. 21)

The brief acknowledged that there were some differences between adults and adolescents with respect to the decision to have an abortion, but noted that they did not reflect on the relative competence of the two groups in making that decision. Instead, the differences "appear[ed] to be related to minors' and adults' differing social situations. For example, adolescents tend to see their decision as more influenced by consideration of its impact on others, and more frequently involve a parent in the decision. They also take more time to reach a decision . . ." (p. 25).

The Decision

In a 6-to-3 opinion, the Supreme Court ruled that the Ohio law "does not impose an undue, or otherwise unconstitutional, burden on a minor seeking an abortion" (*Ohio v. Akron Center for Reproductive Health et al.*, 1990, p. 2974). The restraining order was lifted. Justice Kennedy wrote the majority opinion, concluding that the judicial bypass procedure in the Ohio law complied with the 14th Amendment. The majority opinion did not cite the APA brief, and in fact, the decision totally contradicted its thrust, by concluding that the rights of minors are adequately protected by the law.

The Dissent

Justice Blackmun filed a dissenting opinion in which Justices Brennan and Marshall joined. He wrote: "The constitutional protection against unjustified state intrusion into the process of deciding whether or not to bear a child extends to pregnant minors as well as adult women" (p. 2984). He also argued that the Ohio statute did not protect a minor's right to anonymity: "The decision to terminate a pregnancy is an intensely private one that must be protected in a way that assures anonymity" (p. 2987). The delay of a decision to abort was also a consideration in Justice Blackmun's dissent; he calculated that the law could impose a delay of as much as three weeks.

Evaluation

To conclude that the majority decision in this case ignored input from psychology does not go far enough. Since the emergence of a conservative majority in the Court, its decisions have consistently reflected a set of paternalistic and demeaning assumptions about the competence of children and adolescents. In the case of *H. L. v. Matheson* (1981)—another parental-notification case—the Court said that the "emotional and psychological consequences of an abortion are serious and can be lasting . . . particularly so when the patient is immature" (p. 411). Furthermore, in *Bellotti v. Baird* (1979) the Court concluded that "states validly may limit the freedom of children to choose for themselves in the making of important, affirmative choices with potentially serious consequences" (p. 635). That power was "grounded in the recognition that, during the formative years of childhood and adolescence, minors often lack the experience, perspective, and judgment to recognize and avoid choices that are detrimental to them" (p. 635). That same year, in the case of *Parham v. J. R.* (1979), Chief Justice Burger wrote that "most children, even in adolescence, simply are not able to make sound judgments concerning many decisions, including their need for medical care or treatment. Parents can and must make these judgments" (pp. 603–604).

The APA brief for this case was not ideal; only two studies were cited, and the number of subjects in each was small. Sometimes no tests of the statistical significance of the differences were carried out. Far-reaching claims were made without support; for example, "Parental notification statutes are actually destructive of the family role in child rearing" (1990, p. 26). The brief emphasized the similarity in responses between adolescents and adults and downplayed the differences. One has a feeling, however, that the strongest research findings possible would not have influenced some of the justices, who possessed unshakable views of the competence of minors, combined with reservations about abortion.

LOCKHART V. MCCREE 1986

No case better illustrates a decision that goes out of its way to reject social science conclusions than does *Lockhart v. McCree*. This case is important for several reasons, not the least of which is that it dealt with the death penalty, an issue Justices Brennan and Marshall called "crucial to the administration of capital punishment in this country" (minority opinion in *Wainwright v. Witt*, 1985, p. 861).

The Facts

On the morning of February 14, 1978, a combination gift shop and service station in Camden, Arkansas was robbed; the owner was shot and killed. That afternoon Ardia McCree was arrested in Hot Springs, Arkansas, some 80 miles away, after a police officer saw him driving a car matching an eyewitness's description of the car used in the crime. Upon questioning, McCree admitted that he had been at the crime scene, but he claimed that a tall black stranger had taken a rifle out of the back of McCree's car and used it to kill Evelyn Boughton, the store owner. His story was contradicted by two eyewitnesses, who said that they saw only one person in McCree's car at the time that McCree claimed that the stranger got out of it and walked away with the rifle. Police found McCree's rifle and a bank bag from the shop alongside a dirt road near the crime scene; it was determined that the bullet that killed the store owner had been fired from McCree's gun.

McCree was put on trial for capital murder. During the *voir dire* the judge excluded, for cause, eight prospective jurors who stated that they could not under any circumstances vote for the death penalty. The eventual jury convicted McCree of capital murder, but it rejected the state's request for the death penalty, and instead sentenced him to life in prison without parole.

After unsuccessfully appealing his conviction to the Arkansas Supreme Court, McCree filed a federal habeas corpus petition in which he claimed, among other things, that the removal for cause of the so-called Witherspoon-excludable prospective jurors, *prior to the guilt-determination phase,* violated his right under the 6th and 14th Amendments to have his guilt or innocence determined by a jury that was first, impartial, and second, selected from a representative cross-section of the community.

The federal district court held a hearing in July 1981 in which it received the results of several social science studies, which found that excluding such jurors led to a conviction-prone jury. Three expert witnesses, including two psychologists (Reid Hastie and Craig Haney), testified for McCree. The state of Arkansas presented testimony by another psychologist, Gerald Shure, who criticized the methodologies of the studies. In its decision, announced in August 1983, the district court concluded, that, based on the above evidence, the "death qualification" exclusion produced juries that "were more prone to convict" (quoted in *Lockhart v. McCree*, 1986, p. 1762). The Eighth Circuit Court of Appeals also found "substantial evidentiary support" for the district court's conclusion and its decision to grant McCree habeas relief through a new trial.

The state of Arkansas (with A. L. Lockhart, the director of the Arkansas Department of Corrections, as appellant) appealed the habeas decision to the U.S. Supreme Court, which heard oral arguments for it on January 13, 1986. Sixteen other states submitted *amici* briefs in support of Lockhart as the petitioner.

The Brief

The APA could hardly pass up the opportunity to provide an *amicus* brief to the Supreme Court in this case. As Bersoff (1987) observed: "In few, if any, other cases has the Court so explicitly sought guidance from psychologists and other social scientists as it did in *Witherspoon*; in few, if any, other cases would the quality and force of social science research be so directly at issue as it was likely to be in *Lockhart*" (p. 54). Furthermore, the state of Arkansas and its *amici* had made a wholesale attack on social science and social science research. Its petition argued that the earlier court decision, *Witherspoon v. Illinois*, (1968), had "relied on pseudo-scientific data as circumstantial 'proof' of 'facts' which may not be subject to proof under any methodology now available to social science researchers" (quoted by Bersoff, 1987, p. 54). The Arkansas brief spoke of the "folly" of relying on "such evidence" and argued that "compared to the 'hard' sciences, such as physics, the findings of 'soft' social sciences are ambiguous and subject to radical change with altered methodology. . . . Statistical significance as a measure of proof is better than nothing but not much" (quoted by Bersoff, 1987, p. 54).

The APA brief was written by Donald Bersoff, who is both a lawyer and a psychologist, in collaboration with an attorney, David Ogden, and five psychologists, Phoebe Ellsworth, Craig Haney, Reid Hastie, John Monahan, and Michael Saks. The brief's purpose was to present research findings supporting the argument that death-qualified juries are more pro-prosecution and less representative of the population than are typical criminal juries. The brief noted that in the 1968 *Witherspoon* decision, the Supreme Court declined to rule that death-qualified juries are "less than neutral with respect to guilt" (1968, p. 520) and therefore unconstitutional, because the research data at that time were, in the Court's view, too "tentative and fragmentary" (p. 520). Only three studies had been available to the *Witherspoon* court, and the Court had left open the possibility that it would rule differently if further research "more clearly demonstrated death-qualified juries' non-neutrality" (quoted by the APA brief, p. 2). As Bersoff (1987) has pointed out, it's rare for the Court to invite social scientists to develop data to fill a void on a point of constitutional law, and social scientists responded to the invitation with enthusiasm. Between 1968 and 1986, more than a dozen studies were done. Thompson's (1989) careful review provides the following assessment:

> [These were] increasingly sophisticated studies designed to answer objections the courts had raised to earlier research. Because no single study could answer all these objections, they sought convergent validity through an array of studies looking at the difference between death-qualified and excludable jurors in different ways. The new studies unanimously confirmed previous findings that death-qualified jurors have attitudes more favorable to the prosecution and are more likely to convict than *Witherspoon* excludables. Moreover, differences between death qualified and excludable jurors in jury simulation studies tended to increase as the simulation studies became more realistic. (1989, p. 193)

The APA brief noted that Lockhart's brief had attacked this research on several grounds, and thus the "integrity of the data" (p. 3) became one of the major questions the Supreme Court agreed to answer. The APA brief reviewed a number of studies that showed "without credible exception" (p. 3) that "death-qualified juries are prosecution prone, unrepresentative of the community, and that death qualification impairs proper jury functioning" (p. 3). The brief conceded that the absolutely definitive study had not been done—one that would compare the real-world performance of death-qualified jurors with the performance of typical juries, but that given the three decades of consistent findings, such an experiment would be only marginally useful.

The brief also evaluated the data in light of the petitioner's eight major criticisms of the research and concluded that the objections were either unrelated to the relevant research or mistaken. "The research clearly satisfies the criteria for evaluating the methodological soundness, reliability, and utility of empirical research" the brief concluded (p. 3). Thus, the APA brief was heavily empirical in its orientation, with the empirical issues brought to bear on the constitutional right to due process.

The Decision

The majority opinion of the Court, announced in May 1986, was written by Justice Rehnquist; it was joined by Justices Burger, O'Connor, White, and Powell. Justice Blackmun—usually sympathetic to social science research—concurred inn the result but wrote no opinion, making six votes for the majority. A dissenting opinion was submitted by Justice Marshall, in which Justices Stevens and Brennan joined. The Court held that "the Constitution does not prohibit the States from 'death-qualifying' juries in capital cases" (p. 1764). The postconviction relief given by the earlier courts was overturned and the conviction of Ardia McCree upheld.

Although the majority opinion written by Justice Rehnquist did not cite the APA brief directly, it devoted three pages to an evaluation of the social science evidence. What is most remarkable about this is the placement of the critique at the very beginning of the opinion, before the rationale for the decision is given.

It was noted (Thompson, 1989, p. 195) that Justice Rehnquist examined this body of literature in piecemeal fashion, and whenever he found a "flaw" in a study or group of studies, he dismissed it or them from further consideration. "His analysis treated any study he deemed less than definitive as if it were completely uninformative; [he] never considered that shortcoming in studies of one type might be ruled out by studies of another type" (Thompson, p. 195).

The intensity of Justice Rehnquist's objections is conveyed by the following extended excerpt from his majority opinion in *Lockhart v. McCree*:

> Before turning to the legal issues in the case, we are constrained to point out what we believe to be several serious flaws in the evidence upon which the courts below reached the conclusion that "death qualification" produces "conviction-prone" juries. McCree introduced into evidence some 15 social science studies in support of his constitutional claims, but only 6 of the studies even purported to measure the potential effects of the guilt-innocence determination of the removal from the jury of "*Witherspoon*-excludables." Eight of the remaining nine studies dealt solely with generalized attitudes and beliefs about the death penalty and other aspects of the criminal justice system, and were thus, at best, only marginally relevant to the constitutionality of McCree's conviction. The 15th and final study dealt with the effects on prospective jurors of *voir dire* questioning about their attitudes toward the death penalty, an issue McCree raised in his brief to this Court but that counsel for McCree admitted at oral argument would not, standing alone, give rise to a constitutional violation.
>
> Of the six studies introduced by McCree that at least purported to deal with the central issue in this case, namely the potential effects on the determinations of guilt or innocence of excluding "*Witherspoon*-excludables" from this jury, three were also before this Court when it decided *Witherspoon*. There, this Court reviewed the studies and concluded:
>
> "The data adduced by the petitioner . . . are too tentative and fragmentary to establish that jurors not opposed to the death penalty tend to favor the prosecution in the determination of guilt. We simply cannot conclude, either on the basis of the record now before us or as a matter of judicial notice, that the exclusion of jurors opposed to capital punishment results in an unrepresentative jury on the issue of guilt or substantially increases the risk of conviction. In light of the presently available information, we are not prepared to announce a *per se* constitutional rule requiring the reversal of every conviction returned by a jury selected as this one was." 391 U.S., at 517-518, 88 S. Ct., at 1774-75 [footnote omitted].
>
> It goes almost without saying that if these studies were "too tentative and fragmentary" to make out a claim of constitutional error in 1968, the same studies, unchanged but having aged some 18 years, are still insufficient to make out such a claim in this case.
>
> Nor do the three post-*Witherspoon* studies introduced by McCree on the "death qualification" issue provide substantial support for the "*per se* constitutional rule" McCree asks this Court to adopt. All three of the "new'" studies were

based on the responses of individuals randomly selected from some segment of the population, but who were not actual jurors sworn under the law to the facts of an actual case involving the fate of an actual capital defendant. We have serious doubts about the value of these studies in predicting the behavior of actual jurors. See *Griggs v. Mabry*, 758 F.2d, at 248, n. 7 (J. Gibson, J., dissenting). In addition, two of the three "new" studies did not even attempt to simulate the process of jury deliberation, and none of the "new" studies was able to predict to what extent, if any the presence of one or more "*Witherspoon*-excludables" on a guilt-phase jury would have altered the outcome of the guilt determination.

Finally, and most importantly, only one of the six "death qualification" studies introduced by McCree even attempted to identify and account for the presence of so-called "nullifiers," or individuals who, because of their deep-seated opposition to the death penalty, would be unable to decide a capital defendant's guilt or innocence fairly and impartially. McCree concedes, as he must, that "nullifiers" may properly be excluded from the guilt-phase jury, and studies that fail to take into account the presence of such "nullifiers" thus are fatally flawed. Surely a "*per se* constitutional rule" as far reaching as the one McCree proposes should not be based on the results of the lone study that avoids this fundamental flaw. (*Lockhart v. McCree*, 1986, pp. 1762–1764, footnotes omitted)

Justice Rehnquist's detailed annihilation of research findings was not enough, however. As Bersoff (1987) observed, "Apparently, even if the majority had given the particular research introduced in this case a more respectful (and we believe a more proper) review, it would have made little difference" (p. 56). For Justice Rehnquist added:

Having identified some of the more serious problems with McCree's studies, however, we, will assume for purposes of this opinion that the studies are both methodologically valid and adequate to establish that "death qualification" in fact produces juries somewhat more "conviction-prone" than "non-death-qualified" juries. We hold, nonetheless, that the Constitution does not prohibit the States from "death qualifying" juries in capital cases. (p. 1764)

Two reasons were offered for this startling conclusion. First, with respect to the Sixth Amendment requirement of representatativeness, the courts have interpreted it to mean a representative *venire* (process by which jurors are summoned to try a case), not a specific *jury* that is representative. The Eighth Circuit Court of Appeals had ruled that death qualification violated McCree's rights, but Justice Rehnquist wrote:

We do not believe that the fair-cross-section requirement can, or should, be applied as broadly as that court attempted to apply it. We have never invoked the fair-cross-section principle to invalidate the use of either for-cause or peremptory challenges to prospective jurors, or to require petit juries, as opposed to jury panels or venires, to reflect the composition of the community at large. (p. 1765)

In fact, he noted, it would be a practical impossibility to provide each criminal defendant with a truly representative *petit jury* (ordinary trial jury). Furthermore, in Justice Rehnquist's opinion, "even if we were willing to extend the fair-cross-section requirement to petit juries" (p. 1765), the focus is on a "distinctive" group in the community, and groups "defined solely in terms of shared attitudes that would prevent or substantially impair members of the group from performing one of their duties as jurors . . . are not "distinctive groups' for fair-cross-section purposes" (p. 1765). He later expanded on this point:

> The group of "*Witherspoon*-excludables" involved in the case at bar differs significantly from the groups we have previously recognized as "distinctive. "Death qualification," unlike the wholesale exclusion of blacks, women, or Mexican-Americans from jury service, is carefully designed to serve the State's concededly legitimate interest in obtaining a single jury that can properly and impartially apply the law to the facts of the case at both the guilt and sentencing phases of a capital trial. There is very little danger, therefore, and McCree does not even argue, that "death qualification" was instituted as a means for the State to arbitrarily skew the composition of capital-case juries. (p. 1766)

Justice Rehnquist clearly differed from the APA brief writers with respect to the centrality of such attitudes in prospective jurors. After noting that, in contrast to "blacks, women, and Mexican-Americans, 'Witherspoon-excludables' are singled out for exclusion . . . on the basis of an attribute that is within the individual's control" (p. 1766), Justice Rehnquist stated that "those who firmly believe that the death penalty is unjust may nevertheless serve as jurors in capital cases so long as they state clearly that they are willing to temporarily set aside their own beliefs in deference to the rule of law" (p. 1766). His attitude toward such people seems to surface in this characterization that "the group of 'Witherspoon-excludables' includes only those who cannot or will not conscientiously obey the law with respect to one of the issues in a capital case" (p. 1766).

The second reason for Justice Rehnquist's opinion was his position that McCree presented no evidence that the specific jury which decided his guilt was biased. He wrote: "McCree concedes that the individual jurors who served at his trial were impartial" (p. 1767) and "McCree does not claim that his conviction was tainted by any of the kinds of jury bias or partiality that we have previously recognized as violative of the Constitution" (p. 1767). Instead, McCree argued that "his jury lacked impartiality because the absence of 'Witherspoon-excludables' 'slanted' the jury in favor of conviction" (p. 1767).

Justice Rehnquist concluded that the Court's view of jury impartiality was different; in the *Wainwright v. Witt* (1985) decision, an impartial jury was seen as consisting of nothing more than "*jurors* who will conscientiously apply the law and find the facts" (1985, p. 423, italics in original).

McCree's goal was, in Justice Rehnquist's opinion, "both illogical and hopelessly impractical" (p. 1767). It would require trial judges to undertake "the Sisyphean task of 'balancing' juries, making sure that each contains the proper number of Democrats and Republicans, young persons and old persons, white-collar executives and blue-collar laborers, and so on" (p. 1768).

The Dissent

Justice Marshall's minority opinion, covering 12 pages, supported McCree's claims (it referred to a jury "tilted" in favor of the prosecution, on page 1771) and summarized the conclusions of the psychological studies, the evidence from which it called "overwhelming" (p. 1770). For example, it noted that "The data strongly suggest that death qualification excludes a significantly large subset—at least 11% to 17%—of potential jurors" (p. 1772), including a disproportionate number of Blacks and women. It noted the unanimity of results obtained by researchers using diverse types of subjects and methodologies, and cited specific empirical articles; it concluded that the defendant "presented overwhelming evidence that death-qualified juries are substantially more likely to convict . . . than are juries on which unalterable opponents of capital punishment are permitted to serve" (p. 1771).

Bersoff concludes: "It is very clear that the dissent had carefully read the APA's brief, because much of its critique of the majority's view of the social science evidence relied on, and in some cases, closely paraphrased that brief" (1987, p. 56).

Justice Marshall's dissent faulted the majority for its refusal to take social science evidence into consideration, stating:

> Faced with the near unanimity of authority supporting [the] claim that death qualification gives the prosecution a particular advantage in the guilt phase of capital trials, the majority here makes but a weak effort to contest that proposition. Instead, it merely assumes . . . that "death-qualification" in fact produces juries somewhat more "conviction-prone" than "non-death-qualified" juries . . . and then hold[s] that this result does not offend the Constitution. This disregard for the clear import of the evidence tragically misconstrues the settled constitutional principles that guarantee a defendant the right to a fair trial and an impartial jury whose composition is not biased toward the prosecution. (pp. 1774–1775)

EVALUATION

Bersoff (1987) revealed that the APA, when considering the submission of an *amicus* brief, had recognized that McCree faced an uphill battle in the Supreme Court. Even though the Eighth Circuit Court of Appeals had supported his position and relied on social science research, several other circuit courts had ruled against McCree's position. Bersoff (1986, 1987) has concluded that in cases in which the Supreme Court disregards evidence from the social sciences, the fault sometimes rests upon the social scientists themselves, but in this case, he believed that "the Court itself is primarily responsible" (1987, p. 57). Bersoff's view of the majority's reaction to the research is a generous one:

> The validity of social science evidence in general was not addressed by the majority, although it was urged to do so by the state and its supporting *amici*. And, even though the majority eventually concluded that the social science evidence was not germane to its decision, it did not ignore it either. It gave a respectful hearing and, it must be said, echoed the objective critique APA provided in its *amicus* brief. The Court's emphasis on the admitted lack of perfection in these studies was of far greater import to it, however, than it was to APA. Although I do not agree with the majority's analysis, the opinion does not appear to undermine the usefulness of social science evidence in judicial decision making. It does teach social scientists, however, that if they wish to contribute to constitutional adjudication, they must do so in the most methodologically rigorous and situation-specific way possible. (1987, p. 58)

Bersoff's comments cause us to reconsider: What is the goal of the APA's submission of briefs? Bersoff chose to emphasize that the court could not ignore or dismiss the usefulness of social science evidence, stating that "unlike prior cases in which such evidence was criticized as 'numerology,' the majority (and to a much greater extent, the dissent) was attentive to the import of the findings, even almost grudgingly accepting of them" (1987, p. 58). The decision in this case, Bersoff concluded, while not a victory, was also not a defeat.

William Thompson's review (1989) of Supreme Court decisions on death qualification is much less sanguine than Bersoff's: "If the issue of death qualification was a test of the Court's receptivity to social science, the Court failed the test badly" (p. 215). He noted, however, that tremendous political and practical ramifications would have resulted from declaring death-qualification unconstitutional. Perhaps the Court will be more receptive to social science findings when less is at stake, but Thompson suggested that "the intellectual weakness of the Court's opinions in *Witt* and *McCree* lends support to the cynical conclusion that the majority of the Supreme Court is willing to distort and ignore social science when it supports the 'wrong' conclusion" (p. 215). Thompson's position is elaborated in the following excerpt from his article:

> In sum, the majority opinion in McCree is poorly reasoned and unconvincing both in its analysis of the social science evidence and in its analysis of the legal issue of jury impartiality. If this opinion is forthright and sincere, reflecting the best efforts of the majority of the Court, it should raise serious doubts about the ability of these justices to understand and deal with social science. The Court's piecemeal evaluation of the studies may be explained, perhaps, by a failure to appreciate the concept of convergent validity.

Although this concept was explained in briefs and lower court opinions, the majority of the justices may nevertheless have assumed that a study is unworthy of consideration unless it is designed in a manner that rules out all possible confounds and alternative explanations-an assumption one might call "the myth of the definitive study." The Court's misreading and mischaracterization of several of the studies is more *difficult* to explain, unless it was due simply to intellectual carelessness. This explanation seems unconvincing, however, for several reasons. The research is unusually straightforward and easy to understand. Most of the studies involved simple two-group comparisons. There was no need to understand statistical models to appreciate the results. Finally, the legal and empirical issues were well briefed and had been thoroughly discussed in lower court opinions.

An alternative explanation is that the opinion is not forthright and sincere. Legal realists caution that appellate decisions are often based on pragmatic considerations rather than pure legal analysis. Under this view, the arguments set forth in judicial opinions are often merely the court's effort to provide an acceptable justification for an expedient decision. In *McCree* the Court may have approached the issue of death qualification pragmatically, balancing the perceived rests of eliminating death qualification against the increased protection of defendants' rights that would be afforded by the remedy sought by McCree (i.e., a bifurcated jury trial in capital cases). The decision may ultimately be based on a simple judgment that the increased protections are not worth the trouble of changing a procedure that has been employed for many years. Some of the justices may well believe that capital defendants have enough protection already. Hence, to require the additional protections sought by McCree may have seemed an unnecessary coddling of criminal defendants. Because these pragmatic considerations are not recognized as a legitimate basis for a constitutional holding, they are not reflected in the opinion. Instead, the Court attacked the social science research and shifted to an individual view of jury impartiality in a disingenuous effort to justify a decision reached on the basis of political pragmatism rather than constitutional principle.

An even more cynical view is that the Court was influenced by a desire to avoid reversing the convictions of defendants tried by death qualified juries in previous cases. When *McCree* was decided there were over 1,500 people on death row, and probably an even larger number of individuals serving life sentences, who had been convicted by death qualified juries. In the absence of an innovative and unprecedented holding regarding retroactivity, a finding in McCree's favor would have compelled the Court to reverse these convictions, necessitating new trials in hundreds of murder cases. Perhaps this consideration contributed to the determination of some of the justices to find a way to uphold death qualification. (Thompson, 1989, pp. 202–204, footnotes omitted)

William Thompson's evaluation of the possible rationale for the *McCree* decision returns us to a consideration of the issue in the first half of this book: Are judicial opinions driven by basic values and attitudes? Thompson has suggested that Justice Rehnquist's anti-defendant attitudes influenced the way he evaluated the social science research, much like the way that he responded to Glen Burton Ake's claims of delusions and psychotic behavior.

CONCLUSIONS

The outcome of the cases described in this chapter certainly offers caution to any psychologist who believes that it is sufficient to simply report empirical results to the Court and that that the Court's decision will dutifully reflect their implications. The impact of research can never be assumed, although on occasion it has had its intended effect. Our final chapter seeks to identify just when it is that psychology and social science can have the greatest impact.

10

The Future of the Psychology–
Law Relationship

OVERVIEW

Let us return to the original emphasis of the book—the determinants of judicial decision making—but with a different approach. One conclusion from the first half of the book was that a psychological analysis of judicial decision making is fruitful because judges' values and motives serve as a kind of filter when approaching the issues in a given case. Now we turn to some of the implications of value-influenced decision making, specifically, the impact of values on the sources a judge uses in justifying decisions.

Different judges cite different kinds of sources when justifying their written opinions. The positions of individual justices on the use of various types of sources are reviewed in this chapter, leading to an analysis of organized psychology's obstacles to having an influence on judicial decision making. Some proposals for improving the relationship then are offered.

HISTORICAL PERSPECTIVE REVISITED

Chapters 6 and 7 traversed the sometimes tortuous interaction between psychology and the court system initiated 100 years ago by often arrogant intrusions into the workings of the other discipline, followed by a long period of no contact, and culminating in efforts, with varying degrees of success (and sometimes indeterminate success), to establish a working relationship over the last two decades. Donald Bersoff has commented that if this relationship "were to be examined by a Freudian, the analyst would no doubt conclude that it is a highly neurotic, conflict-ridden affair (. . . it is certainly no marriage)" (1986, p. 155).

Prior to active involvement by Munsterberg and others near the beginning of the twentieth century, social science did have an impact on the courts, but it was more subtle. History was the only social science upon which the courts of the 1800s would explicitly rely on for extralegal facts (Kerr, 1986); rulings could, however, be premised upon strongly entrenched sociological and psychological assumptions, such as the belief that segregation was not oppressive to Blacks and that Blacks were inherently inferior to Whites. As noted in Chapter 6, although the conclusion of Tomkins and Oursland (1991) that the Supreme Court decisions in the nineteenth century—particularly *Dred Scott v. Sandford* (1857) and *Plessy v. Ferguson* (1896)—were congruent with conventional social science thinking at that time, the impact of such perspectives was often not easily demonstrated. Things have changed in one century; the relationship between social science and the courts has grown more complex. For example, the shift in the Court's position on the rights of homosexual persons from the 1986 *Bowers v. Hardwick* decision to the 1996 *Romer v. Evans* decision *may* reflect increased societal awareness of the psychological research conclusion that sexual orientation is unrelated to pathology or deviance, but it is hard to see any congruence between social science thinking and recent decisions about defendants' rights or the death penalty.

Uses and Misuses of Psychological Research Findings

It is true that in several recent decisions, social science perspectives have had an impact on Supreme Court decisions, as Chapter 8 illustrates, and some previous justices, particularly Thurgood Marshall and Harry Blackmun, were quite sympathetic to this perspective. Justice Blackmun cited social science research extensively in his *Ballew v. Georgia* decision and in some of his dissents, notably *Bowers v. Hardwick*. In his arguments against the death penalty in *Furman v. Georgia* (1972), Justice Marshall cited numerous empirical studies relevant to a claim that the death penalty has a deterrent effect on violent crime, as well as studies indicating a racial bias in the assignment of death sentences.

But when psychological research is cited, it is sometimes misinterpreted. Norbert Kerr's 1986 review gave several examples in which the Court used social science results in inappropriate ways. For example, some Court opinions showed a poor understanding of basic statistical concepts. The 1970 *Williams v. Florida* decision concluded that any difference in the representativeness of 12-person versus 6-person juries would be negligible. In the 1977 *Castaneda v. Partida* decision, the opinion by Justice Blackmun confused the terms *standard deviation and standard error.*

On occasion, the Court's decision dismisses conclusions of a statistically significant difference between groups. For example, *Craig v. Boren* (1976) dealt with an Oklahoma law that permitted females, but not males, between the ages of 18 and 21 years of age to purchase 3.2% beer. In support of this law, the state presented empirical evidence to the Court that 2% of 18–21-year-old males were cited for drunk driving, while only 0.18% of females were. The Court acknowledged these data, but concluded that this statistically significant difference was, in effect, irrelevant because the overriding principle at issue was equal protection before the law.

Relying on weak data is another type of misuse, which fails to distinguish between good research and poor research. Chapter 6 described the studies used to support the conclusion that jury size was immaterial in the *Williams v. Florida* decision. In the follow-up decision, *Colgrove v. Battin* (1973), which applied to civil trials, the Court reaffirmed its ruling by relying on four poorly empirical studies.

LEE V. WEISMAN 1992

A detailed examination of the misuse of social science knowledge in one case is provided by Bersoff and Glass (1995); the case, *Lee v. Weisman* (1992), involved the legality of including a prayer as part of a public school graduation ceremony. The court action (a request for a temporary restraining order) was initiated by the father of 14-year-old Deborah Weisman 4 days before her graduation from middle school; he sought to bar the school board from the practice of inviting members of the clergy to give invocations and benedictions at the high school and middle school ceremonies. The Constitution, of course, prohibits the establishment of a state religion. Did this qualify?

The federal district court denied Weisman's motion, saying it did not have enough time to consider the temporary restraining order. At the graduation, which Deborah and her family attended, a rabbi selected by the school principal gave a nonsectarian religious invocation and benediction. The graduates sat together, apart from their families.

The case eventually made its way to the U.S. Supreme Court, which ruled that prayer in the public schools carries an acute risk of indirect and subtle coercion (p. 2656) and that high school students who wished to abstain would suffer real injury if forced to pray in a way antithetical to their consciences (p. 2658). The majority decision bolstered this "common assumption" (p. 2659) with three research articles from prominent psychological journals, claiming that the articles showed that "adolescents are often susceptible to pressure from their peers toward conformity, and that the influence is strongest in matters of social convention" (p. 2659). Justice Kennedy wrote the majority opinion; he was joined by Justices Blackmun, Stevens, O'Connor, and Souter. He based his opinion on three main "facts": First, that it was a public official who decided that the invocation and benediction would be given; actually, it was the principal. Second, that even for students who objected to the religious exercise, attendance and participation were in a real sense obligatory even though attendance was not a requirement for receiving a diploma (p. 2660). Third was the "fact" of the aforementioned potential psychological harm from indirect coercion.

Two of the justices in the majority wrote concurring opinions. Justice Blackmun, joined by Justices O'Connor and Stevens, agreed that such religious invocations and benedictions violated the Establishment Clause of the First Amendment, but could not go along with Justice Kennedy on the issue of coercion. It was not that Justice Blackmun believed that no coercion was present, but rather that a finding of coercion wasn't necessary to conclude that the practice was unconstitutional. Justice Souter, in a concurring opinion joined by Justices Stevens and O'Connor, argued that the Establishment Clause forbade public school practices that supported religion in general as well as those favoring one religion over others.

A dissenting opinion by Justice Scalia endorsed the position that some forms of governmental support for religion were an accepted part of our political and cultural heritage (p. 2678). He also rejected the assertion that students were obligated to participate in the invocation and benediction; the fact that dissenting students were asked to stand with their classmates did not necessarily means that they had to join in the prayers (pp. 2681–2682).

Justice Scalia had some sharp remarks for the majority's opinion on what he called "psycho-coercion" (p. 2685; Bersoff & Glass, 1995). Calling it a "jurisprudential disaster," (p. 2685), he felt that Justice Kennedy had completely misunderstood the nature of religious coercion. He argued that historically coercion meant requiring colonists to adopt a particular religious orthodoxy and to provide financial support to a state church under threat of a penalty (p. 2683). That brand of coercion, he added, "is readily discernible to those of us who have made a career of reading the disciples of Blackstone rather than of Freud" (p. 2684). Thus, he concluded, the majority's coercion test "suffers from the double disability of having no roots whatever in our people's historic practice, and being as infinitely expandable as the reasons for psychotherapy itself" (p. 2685). This is not the only time, as we will see, that Justice Scalia has gratuitously attacked psychology.

Bersoff and Glass (1995) provide a detailed critique of the applicability of the three empirical studies used by Justice Kennedy in his majority opinion; recall that these were cited to bolster the "common assumption" that adolescents are especially susceptible to conformity as a result of peer pressure, and that as a result, they must be protected from the harm that such pressure can cause (p. 2659). The psychologists conclude that "overall, the studies, at best, marginally support the Court's opinion" (Bersoff & Glass, 1995, p. 289). The procedures and results of the studies are as follows:

C. V. Brittain (1963) presented hypothetical vignettes to 280 girls in Alabama and Georgia middle and high schools. In each one, a female adolescent had to choose between alternatives favored by her parents and those favored by her friends. Examples included what dress to wear to a party, whether to report a classmate who had participated in vandalism, and which part-time job to take. The results indicated that the girls' choices were affected by the type of situation in which guidance was sought. They relied on peers more in vignettes dealing with dress, appearance, and attendance at social gatherings, whereas parents were more often the reference group for decisions involving personal values or choice of a job. The study had no direct indication of *how much* adolescent girls conformed to either reference group.

Clasen and Brown (1985) used a sample of 689 students in grades 7 through 12 in two Midwestern communities to study adolescent perceptions of peer pressure. Each student completed a questionnaire indicating the level of pressure felt in a variety of situations. These adolescents reported a high degree of peer pressure with regard to issues involving peers and school but less pressure for issues regarding misconduct. Respondents in the higher grades reported fewer conformity pressures from friends than did the younger (seventh- and eighth-grade) students. Again, the study provides no direct evidence of the extent of conformity.

Brown, Clasen, and Eicher (1986) used the same measure of perceived peer pressure as the above study, with 1027 students from middle and high schools. Results were similar to the previous study. Additionally, the study found that peer pressure accounted for only a small part of self-reported behavior. Thus the authors explicitly cautioned against "inferring adolescents' conformity behavior strictly from measures of conformity dispositions" (p. 529).

Bersoff and Glass provided a list of criticisms about the conclusions that Justice Kennedy's opinion drew from the studies, which included:

- It is improper to generalize from these three studies to adolescents' compliance with peer pressure in a situation involving school prayer. They noted that "to provide empirical support for the argument that peer pressure could cause students to be coerced into participating in religious graduation exercises, the majority should have cited research that studied adolescents in these specific situations" (p. 290). Bersoff and Glass reported conducting an extensive search of relevant social science databases, and said they could find no such studies. Applying research that questions adolescents about their expected reactions in everyday situations to a "ceremonial, one-time, highly important life event implicating factors central to the integrity of the family" (p. 291) showed that the Supreme Court opinion "overgeneralized the range of application of the cited research, inappropriately stretched the research to fit the facts, and seriously diminished the validity of its ultimate opinion" (p. 291).

- The opinion overlooked consistent findings that in later adolescence, the perceived pressures to meet group norms become less important.
- The data show that older adolescents' ability to make important decisions is comparable to that of adults. This research-based conclusion, which conflicts with "common assumptions," was exemplified in the section of Chapter 9 dealing with adolescent abortion cases.
- "social science research indicates that the effects of peer pressure are often mediated by parental influence, depending on the specific situation" (Bersoff and Glass, 1995, pp. 292–293). Especially in situations involving weighty issues such as values and lifestyle, parental input carries more weight than input from peers.

The overall evaluation by Bersoff and Glass seems fitting:

> In sum, the serial science research the majority cites fails to substantiate a theory of psychological coercion, at least as applied to the facts of this case. Justice Kennedy's social science support is under-researched and overgeneralized. Although there is a reasonably large literature on the topic of per pressure and conforming behavior, Justice Kennedy cited only three isolated, marginally analogous studies from which he drew conclusions that were unwarranted and went far beyond those to which the authors of the studies themselves came. (Bersoff & Glass. 1995, p. 293)

What kind of judge cites social science research? Every judicial opinion must have a justification. Traditionally, of course, the justification has come from interpretations of the Constitution, the laws, and past court decisions. But as we have seen, judges and justices may cite other sources. What accounts for a judge citing other sources? Do some judges do so more consistently than others?

PRIMARY VERSUS SECONDARY SOURCES

A distinction can be made between two types of sources (Hafemeister & Melton, 1987). *Primary sources* come directly from the law: cases, statutes, and regulations. *Secondary sources* may be further divided into two types, *legal* secondary sources, or legal commentaries published in law reviews, legal treatises, and legal reference books; and *nonlegal* or *extralegal* secondary sources, which and books include social science journals and books, as well as a variety of other sources.

Our interest centers on the citation of social science sources. Rosenblum's 1975 survey, described in Kerr's 1986 review, indicated that during the 1950s, such sources were infrequently cited in Supreme Court rulings—only 5.8% of the decisions in 1954 did so, for example—but from the mid-1950s through the mid-1970s the percentage rose steadily, to 12% of cases in 1974.

The citations were typically quite brief; more than a third of them in Rosenblum's survey involved only a single source, and direct quotations were not common (18 of 148 uses), nor were the presentation or analysis of original data (5 of 148 instances). Of special importance is the finding that the source publication was typically *not* a social science journal, and that most of the articles cited were written by lawyers or law professors (1975).

The material was generally presented in "a fairly cursory manner" (Kerr, 1986, p. 64) and usually escaped critical evaluation; in about a third of Rosenblum's cases, the source was cited without any comment. Though there were noteworthy exceptions—some of which are described in this book—the opinion generally devoted no more than two sentences to such sources, and their validity was "usually assumed without question" (Kerr, 1986, p. 64).

As one would expect, certain topics and types of cases were more likely to have this kind of reference. Rosenblum's 1975 survey found social science sources more likely to be mentioned in decisions in which the topic was apportionment and election law, racial discrimination, or criminal procedure. Also, cases raising constitutional issues were more likely to have referred to social science findings than cases not raising such issues. (Some cases the Court must decide even though there is no constitutional issue in dispute are jurisdictional matters—not likely to call on social science research for resolution.) The constitutional issues that referred to social science sources were primarily equal protection, due process, and self-incrimination, Rosenblum proposed that when justices are concerned with communicating to the general public, they are more likely to refer to social science findings and conclusions. As evidence of this, he noted that social science citations occur more often in cases with multiple opinions; Kerr's 1986 analysis indicated that this effect extends beyond the expected increase from the number of opinion writers involved.

JUDICIAL PHILOSOPHY AND SOCIAL SCIENCE RESEARCH CITATION

In their review of social science research citations, Hafemeister and Melton (1987) concluded that citation of secondary sources was correlated with the judicial philosophy of individual justices. Such a conclusion is logical; a "strict constructionist" is more likely to cite the wording of the Constitution and less likely to rely on an article from a social science journal. Does this difference extend to political orientation? In previous chapters we saw examples of opinions by Marshall, Blackmun, and Brennan—justices who composed the "liberal wing" in the 1980s—that relied on social science to justify their opinions. But we also saw decisions by O'Connor and Kennedy—the current "swing votes"—that do the same.

Although analyses of the Court that go back more than 30 years (Daniels, 1983; Newland, 1961; Rosen, 1972) suggest that politically liberal justices were more likely to cite social science material, Rosenblum's thorough 1975 analysis, reported by Kerr (1986), found no striking differences between liberals and conservatives. Clearly there were individual differences; some justices rarely referred to social science (for example, only 2.3% of the sampled opinions of Justice Rehnquist), whereas others did so more often (18.4% for Justice Frankfurter). Individual differences also extended to how the justices used this evidence—some when they were in the majority (Chief Justice Burger was an example here), others (such as Justice Stewart) were more often when in the minority. For some justices, the citation of such sources was an important part of the opinion; for others, it was less so. Rosenblum noted that although Justice Stewart made relatively frequent use of social science sources, he rarely employed them in a significant manner.

INDIVIDUAL JUDGES' ATTITUDES TOWARD PSYCHOLOGY

The attitude of a judge regarding social science may predict his or her degree of reliance on its findings. Examples of specific judges' reactions provide examples.

Blackmun versus Powell

Two justices facing the same set of facts in a case can interpret them differently, as Chapter 2 illustrated with Justices Marshall and Rehnquist in *Ake v. Oklahoma*, but they can also differ concerning the appropriateness of relying on psychology or social science findings. When Justice Blackmun, in *Ballew v. Georgia*, reviewed the research on jury size, Justice Powell had this response:

> I have reservations as to the wisdom-as well as the necessity—of Mr. Justice Blackmun's heavy reliance on numerology derived from statistical studies. Moreover, neither the validity nor the methodology employed by the studies cited was subjected to the traditional testing mechanisms in the adversary process. The studies relied on merely represent unexamined findings of persons interested in the jury system. (*Ballew v. Georgia*, 1978, p. 246).

Justice Blackmun's justification:

> We have considered [empirical and statistical studies] carefully because they provide the only basis, besides judicial hunch, for a decision about whether smaller and smaller juries will be able to fulfill the purpose and functions of the Sixth Amendment. Without an examination about how juries and small groups actually work, we would not understand the basis for the conclusion of Mr. Justice Powell that "a line has to be drawn somewhere." (*Ballew v. Georgia*, 1978. p. 231, n.10)

Justice Scalia

"Where does community sentiment stand on the death penalty for juveniles?" This is seemingly an empirical question, and most psychologists would suggest that the way to answer it is to conduct an opinion poll. Justice Scalia, however, has favored another procedure: the courts should focus on what he calls "objective indicia" ("indicia" meaning signs or indications). Examples of indicia are legislation and jury decisions about sentences in capital cases, that is, when faced with the question of the legitimacy of assigning the death penalty to a juvenile, or to a rapist, or to a mentally retarded person, Justice Scalia would defer to the state legislature as the representative of the public will, rather than to a public opinion poll. In fact, when cases have come before the Supreme Court appealing death sentences for an adolescents (examples are *Thompson v. Oklahoma*, 1988, and *Stanford v. Kentucky*, 1989), Justice Scalia has consistently held that the determinant should be what that state's statutes do and do not permit (Finkel, 1995).

OBSTACLES TO PSYCHOLOGY'S INFLUENCE ON THE LAW

Psychology, in contrast to law, is generally committed to the concept of an objectifiable world of experience that can be best understood by unwavering adherence to the rules of science, including systematic testing of hypotheses by observation and experimental methodology. As scientists, psychologists strive for a public, objective pursuit of truth, using methods that can be repeated by others, and generally, they follow predetermined procedures in interpreting their results. It should be clear by now that what psychologists consider acceptable research and clear-cut findings are not enough to guarantee acceptance by the legal system. In psychological training the credo is "The data speak for themselves," but this credo does not carry over to a world where another discipline has made up the rules.

Each discipline approaches the generation of knowledge and the standards for decision making in its own way. An attorney and a psychologist will see the same event from different perspectives because of their specialized training. It is not that one approach is right and the other wrong; they are different. Psychologists sometimes do not realize how this other world may see them. Consider the reaction of Senator Orrin Hatch, who is not a judge, but (under a Republican-controlled Senate) is the chair of a committee that acts upon presidential recommendations for federal judgeships. He wrote (in the *American Psychologist,* no less) that psychologists risk being perceived as "a group on the fringe of social normality who are promoting social deviance" (1982, p. 1035). In light of the APA's *amicus* brief in *Bowers v. Hardwick*, his comments are disturbing: "When clinical psychologists vote to consider homosexuality as a normal sexual preference, what steps do they take to reassure those portions of society who are irrevocably opposed to that view?" (p. 1035). His observation serves as an example of an obstacle to judicial influence faced by the social sciences.

JUDGES' VALUES REVISITED

Judges' values differ from those of psychologists. Ewing concludes that judicial reasoning "is driven more by moral intuition and concern for public safety than by empirical fact" (1991, p. 159). What judges see as "common sense" is often more determinative than a raft of empirical results. For example, on the issue of predicting future dangerousness, Justice White, in the 1983 *Barefoot v. Estelle* case, was more willing to place his trust in the jury's ability to detect dangerousness than to rely on cautions from psychological evidence. Chapter 9 documented that research showing the maturity of adolescent decisions about abortion had no impact when it ran counter to judges' values.

WHEN DO JUSTICES CITE THE RESEARCH?—A CYNICAL VIEW

A recurring theme in the reactions of political scientists and psychologists who observe the courts is that judges use social science research findings in a self-serving way. If research conclusions support a decision already made by the judge on other grounds, the written opinion will cite and endorse these findings. If not, they are ignored. This impression extends back to Chief Justice Warren's use of the Clark doll study and the social scientist statement in the 1954 *Brown v. Board of Education* decision.

Kerr has pulled together the observations of a number of social scientists on this theme. "Justices will use social science findings," says Kerr (1986, pp. 64–65) when:

- They reaffirm the judges' position (Wasby, 1981, p. 16)
- "[They] recommend something which the judges already want to do,

because it will then be used by the courts to provide a rationale for a decision which was actually reached on other grounds" (Grofman & Scarrow, 1980, p. 118)

Further examples from Kerr's compilation include:

> • When social science data support or coincide with [the justices'] value system, they are looked upon with favor in the opinion, but when such data . . . do not coincide with their beliefs or systems of values, the preconceived theory held by the majority prevails over the data. (Davis, 1973, p. 113)
> • [When] facts, however stubborn, are confronted by a "stubborn theory," it is the latter that usually wins. . . . "Facts," as Professor Morris K. Cohen has well said, "are more pliable than stubborn theories. Facts can be ignored, explained away, or denied. But theories are mental habits which cannot be changed at will." (Mason. 1931, p. 114)
> • It is plausible to interpret these data to support the proposition that citations at the Court's own initiative are frequently post hoc efforts by justices or clerks to find whatever support might be available to bolster the position taken. (Rosenblum, 1975, p. 72)

More recently, Donald Bersoff dramatically made the same point: "Like an insensitive scoundrel involved with an attractive but fundamentally irksome lover who too much wants to be courted, the judiciary shamelessly uses the social sciences" (1986, pp. 155–156). Can the methodology of the social sciences be applied to evaluate these conjectures? Rosenblum's (1975) survey offers some support:

- Most citations of social science findings were cursory, indicating limited importance for case outcome.
- Rosenblum had coders rate each social science citation for its relevance to the proposition for which it was cited; they also rated the importance of that proposition for the outcome of the case. Only a third of the citations were considered highly relevant to their proposition, and only 16% of those were rated as highly important to the outcome.
- Majority opinions more often accepted social science findings uncritically; minority opinions were more critical of the findings they cited. For example, consider the position of Chief Justice Burger and Justice Rehnquist on cases involving jury size. In *Williams v. Florida* (1970), both justices "uncritically embraced the opinions of several court officials (unsupported by data) that variations in jury size had no effect on juries" (Kerr, 1986, pp. 65–66). But when the *Ballew v. Georgia* case was decided, they rejected better empirical evidence cited by Justice Blackmun, instead joining in Justice Powell's dissent that labeled such evidence "numerology."

CONCLUSIONS

Given the obstacles to having influence, how should organized psychology proceed with the courts? Several prominent and thoughtful psychologists have offered suggestions.

Shari Diamond (1989), in her presidential address to the American Psychology–Law Society, encouraged psychologists to focus on the "trouble cases," cases for which legal doctrine does not provide the court with clear guidance, because courts are more likely to be receptive to social science research in unsettled cases.

Psychology must be careful, however, not to exceed its empirical domain. Psychology's expertise is not in constitutional analysis; it is in analysis of human behavior (Grisso & Saks, 1991). Psychology can best serve the courts by "being a reliable, credible informant regarding human behavior, addressing what is known and not known about it, how this is probative for the legal question, and what psychology's legal theories and data suggest will be the effects of various legal decisions on behavior" (p. 210).

Charles Ewing (1991) reaffirmed the admonition of Grisso and Saks: To influence the courts, research must be both methodologically and conceptually sound. But he emphasized that there are limits to the impact of research conclusions:

> Behavioral scientists need to recognize that many constitutional issues, particularly those dealing with the rights of criminal defendants and convicts, are unlikely ever to be resolved simply on the basis of empirical evidence. The law's treatment of alleged and convicted criminal defendants reflects, first or foremost, deeply held beliefs about human nature, freedom, and public safety. While many of these beliefs can and should be tested empirically, neither their foundation nor their influence with the courts is likely to be readily shaken by even the most solid and clearly relevant empirical research. (1991, p. 158)

Thus, as Shari Diamond noted in her address, psychologists need to choose wisely among the many possible cases that seem relevant.

Why is psychology so often treated cavalierly by the courts? Conflict over the basis fur making decisions is one reason, of course; as Bersoff (1986) observes, the courts, unlike psychology, do not find empirical data so determinative in deciding critical issues. This was made pungently clear in the majority opinion in *Craig v. Boren* (1976): "Proving broad sociological propositions by statistics is a dubious business, and one that inevitably is in tension with the normative philosophy that underlies the Equal Protection Clause" (p. 204).

Such tension will always exist, but psychologists can reduce misunderstandings by educating the courts on the purposes and benefits of social science research. Misunderstanding cannot be corrected overnight, however. One solution is through training—training that begins in law school. Scientific methodology should be a legitimate topic for study in law schools. Not only judges, but trial lawyers too, often do not appreciate the difference in research between results and conclusions, Whereas psychologists and scientists may disagree about conclusions they rarely disagree on the results themselves.

Law students, lawyers, and judges need to appreciate the cumulative nature of scientific knowledge and understand that as knowledge increases, conclusions are modified or qualified. Furthermore, as illustrated in Justice Rehnquist's opinion in *Lockhart v. McCree* (1906), we need to educate judges that no single study is final, but that a variety of studies can approach certainty by reflecting a consistency of results based on the use of multiple methodologies and populations.

Like the rest of us, judges cannot escape the role of personal values when deciding cases, but increasing sophistication about the methods and contributions of psychology can increase psychology's relevance to judicial decision making.

References

Adler, R. (1987, September 14 and 21). Coup at the court. *New Republic*, pp. 37–48.

Ake v. Oklahoma, 105 S.Ct. 1087 (1985).

Allport, F. H. et al. (1953). The effects of segregation and the consequences of desegregation: A social science statement. *Minnesota Law Review, 37*, 427–439.

Ambuel, B., & Rappaport, J. (1992). Developmental trends in adolescents' psychological and legal competence to consent to abortion. *Law and Human Behavior, 16*, 129–154.

American Psychological Association. (1984). *Amicus curiae* brief, Ake v. Oklahoma. Washington, DC: American Psychological Association.

American Psychological Association. (1986). *Amicus curiae* brief, Bowers v. Hardwick. Washington, DC: American Psychological Association.

American Psychological Association. (1986). *Amicus curiae* brief, Ford v. Wainwright. Washington, DC: American Psychological Association.

American Psychological Association. (1993). *Amicus curiae* brief, Harris v. Forklift Systems, Inc. Washington, DC: American Psychological Association.

American Psychological Association. (1986). *Amicus curiae* brief, Lockhart v. McCree. Washington, DC: American Psychological Association.

American Psychological Association. (1990). *Amicus curiae* brief, Ohio v. Akron Center for Reproductive Health et al. Washington, DC: American Psychological Association.

American Psychological Association. (1989). *Amicus curiae* brief, Penry v. Lynaugh. Washington, DC: American Psychological Association.

American Psychological Association. (1987). *Amicus curiae* brief, Price Waterhouse v. Ann B. Hopkins. Washington, DC: American Psychological Association.

Asch, S. E. (1958). Effects of group pressure upon modification and distortion of judgments. In E. E. Maccoby, T. M. Newcomb, & E. L. Hartley (Eds.), *Readings in social psychology* (pp. 174–183). New York: Holt.

Associated Press. (1996, May 18.). Chief justice bashes grandstanding lawyers. *Lawrence Journal-World*, p. 7A.

Associated Press. (1996, August 26). Cuckold's coldcock gets five minutes of probation. *National Law Journal*, p. A23.

Baehr v. Lewin, 852 P.2d 44 (Hawaii Supreme Court 1993).

Bailey v. Drexel Furniture Co., 259 U.S. 20 (1922).

Baldus, D., Woodworth, G., & Pulaski, C. (1990). *Equal justice and the death penalty: A legal and empirical analysis.* Boston: Northeastern University Press.

Baldus, D. C., Woodworth, G., & Pulaski, C. A., Jr. (1992). Law and statistics in conflict: Reflections on *McClesky v. Kemp.* In D. K. Kagehiro & W. S. Laufer (Eds.), *Handbook of psychology and law* (pp. 251–271). New York: Springer-Verlag.

Bales, R. F. (1953). The equilibrium problem in small groups. In T. Parsons, R. F. Bales, & E. A. Shils (Eds.), *Working papers in the theory of action* (pp. 111–161). Glencoe, IL: Free Press.

Bales, R. F. (1958). Task roles and social roles in problem-solving groups. In E. E. Maccoby, T. M. Newcomb, & E. L. Hartley (Eds.), *Readings in social psychology* (3rd ed., pp. 396–413). New York: Holt, Rinehart and Winston.

Ball, H. (1978). *Judicial craftsmanship or fiat: Direct overturn by the United States Supreme Court.* Westport, CT: Greenwood Press.

Ballew v. Georgia, 435 U.S. 223 (1978).

Barbash, F. (1983, December 5). Brennan, Marshall keep vigil against death penalty. *Washington Post*, p. A–10.

Barefoot v. Estelle, 463 U.S. 880 (1983).

Barnum, D. G. (1985). The Supreme Court and public opinion: Judicial decision making in the post-New Deal period. *Journal of Politics, 47*, 652–665.

Barrett, G. V., & Morris, S. B. (1991). The American Psychological Association's *amicus curiae* brief in Price Waterhouse v. Hopkins: The values of science versus the values of the law. *Law and Human Behavior, 17*, 201–215.

Baum, L. (1985). *The Supreme Court* (2nd ed.). Washington, DC: Congressional Quarterly Press.

Baum, L. (1992). *The Supreme Court* (4th ed). Washington, DC: Congressional Quarterly Press.

Baum, L. (1998). *The puzzle of judicial behavior.* Ann Arbor, MI: University of Michigan Press.

Baxter, L. A. (1984). An investigation of compliance-gaining as politeness. *Human Communication Research, 10*, 427–456.

Bellotti v. Baird, 443 U.S. 622 (1979).

Berger, C. R. (1985). Social power and interpersonal communication. In M. L. Knapp & G. R. Miller (Eds.), *Handbook of interpersonal communication* (pp. 439–499). Thousand Oaks, CA: Sage.

Berkman, H. (1994, June 13). No racial bias found in federal death suits. *National Law Journal*, p. A12.

Berkman, H. (1997, July 7). Experts miss mark on line item veto. *National Law Journal*, p. A10.

Berkman, H., & MacLachlan, C. (1996, October 21). Clinton's picks—Not so liberal. *National Law Journal*, pp. A1, A21.

Bermant, G. (1986). Two conjectures about the issue of expert testimony. *Law and Human Behavior, 10*, 97–100.

Bersoff, D. N. (1986). Psychologists and the judicial systems: Broader perspectives. *Law and Human Behavior, 10*, 151–165.

Bersoff, D. N. (1987). Social science data and the Supreme Court: *Lockhart* as a case in point. *American Psychologist, 42*, 52–58.

Bersoff, D. N., & Glass, D. J. (1995). The not-so *Weisman*: The Supreme Court's continuing misuse of social science research. *Roundtable: A Journal of Interdisciplinary Legal Studies, 2*, 279–302.

Bersoff, D. N., & Ogden, D. W. (1991). APA *amicus curiae* briefs: Furthering lesbian and gay male civil rights. *American Psychologist, 46*, 950–956.

Binet, A. (1900). *La suggestibilite.* Paris: Schleider Freres. (Cited by Wells and Loftus, 1984).

Bird, C. (1940). *Social psychology.* New York: Appleton-Century-Crofts.

Biskupic, J. (1995, May 8–14). The two worlds of Ms. Justice Ginsburg. *Washington Post National Weekly Edition,* p. 32.

Biskupic, J. (1996, July 15–21). Erasing the lines of distinction. *Washington Post National Weekly Edition,* p. 32.

Bolick, C. (1996, April 4). Clinton judges hold pro-defendant record. *USA Today,* p. 13A.

Boster, F. J., & Stiff, J. B. (1984). Compliance-gaining message selection behavior. *Human Communication Research, 10,* 539–556.

Bowen v. Kendrick, 108 S.Ct. 2562 (1988).

Bowers v. Hardwick, 106 S. Ct. 2841 (1986).

Bradley, R. C., & Maveety, N. (1992). Reductionist conservatism: The judicial ideology of Sandra Day O'Connor. *Quarterly Journal of Ideology, 15,* 45–62.

Brenner, S. (1980). Fluidity on the United States Supreme Court: A reexamination. *American Journal of Political Science, 24,* 526–535.

Brenner, S. (1982a). Fluidity on the Supreme Court: 1956–1967. *American Journal of Political Science, 26,* 388–390.

Brenner, S. (1982b). Ideological voting on the U.S. Supreme Court: A comparison of the original vote on the merits with the final vote. *Jurimetrics Journal, 22,* 287–292.

Brenner, S. (1989). Ideological voting on the Vinson Court: A comparison of original and final votes on the merits. *Polity, 22,* 157–164.

Brenner, S., Hagle, T., & Spaeth, H. J. (1990). Increasing the size of minimum winning original coalitions on the Warren Court. *Polity, 23,* 309–318.

Brenner, S., Caporale, T., & Winter, H. (1996). Fluidity and coalition sizes on the Supreme Court. *Jurimetrics Journal, 36,* 245–254. (Cited by Baum, 1998).

Brenner, S., & Dorff, R. H. (1992). The attitudinal model and fluidity voting on the United States Supreme Court: A theoretical perspective. *Journal of Theoretical Politics, 4,* 195–205.

Brenner, S., & Spaeth, H. J. (1988). Majority opinion assignments and the maintenance of the original coalition on the Warren Court. *American Journal of Political Science, 32,* 72–81.

Breyer, S. (1997, January 9). Q&A with high-school students. C-SPAN television broadcast.

Brittain, C. V. (1963). Adolescent choice and parent–peer cross pressures. *American Sociological Review, 28,* 385–391.

Brown, B. B., Clasen, D. R., & Eicher, S. A. (1986). Perceptions of peer pressure, peer conformity dispositions, and self-reported behavior among adolescents. *Developmental Psychology, 22,* 521–530.

Brown v. Board of Education of Topeka, Kansas, 347 U.S. 483 (1954).

Bugliosi, V. (1998). *No island of sanity.* New York: Ballantine Publishing Group.

Burka, P. (1996, July). State secrets. *Texas Monthly,* p. 160.

Burtt, H. (1931). *Legal psychology.* Englewood Cliffs, NJ: Prentice Hall.

Caldeira, G. A. (1987). Public opinion and the Supreme Court: FDR's court-packing plan. *American Political Science Review, 81,* 1139–1154.

Caldeira, G. A., & Wright, J. R. (1988). Organized interests and agenda setting in the U. S. Supreme Court. *American Political Science Review, 82,* 1109–1128.

Caldeira, G.A., & Wright, J.R. (1990). Amici curiae participation before the Supreme Court: Who participates, when, and how much? *Journal of Politics, 52,* 782–806.

Caldeira, G. A., & Wright, J. R. (1994, April). *Nine little law firms? Justices, organized interests, and agenda-setting in the Supreme Court.* Paper presented at the meetings of the Midwest Political Science Association, Chicago.

Caplan, L. (1987). *The tenth justice: The solicitor general and the rule of law.* New York: Random House.

Cardozo, B. N. (1921). *The nature of the judicial process.* New Haven, CT: Yale University Press.

Carelli, R. (1997, June 29). Court flexed its muscles. *Kansas City Star,* pp. A16, A17.

Cartwright, D., & Zander, A. (1960). Leadership and group performance: Introduction. In D. Cartwright & A. Zander (Eds.), *Group dynamics* (2nd ed., pp. 487–510). New York: Row–Peterson.

Casper, J. (1972). *Lawyers before the Warren Court.* Urbana, IL: University of Illinois Press.

Castaneda v. Partida, 430 U.S. 482 (1977).

Cattell, J. McK. (Ed.). (1894). *Proceedings of the American Psychological Association.* New York: Macmillan.

Charen, M. (1996, May 28). Justices act like politicians. *Lawrence Journal-World,* p. 7B.

Chemers, M. M. (1997). *An integrative theory of leadership.* Mahwah, NJ: Erlbaum.

Chi, M. T. H., Glaser, R., & Farr, M. J. (Eds.). (1988). *The nature of expertise.* Hillsdale, NJ: Erlbaum.

Chisholm v. Georgia, 2 Dallas 419 (1793).

Christie, R., & Geis, F. L. (1970). *Studies in Machiavellianism.* Orlando, FL: Academic Press.

Clark, H. R. (1995) *Justice Brennan: The great conciliator.* New York: Birch Lane Press

Clark, K. B., & Clark, M. P. (1952). Racial identification and preference in Negro children. In G. E. Swanson, T. M. Newcomb, & E. L. Hartley (Eds.), *Readings in social psychology* (revised edition) (pp. 551–560). New York: Holt.

Clasen, D. R., & Brown, B. B. (1985). The multidimensionality of peer pressure in adolescence. *Journal of Youth and Adolescence, 14,* 451–468.

Clay, R. A. (1997, February). Psychology informs debate on same-gender marriages. *APA Monitor,* p. 40.

Clinton v. City of New York, No. 97–1374 (1998).

Clinton v. Jones, No. 95–1853 (1996).

Colgrove v. Battin, 413 U.S. 149 (1973).

Congressional Research Service. (1982). *The Constitution of the United States of America: Analysis and interpretation.* Washington, DC: U.S. Government Printing Office.

Cook, S. W. (1979). Social science and school desegregation: Did we mislead the Supreme Court? *Personality and Social Psychology Bulletin, 5,* 420–434.

Cook, S. W. (1984a). The 1954 social science statement and school desegregation: A reply to Gerard. *American Psychologist, 39,* 819–832.

Cooper, P. J. (1995). *Battles of the bench: Conflict inside the Supreme Court.* Lawrence, KS: University Press of Kansas.

Coy v. Iowa, 108 S. Ct. 2798 (1988).

Coyle, M. (1994, July 4.) O. J. case highlights death row debate. *National Law Journal,* pp. A6–A7.

Coyle, M. (1996a, June 3). Court: 'animus' in Colo. gay law. *National Law Journal,* p. A11.

Coyle, M. (1996b, July 8). High court goes for 'skeptical' scrutiny on gender. *National Law Journal,* p. A12.

Coyle, M. (1996c, July 15). Court ducks affirmative action case. *National Law Journal,* p. A10.

Coyle, M. (1997, June 9). Line-item veto: Who'll vote how. *National Law Journal,* pp. A1, A22–A23.

Craig v. Boren, 429 U.S. 190 (1976).

Cray, E. (1997). *Chief Justice: A biography of Earl Warren.* New York: Simon & Schuster.

Danelski, D. J. (1979). The influence of the chief justice in the decisional process. In W. F. Murphy & C. H. Pritchett (Eds.), *Courts, judges, and politics* (pp. 497–508). New York: Random House.

Daniels, W. (1983). "Far beyond the law reports": Secondary source citations in the United States Supreme Court opinions, October terms 1900, 1940, and 1978. *Law Library Journal, 76,* 1–47.

Darley, J. M., & Gross, P. H. (1983). A hypothesis–confirming bias in labeling effects. *Journal of Personality and Social Psychology, 44,* 20–33.

Daubert v. Merrell Dow Pharmaceuticals, 113 S.Ct. 2786 (1993).

Davis, A. L. (1973). *The United States Supreme Court and the uses of social science data.* New York: MSS Information Corp.

Davis, J. H. (1989). Psychology and the law: The last 15 years. *Journal of Applied Social Psychology, 19,* 199–230.

Davis, R. (1994). *Decisions and images: The Supreme Court and the press.* Englewood Cliffs, NJ: Prentice Hall.

Davis, S. (1989). *Justice Rehnquist and the Constitution.* Princeton, NJ: Princeton University Press.

Davis, S. (1990). Power on the Court: Chief Justice Rehnquist's opinion assignments. *Judicature, 74,* 66–72.

DeAngellis, T. (1993, August). APA files *amicus* brief in sex harassment case. *APA Monitor,* pp. 19–20.

Dennis v. United States, 341 U.S. 494 (1951).

Deutsch, M., & Gerard, H. B. (1955). A study of normative and informational social influence upon individual judgment. *Journal of Abnormal and Social Psychology, 51,* 629–636.

Diamond, S. S. (1989). Using psychology to control law: From deceptive advertising to criminal sentencing. *Law and Human Behavior, 13,* 239–252.

Dillard, J. P., & Burgoon, M. (1985). Situational influences on the selection of compliance-gaining messages: Two tests of the predictive utility of the Cody-McLaughlin typology. *Communication Monographs, 52,* 289–304.

Dorff, R. H., & Brenner, S. (1992). Conformity voting on the United States Supreme Court. *Journal of Politics, 54,* 762–775.

Douglas, W. O. (1980). *The Court years 1939–1975: The autobiography of William O. Douglas.* New York: Random House.

Dred Scott v. Sandford, 60 U.S. (19 How.) 393 (1857).

Dunlap, D. W. (1996a, March 6). Fearing a toehold for gay marriages, conservatives rush to bar the door. *New York Times,* p. A7.

Dunlap, D. W. (1996b, September 20.) Gay partners of I.B.M. workers to get benefits. *New York Times,* p. A10.

Eagly, A. H., & Chaiken, S. (1998). Attitude structure and function. In D. T. Gilbert, S. T. Fiske, & G. Lindzey (Eds.), *Handbook of social psychology* (4th Ed., Vol. 1, pp. 269–322). New York: Oxford University Press.

Ebbinghaus, H. E. (1885). *Memory: A contribution to experimental psychology.* New York: Dover.

Eisenstein, J., & Jacob, H. (1977). *Felony justice: An organizational analysis of criminal courts.* Boston: Little, Brown.

Eisler, K. I. (1993). *A justice for all: William J. Brennan, Jr. and the decisions that transformed America.* New York: Simon & Schuster.

Elliott, R. (1991). Social science data and the APA: The *Lockhart* brief as a case in point *Law and Human Behavior, 15,* 59–76.

Elliott, R. (1993). Expert testimony about eyewitness identification: A critique. *Law and Human Behavior, 17,* 423–438.

Ellison v. Brady, 924 F.2d 871 (9th Cir. 1991).

Ellsworth, P. C. (1991). To tell what we know or wait for Godot? *Law and Human Behavior, 15,* 77–90.

Epstein, L. (1991). Courts and interest groups. In J. B. Gates & C. A. Johnson (Eds.), *The American courts: A critical assessment* (pp. 335–371). Washington, DC: Congressional Quarterly Press.

Epstein, L., & Knight, J. (1998). *The choices judges make.* Washington, DC: Congressional Quarterly Press.

Epstein, L., & Rowland, C. K. (1991). Debunking the myth of interest group invincibility in the courts. *American Political Science Review, 85,* 205–217.

Eshleman, A. (1997). *Desegregation and deception: An analysis of "well-meaning rhetoric."* Unpublished manuscript, Department of Psychology, University of Kansas, Lawrence, KS.

Eskridge, W. (1996a, June 17). Credit is due. *New Republic,* p. 11.

Eskridge, W. N., Jr. (1996b). *The case for same sex marriage.* New York: Free Press.

Estrich, S. (1995, December 14). Justice Stevens, a hero to me. *USA Today,* p. A11.

Evans, R. I. (1980). *The making of social psychology: Discussions with creative contributors.* New York: Gardner Press.

Ex parte Quirin, 317 U.S. 1 (1942).

Ewing, C. P. (1991). Preventive detention and execution: The constitutionality of punishing future crimes. *Law and Human Behavior, 15,* 139–163.

Falbo, T. (1977). Multidimensional scaling of power strategies. *Journal of Personality and Social Psychology, 35,* 537–547.

Felitti, E. M. (1995). The Honorable Jacqueline Taber: An oral history. *Western Legal History, 8,* 91–113.

Fiedler, F. E. (1964). A contingency model of leadership effectiveness. In L. Berkowitz (Ed.), *Advances in experimental social psychology* (Vol. 1, pp. 149–190). New York: Academic Press.

Fiedler, F. E. (1967). *A theory of leadership effectiveness.* New York: McGraw-Hill.

Fiedler, F. E. (1969). Style or circumstance: The leadership enigma. *Psychology Today, 2*(10), 38–43.

Fiedler, F. E. (1971). Validation and extension of the contingency model of leadership effectiveness: A review of empirical findings. *Psychological Bulletin, 76,* 128–148.

Fiedler, F. E., & Garcia, J. E. (1987). *New approaches to effective leadership: Cognitive Resourses and organizational performance.* New York: John Wiley.

Finkel, N. J. (1995). Prestidigitation, statistical magic, and Supreme Court numerology in juvenile death penalty cases. *Psychology, Public Policy, and Law, 1,* 612–642.

Fiske, S. T., & Taylor, S. E. (1991). *Social cognition.* New York: McGraw-Hill.

Fiske, S. T., Bersoff, D. N., Borgida, E., Deaux, K., & Heilman, M. E. (1991). Social science research on trial: Use of sex stereotyping research in *Price Waterhouse v. Hopkins. American Psychologist, 46,* 1049–1060.

Fiske, S. T., Bersoff, D. N., Borgida, E., Deaux, K., & Heilman, M. E. (1993). What constitutes a scientific review: A majority retort to Barrett and Morris. *Law and Human Behavior, 17,* 217–233.

Fiss, O., & Krauthammer, C. (1982). The Rehnquist court. *New Republic,* pp. 14–21.

Fitzpatrick, M. A., & Winke, J. (1979). You always hurt the one you love: Strategies and tactics in interpersonal conflict. *Communication Quarterly, 27,* 1–11.

Fleishman, E. A., Harris, E. F., & Burtt, H. E. (1955). *Leadership and supervision in industry.* Columbus, OH: Ohio State University Press.

Florida v. Royer, 460 U.S. 491 (1983).

Foley, L. A. (1993). *A psychological view of the legal system.* Madison, WI: Brown and Benchmark.

Foote, W. E. (1998, August). *APA and the amicus process: COLI's perspective.* Symposium paper presented at the meetings of the American Psychological Association, San Francisco.

Ford v. Wainwright, 474 U.S. 699 (1986).

Fortas, A. (1975). Chief Justice Warren: The enigma of leadership. *Yale Law Journal, 84,* 405–412.

Frank, J. (1930). *Law and the modern mind.* New York: Coward McCann.

Frank, J. (1949). *Courts on trial: Myth and reality in American justice.* Princeton, NJ: Princeton University Press.

Freund, P. (1967). Charles Evans Hughes as Chief Justice. *Harvard Law Review, 81,* 4–43.

Furman v. Georgia, 408 U.S. 238 (1972).

George, T. E., & Epstein, L. (1992). On the nature of Supreme Court decision making. *American Political Science Review, 86.* 323–337

Gerard, H. (1983). School desegregation: The social science role. *American Psychologist, 38,* 869–877.

Gibb, C. A. (1969). Leadership. In G. Lindzey & E. Aronson (Eds.), *Handbook of social psychology* (Vol. IV, 2nd ed., pp. 205–282). Reading, MA: Addison–Wesley.

Gibbons v. Ogden, 22 U.S. 1 (1824).

Gibson, J. L. (1983). From simplicity to complexity: The development of theory in the study of judicial behavior. *Political Behavior, 5,* 7–49.

Gideon v. Wainwright, 372 U.S. 335 (1963).

Glaser, R., & Chi, M. T. H. (1988). Overview. In M. T. H. Chi, R. Glaser, & M. J. Farr (Eds.), *The nature of expertise* (pp. xv–xxvii). Hillsdale, NJ: Erlbaum.

Goodman, G. S., Levine, M., Melton, G. B., & Ogden, D. W. (1991). Child witnesses and the confrontation clause: American Psychological Association brief in Maryland v. Craig. *Law and Human Behavior, 15,* 13–29.

Goodman, G. S., Levine, M., & Melton, G. B. (1992). The best evidence produces the best law. *Law and Human Behavior, 16,* 244–251.

Goodman, J. (1993). Evaluating psychological expertise on questions of social fact: The case of Price Waterhouse v. Hopkins. *Law and Human Behavior, 17,* 249–255.

Goodman, J., & Croyle, R. T. (1989). Social framework testimony in employment discrimination cases. *Behavioral Sciences & the Law, 7,* 227–241.

Greenberg, P., & Gasman, G. B. (1996, June 3). Federal, state bills challenge same–sex marriages. *National Law Journal,* p. B8.

Greenhouse, L. (1993, March 3). High court to decide burden of accusers in harassment cases. *New York Times,* pp. A1, A11.

Greenhouse, L. (1996a, May 21). Gay rights laws can't be banned, high court rules. *New York Times,* pp. A1, C19.

Greenhouse, L. (1996b, June 27). Military college can't bar women, high court rules. *New York Times,* pp. A1, C18.

Greenwald, A. G. (1980). A totalitarian ego: Fabrication and revision of personal history. *American Psychologist, 35,* 603–618.

Gregg v. Georgia, 428 U.S. 153 (1976).

Gregory v. Ashcroft, 115 L Ed 2d 410 (1991).

Griggs v. Mabry, 758 F. 2d 226 (1985).

Grisso, T., & Saks, M. J. (1991). Psychology's influence on constitutional interpretation: A comment on how to succeed. *Law and Human Behavior, 15,* 205–211.

Grofman, B., & Scarrow, H. (1980). Mathematics, social science, and the law. In M. J. Saks & C. H. Baron (Eds.), *The use/nonuse/misuse of applied social research in the courts* (pp. 117–127). Cambridge, MA: Abt Books.

Gruenfeld, D. H. (1995). Status, ideology, and integrative complexity in the U.S. Supreme Court: Rethinking the politics of political decision making. *Journal of Personality and Social Psychology, 68,* 5–20.

Gunther, J. (1947). *Inside U.S.A.* New York: Harper.

H. L. v. Matheson, 450 U.S. 398 (1981).

Hafemeister, T. L., & Melton, G. B. (1987). The impact of social science research on the judiciary. In G. B. Melton (Ed.), *Reforming the law: Impact of child development research* (pp. 27–59). New York: Guilford Press.

Hale, M., Jr. (1980). *Human science and social order: Hugo Munsterberg and the origins of applied psychology.* Philadelphia: Temple University Press.

Halpin, A. W. (1966). *Theory and research in administration.* New York: Macmillan.

Halpin, A. W., & Winer, B. J. (1952). *The leadership behavior of the airplane commander.* Columbus, OH: Ohio State University Research Foundation.

Hammer v. Dagenhart, 247 U.S. 251 (1918).

Harlan, J. M., III. (1955). What part does the oral argument play in the conduct of an appeal? *Cornell Law Quarterly, 41,* 6–11.

Harris, A. (1986, August 21). The unintended battle of Michael Hardwick. *Washington Post,* pp. C1, C4.

Harris v. Forklift Systems, Inc., 114 S.Ct. 367 (1993).

Hatch, O. G. (1982). Psychology, society, and politics. *American Psychologist, 37,* 1031–1037.

Hodgson et al. v. Minnesota, 110 S. Ct. 2926 (1990).

Hoeflich, M. (1996, March 27). Judges, clerks have special tie. *Lawrence Journal-World,* p. 7B.

Holbrook, S. H. (1987). *Dreamers of the American dream.* Garden City, NY: Doubleday.

Holt, E. B. (1915). *The Freudian wish and its place in ethics.* New York: Henry Holt.

Hopkins v. Price Waterhouse, 618 F.Supp. 1109 (1985).

Hopwood v. State of Texas, 78 F.3d 932 (5th Cir.1996).

Hovenkamp, H. (1985). Social science and segregation before *Brown. Duke Law Journal, 1985,* 624–672.

Howard, A. E. D. (1997, June 30). Shaking up the high court. *Washington Post National Weekly Edition,* p.33.

Howard, J. W., Jr. (1968). On the fluidity of judicial choice. *American Political Science Review, 62,* 43–56.

Hull, A. (1997). *Strategic interaction and schema: An integration and study of judicial decision-making models.* Unpublished manuscript, Department of Political Science, University of Kansas, Lawrence, KS.

Hutchins, R. M., & Slesinger, D. (1928a). Some observations on the law of evidence—spontaneous exclamations. *Columbia Law Review, 28,* 432–440.

Hutchins, R. M., & Slesinger, D. (1928b). Some observations on the law of evidence—memory. *Harvard Law Review, 41,* 860–873.

INS v. Chadha, 462 U.S. 919 (1983).

Jeffries, J. C., Jr. (1994). *Justice Lewis F. Powell, Jr.* New York: Charles Scribner's Sons.

Jenkins v. United States, 307 F.2d 637 (1962).

Jerome, R. (1996, August 26). No reprieve. *People,* pp. 42–49.

Johnson v. Transportation Agency, Santa Clara County, California, 480 U.S. 616 (1987).

Johnson. J. W. (1997). *The struggle for student rights.* Lawrence, KS: University Press of Kansas.

Jones v. Hallahan, 501 S.W.2d 588 (Kentucky Court of Appeals, 1973).

Kadish, M. R., & Kadish, S. H. (1971). The institutionalization of conflict: jury acquittals. *Journal of Social Issues, 27*(2), 199–218.

Kalven, H., & Zeisel, H. (1966). *The American jury.* Boston: Little, Brown.

Kargon, R. (1986). Expert testimony in historical perspective. *Law and Human Behavior, 10,* 15–27.

Kassin, S. M., Ellsworth, P. C., & Smith, V. L. (1989). The "general acceptance" of psychological research on eyewitness testimony: A survey of the experts. *American Psychologist, 44,* 1089–1098.

Kassin, S.M., & Wrightsman, L.S. (1983). The construction and validation of a juror bias scale. *Journal of Research in Personality, 17,* 423–441.

Katz, D. (1960). The functional approach to the study of attitudes. *Public Opinion Quarterly, 24,* 163–204.

Katz, D. (1968). Consistency for what? The functional approach. In R. P. Abelson et al. (Eds.), *Theories of cognitive consistency: A source book* (pp. 179–191). Chicago: Rand-McNally.

Katz, D., & Stotland, E. (1959). A preliminary statement to a theory of attitude structure and change. In S. Koch (Ed.), *Psychology: A study of a science* (Vol. 3, pp. 423–475). New York: McGraw-Hill.

Keiter, R. B. (1982). Privacy, children, and their parents: Reflections on and beyond the Supreme Court's approach. *Minnesota Law Review, 66,* 459–518.

Kelman, H. C. (1958). Compliance, identification, and internalization: Three processes of opinion change. *Journal of Conflict Resolution, 2,* 51–60.

Kennedy, D. M. (1995, July). How FDR derailed the New Deal. *Atlantic Monthly,* pp. 87–92.

Kerr, N. L. (1986). Social science and the U.S. Supreme Court. In M. F. Kaplan (Ed.), *The impact of social psychology on procedural justice* (pp. 56–79). Springfield, IL: Charles C Thomas.

Kiesler, C. A., Collins, B. E., & Miller, N. (1969). *Attitude change: A critical analysis of theoretical approaches.* New York: Wiley.

Kimmel, P. R. (1994, July). SPSSI and *Brown v. Board of Education. SPSSI Newsletter,* pp. 5, 16.

Klineberg, O. (1986). SPSSI and race relations, in the 1950s and thereafter. *Journal of Social Issues, 42,* 53–59.

Kluger, R. (1975). *Simple justice: The history of Brown v. Board of Education and Black America's struggle for equality.* New York: Alfred A. Knopf.

Kobylka, J. (1987). A court–created context for group litigation: Libertarian groups and obscenity. *Journal of Politics, 49,* 1061–1078.

Kolasa, B. J. (1972). Psychology and law. *American Psychologist, 27,* 499–503.

Konecni, V. J., & Ebbesen, E. B. (1986). Courtroom testimony by psychologists on eyewitness identification issues: Critical notes and reflections. *Law and Human Behavior, 10,* 117–126.

Krislov, S. (1963). The *amicus curiae* brief: From friendship to advocacy. *Yale Law Journal, 72,* 694–721.

Kruglanski, A. W. (1980). Lay epistemology process and contents. *Psychological Review, 87,* 70–87.

Kull, A. (1996, January 22). The stealth revolution. *New Republic,* pp. 38–41.

Kunda, Z. (1990). The case for motivated reasoning. *Psychological Bulletin, 108,* 480–498.

Lash, J. P. (Ed.). *From the diaries of Felix Frankfurter.* New York: W. W. Norton.

Lazarus, E. (1998). *Closed chambers.* New York: Random House.

Lee v. Weisman, 112 S. Ct. 2649 (1992).

Leo, J. (1993, November 29). An empty ruling on harrassment. *U.S. News and World Report,* p. 20.

Leuchtenburg, W. E. (1995). *The Supreme Court reborn: The constitutional revolution in the age of Roosevelt.* New York: Oxford University Press.

Lewin, K. (1951). *Field theory in social science.* New York: Harper.

Lewis v. United States, 116 S.Ct. 2163 (1996).

Lewis, A. (1980). A comparison of minors' and adults' pregnancy decisions. *American Journal of Orthopsychiatry, 50,* 446–453.

Lewis, A. (1981). A public right to know about public institutions. In P. B. Kurland & G. Casper (Eds.), *The Supreme Court review 1980* (pp. 1–25). Chicago: University of Chicago Press.

Liles v. Oregon, 425 U.S. 863 (1976).

Llewellyn, K. N. (1925). The effect of legal institutions upon economics. *American Economic Review, 15,* 665–683.

Lockhart v. McCree, 106 S. Ct. 1758 (1986).

Lofgren, C. (1987). *The Plessy case: A legal–historical interpretation.* New York: Oxford University Press.

Loftus, E. F. (1979). *Eyewitness testimony.* Cambridge, MA: Harvard University Press.

Loftus, E. F., Schooler, J. W., Boone, S. M., & Kline, D. (1986). *Time went by so slowly: Overestimation of event duration by males and females.* Unpublished manuscript, University of Washington, Seattle.

Loftus, E. F. (1975). Leading questions and the eyewitness report. *Cognitive Psychology, 7,* 560–572.

Loftus, E. F. (1986). Experimental psychologist as advocate or impartial educator. *Law and Human Behavior, 10,* 63–78.

Loh, W. D. (1981). Perspectives on psychology and law. *Journal of Applied Social Psychology, 11,* 314–355.

Louisell, D. W. (1955). The psychologist in today's legal world. *Minnesota Law Review, 39,* 235–272.

Loving v. Virginia, 388 U.S. 1 (1967).

Lubet, S. (1995, August 21). Recusal can deny cert. *National Law Review,* pp. A19–A20.

Lukas, J. A. (1997). *Big trouble: A murder in a small Western town sets off a struggle for the soul of America.* New York: Simon & Schuster.

Maltzman, F., & Wahlbeck, P. J. (1996a). May it please the Chief? Opinion assignments in the Rehnquist Court. *American Journal of Political Science, 40,* 421–443

Maltzman, F., & Wahlbeck, P. J. (1996b). Strategic policy considerations and voting fluidity on the Burger Court. *American Political Science Review, 90,* 581–592.

Mann, J. (1983, September). Year-end salute. *American Lawyer,* p. 94.

Mapp v. Ohio. 367 U.S. 643 (1961).

Marshall, S. (1994, March 16). 10 blacks on federal death row. *USA Today,* p. 3A.

Marshall, T. (1989). *Public opinion and the Supreme Court.* New York: Longman.

Marwell, G., & Schmitt, D. R. (1967). Dimensions of compliance–gaining behavior: An empirical analysis. *Sociometry, 30,* 350–364.

Maryland v. Craig, 110 S.Ct. 3157 (1990).

Mason, A. T. (1931). *Brandeis: Lawyer and judge in the modern state.* Princeton, NJ: Princeton University Press.

Mason, A. T. (1965). *William Howard Taft: Chief Justice.* New York: Simon & Schuster.

Mauro, T. (1996, August 27). Thomas' role in case questioned. *USA Today,* p. 3A.

Mauro, T. (1997, June 2). Justices' private holdings can affect their public duty. *USA Today,* pp. 1A–2A.

Mauro, T. (1998, March 13–15). Justices give pivotal role to novice lawyers. *USA Today,* pp. 1A–2A.

Maveety, N. (1996). *Sandra Day O'Connor: Strategist on the Supreme Court.* Lanham, MD: Rowman and Littlefield.

McCandless, S. R., & Sullivan, L. P. (1991, May 6). Two courts adopt new standard to determine sexual harassment. *National Law Journal,* pp. 18–20.

McCleskey v. Kemp, 481 U.S. 279 (1987).

McCloskey, M. E., & Egeth, H. E. (1983). Eyewitness identification: What can a psychologist tell a jury? *American Psychologist, 38,* 550–563.

McCloskey, M., Egeth, H., & McKenna, J. (1986). The experimental psychologist in court: The ethics of expert testimony. *Law and Human Behavior, 10,* 1–14.

McGuire, K. T. (1996, November). *Explaining executive success in the U.S. Supreme Court.* Paper presented at the conference on the Scientific Study of Judicial Politics, St. Louis.

McHugh, J. L., Jr. (1988, August). *APA and the amicus process: The General Counsel's role.* Symposium paper presented at the meetings of the American Psychological Association, San Francisco.

McIntosh, W. V. (1991). Courts and socioeconomic change. In J. B. Gates & C. A. Johnson (Eds.), *The American courts: A critical assessment* (pp. 281–301). Washington, DC: Congressional Quarterly Press.

McLauchlan, W. P. (1972). Research note: Ideology and conflict in Supreme Court opinion assignment. *Western Political Quarterly, 25.* 16–27.

Melton, G. B. (1989). Public policy and private prejudice: Psychology and law on gay rights. *American Psychologist, 44,* 933–940.

Menez, J. F. (1984). *Decision making in the Supreme Court of the United States: A political and behavioral view.* Lanham, MD: University Press of America.

Mennel, R. M., & Compston, C. L. (Eds.), (1996). *Holmes and Frankfurter: Their correspondence, 1912–1934.* Hanover, NH.: University of New Hampshire/University Press of New England.

Meritor Savings Bank v. Vinson, 106 S.Ct. 2399 (1986).

Miller, G. R., & Parks, M. R. (1982). *Communication in dissolving relationships.* In S. Duck (Ed.), *Personal relationships 4: Dissolving relationships* (pp. 127–154). Orlando, FL: Academic Press.

Minersville School District v. Gobitis, 310 U.S. 586 (1940).

Mirsky, C. L. (1996, February 26). The exclusionary rule was appropriately used. *National Law Journal,* pp. A21, A23.

Mitchell, A. (1996, April 3). President defends his criticism of ruling by a New York judge. *New York Times,* p. C18.

Monahan, J., & Walker, L. (1988). Social science in law: A new paradigm. *American Psychologist, 43,* 465–472.

Monahan, J., & Walker, L. (1991). Judicial use of social science research. *Law and Human Behavior, 15,* 571–584.

Muller v. Oregon, 208 U.S. 412 (1908).

Munn v. Illinois, 94 U.S. 113 (1877).

Munsterberg, H. (1908). *On the witness stand.* Garden City, NY: Doubleday.

Murphy, W. F. (1964). *Elements of judicial strategy.* Chicago: University of Chicago Press.

National Labor Relations Board v. Jones and Laughlin Steel Corp., 301 U.S. 1 (1937).

Newland, C. A. (1961). Innovation in judicial techniques: The Brandeis opinion. *Southwestern Social Science Quarterly, 42,* 24–31.

Northouse. P. G. (1997). *Leadership: Theory and practice.* Thousand Oaks, CA: Sage.

Novak, L. (1980). The precedential value of Supreme Court plurality decisions. *Columbia Law Review, 80,* 756–781.

Ohio v. Akron Center for Reproductive Health et al., 110 S. Ct. 2972 (1990).

Oregon v. Mitchell, 400 U.S. 112 (1970).

Oregon v. Miller, 300 Or. 203, 709 P.2d 225 (1985).

O'Brien, D. M. (1993). *Storm center: The Supreme Court in American politics* (3rd ed.). New York: W.W. Norton.

O'Brien, D. M. (Ed.). (1997). *Judges on judging: Views from the bench.* Chatham, NJ: Chatham House Publishers.

O'Connor, K. (1983). The *amicus curiae* role of the U. S. Solicitor General in Supreme Court litigation. *Judicature, 66,* 256–264.

O'Connor, K., & Epstein, L. (1983). Court rules and workload: A case study of rules governing *amicus curiae* participation. *Justice System Journal, 8,* 35–45.

Page, B. I., & Shapiro, R. Y. (1983). Effects of public opinion on policy. *American Political Science Review, 77,* 175–190.

Parham v. J. R.., 442 U.S. 584 (1979).

Patterson v. McLean Credit Union, 491 U.S. 164 (1989).

Payne v. Tennessee, 115 L Ed 2d 720 (1991).

Pear, R. (1997, June 27). Court allows Clinton the line-item veto. *New York Times,* p. A17.

Perkins, D. D. (1988). The use of social science in public interest litigation: A role for community psychologists. *American Journal of Community Psychology, 46,* 465–485.

Perloff, R. M. (1993). *The dynamics of persuasion.* Hillsdale, NJ: Lawrence Erlbaum Associates.

Perry, H. W., Jr. (1991). *Deciding to decide: Agenda setting in the United States Supreme Court.* Cambridge, MA: Harvard University Press.

Peters, L. H., Hartke, D. D., & Pohlmann, J. T. (1985). Fiedler's contingency theory of leadership: An application of the meta-analysis procedures of Schmidt and Hunter. *Psychological Bulletin, 47,* 274–285.

Peterson, S. A., Schubert, J. N., Schubert, G., & Wasby, S. (1991). Patterns in Supreme Court oral argument. Paper presented at the meetings of the Law and Society Association, Amsterdam, The Netherlands.

Pitts, L., Jr. (1996, February 8). Judicial homophobia led to bizarre custody decision favoring killer dad. *Kansas City Star*, p. C–13.

Planned Parenthood v. Danforth, 428 U.S. 52 (1976).

Planned Parenthood v. Casey, 112 S. Ct. 2791 (1992).

Plessy v. Ferguson, 163 U.S. 537 (1896).

Plevan, B. P. (1993, December 6). Harris won't end harassment questions. *National Law Journal*, pp. 19–20.

Pollock v. Farmers' Loan and Trust Co., 157 U.S. 429 (1895).

Posner, R. A. (1996, December 15). Poetic justice. *New York Times Book Review*, pp. 16–17.

Pound, R. (1912). The scope and purpose of sociological jurisprudence, Part 3. *Harvard Law Review, 25*, 489–562.

Price Waterhouse v. Hopkins, 109 S. Ct. 1775, 490 U.S. 228 (1989).

Price Waterhouse v. Hopkins, 825 F.2d 458 (D.C. Cir. 1987).

Pritchett, C. H. (1948). *The Roosevelt Court: A study in judicial politics and values, 1937–1947.* New York: Macmillan.

Provine, D. M. (1980). *Case selection in the United States Supreme Court.* Chicago: University of Chicago Press.

Puro, S. (1981). The United States as *amicus curiae*. In S. S. Ulmer (Ed.), *Courts, law and judicial processes* (pp. 220–229). New York Free Press.

Pusey, M. J. (1951). *Charles Evans Hughes.* New York: Macmillan

Pyszczynski, T., & Greenberg, J. (1987). Toward an integration of cognitive and motivational perspectives on social influence: A biased hypothesis-testing model. In L. Berkowitz (Ed.), *Advances in experimental social psychology* (Vol. 20, pp. 297–340). Orlando, FL: Academic Press.

Raines v. Byrd, No. 96–1671 (1997).

Rathjen, G. J. (1974). Policy goals, strategic choice, and majority opinion assignments in the U.S. Supreme Court: A replication. *Midwest Journal of Political Science, 18*, 713–724.

Regents of University of California v. Bakke, 438 U.S. 265 (1978).

Rehnquist, W. H. (1987). *The Supreme Court: How it was, how it is.* New York: William Morrow.

Reynolds v. Sims, 377 U. S. 533 (1964).

Rich, F. (1996a, March 12). Beyond the birdcage. *New York Times*, p. A15.

Rich, F. (1996b, May 21). A gay-rights victory muffled. *New York Times*, p. A11.

Richmond Newspapers, Inc. v. Virginia, 448 U.S. 555 (1980).

Ring, K. (1979). *Let's get started: An appeal to what's left in psychology.* Unpublished manuscript, University of Connecticut.

Rizzo v. Goode, 420 U.S. 663 (1976).

Robinson v. Jacksonville Shipyards, 59 LW 2470 (February 12, 1991).

Robinson, E. (1935). *Law and the lawyers.* New York: Macmillan.

Roe v. Wade, 410 U.S. 113 (1973).

Roesch, R., Golding, S. L., Hans, V. P., & Reppucci, N. D. (1991). Social science and the courts: The role of *amicus curiae* briefs. *Law and Human Behavior, 15*, 1–11.

Rohde, D. W. (1972). Policy goals, strategic choice, and majority opinion assignments in the U.S. Supreme Court. *American Journal of Political Science, 16*, 652–682.

Rohde, D. W., & Spaeth, H. J. (1976). *Supreme Court decision making.* San Francisco: W. H. Freeman.

Rohde, D. W., & Spaeth, H. J. (1989). Ideology, strategy, and Supreme Court decisions: William Rehnquist as Chief Justice. *Judicature, 72(4)*, 247–250.

Romer v. Evans, 64 U.S.L.W. 4353 (1996).

Rosen, J. (1993a, November 1). Reasonable women. *New Republic*, pp. 12–13.

Rosen, J. (1993b, November 16). Fast-food justice. *New York Times*, p. A15.

Rosen, J. (1996, June 24). What right to die? *New Republic*, pp. 28–31

Rosen, P. L. (1972). *The Supreme Court and social science*. Urbana, IL: University of Illinois Press.

Rosenblum, V. G. (1975). Report on the uses of social sciences in judicial decision making. Final report on NSF Grant #74–17572 to the Panel on Law and Social Sciences, National Science Foundation. (Cited in Kerr, 1986).

Rowland, C. K., & Carp, R. A. (1996). *Politics and judgment in federal district courts*. Lawrence, KS: University Press of Kansas.

Rowley, J. (1997, May 20). Vacancies on federal bench hit century mark. *USA Today*, p. 4A.

Rubin, J. H. (1989, March 12). How much does public opinion sway the court? *Lawrence Journal-World*, p. 7A.

Russell, G. D. (1994). *The death penalty and racial bias: Overturning Supreme Court assumptions*. Westport, CT: Greenwood Press.

Saks, M. J. (1977). *Jury verdicts*. Lexington, MA; D.C. Heath.

Saks, M. (1993). Improving APA science translation *amicus* briefs. *Law and Human Behavior, 17*, 235–247.

Saks, M., & Marti, M. W. (1997). A meta–analysis of the effects of jury size. *Law and Human Behavior, 21*, 451–467.

Salokar, R. M. (1992). *The Solicitor General: The politics of law*. Philadelphia: Temple University Press.

San Antonio v. Rodriquez, 411 U.S. 1 (1973).

Scalia, A. (1994). The dissenting opinion. *Journal of Supreme Court History, 1994*, 33–44.

Schechter Poultry Corporation v. United States, 295 U.S. 495 (1935).

Schenck-Hamlin, W. J., Wiseman, R. L., & Georgacarakos, G. N. (1982). A model of properties of compliance-gaining strategies. *Communication Quarterly, 30*, 92–100.

Schubert, G. (1965a). *Judicial policy-making*. Glenview, IL: Scott, Foresman.

Schubert, G. (1965b). *The judicial mind: Attitudes and ideologies of Supreme Court justices, 1946–1963*. Evanston, IL: Northwestern University Press.

Schubert, G. (1974). *The judicial mind revisited: Psychometric analysis of Supreme Court ideology*. New York: Oxford University Press.

Schwattz, B. (1983). *Super Chief: Earl Warren and his Supreme Court: A judicial biography*. New York: New York University Press.

Schwartz, B. (1988). *Behind Bakke: Affirmative action and the Supreme Court*. New York: New York University Press.

Schwartz, B. (1996). *Decision: How the Supreme Court decides cases*. New York: Oxford University Press.

Schwartz, H. (1988). *Packing the courts: The conservative campaign to rewrite the Constitution*. New York: Charles Scribner's Sons

Scigliano, R. (1971). *The Supreme Court and the Presidency*. New York: Free Press.

Scott v. Sandford, 19 Howard 393 (1857).

Segal, J. A., & Reedy, C. D. (1988). The Supreme Court and sex discrimination: The role of the Solicitor General. *Western Political Quarterly, 41*, 553–568.

Segal, J. A., & Spaeth, H. J. (1993). *The Supreme Court and the attitudinal model*. New York: Cambridge University Press.

Selective Draft Law Cases, 245 U.S. 366 (1918).

Shapiro v. Thompson, 394 U.S. 618 (1969).

Shaw, M.E. (1963). *Scaling group tasks: A method for dimensional analysis*. Unpublished manuscript, University of Florida.

Silberman, L. (1996, April 11). Hawaii decision on gay marriages should affect only Hawaii. *New York Times*, p. A14.

Silvia, P. (1997). *Straw polls and fluidity on the Supreme Court*. Unpublished paper, Department of Psychology, University of Kansas.

Simon, J. F. (1995). *The center holds: The power struggle inside the Rehnquist Court*. New York: Simon & Schuster.

Smith, J. E. (1996). *John Marshall: Definer of a nation*. New York: Henry Holt.

Smith, M. B., Bruner, J., & White, R. W. (1956). *Opinions and personality*. New York: Wiley.

Smolla, R. A. (1995). Introduction: Personality and process. In R. A. Smolla (Ed.), *A year in the life of the Supreme Court* (pp.1–29). Durham, NC: Duke University Press.

Smolowe, J. (1994, August 1). Race and the O. J. Case. *Time*, pp. 24–26.

Snow, T. (1994, April 25). Lower penalty for murdering blacks? *USA Today*, p. 11A.

Songer, D. R., & Sheehan, R. S. (1993). Interest group success in the courts: *Amicus* participation in the Supreme Court. *Political Research Quarterly, 46*, 339–354.

Spencer, J. R., & Flin, R. (1990). *The evidence of children*. London: Blackstone.

Sporer, S. L. (1981). *Toward a comprehensive history of legal psychology*. Unpublished manuscript, University of Erlagen–Nurnberg. (Cited by Wells and Loftus, 1984).

Stanford v. Kentucky, 492 U.S. 361 (1989).

Steamer, R. J. (1986). *Chief Justice: Leadership and the Supreme Court*. Columbia, SC: University of South Carolina Press.

Stephens v. Hopper, 58 L.Ed 2d 667 (1979).

Stern, L. W. (1903). *Beitrage Zur Psychologie der Aussage*. (Contributions to the Psychology of Testimony). Leipzig: Verlag Barth.

Stern, R. L., & Gressman, E. (1962). *Supreme Court practice* (3rd ed.). Washington, DC: Bureau of National Affairs.

Stern, R. L., & Gressman, E. (1978). *Supreme Court practice* (5th ed.). Washington, DC: Bureau of National Affairs.

Stogdill, R. M. (1950). Leadership, membership, and organization. *Psychological Bulletin, 47*, 1–14.

Strube, M., & Garcia, J. (1981). A meta-analysis investigation of Fiedler's contingency model of leadership effectiveness. *Psychological Bulletin, 90*, 307–321.

Strum, P. (1984). *Louis D. Brandeis: Justice for the people*. New York: Schocken Books.

Tanenhaus, J., Schick, M., Muraskin, M., & Rosen, D. (1978). *The Supreme Court's certiorari jurisdiction: Cue theory*. In S. Goldman & A. Sarat (Eds.), *American court systems: Readings in judicial process and behavior* (pp. 130–143). San Francisco: W. H. Freeman.

Tanke, E. D., & Tanke, T. J. (1977). The psychology of the jury: An annotated bibliography. *JSAS Catalog of Selected Documents in Psychology, 7*, 108 (MS. No. 1591).

Tanke, E. D., & Tanke, T. J. (1979). Getting off a slippery slope: Social science in the judicial process. *American Psychologist, 34*, 1130–1138.

Tapp, J. L. (1976). Psychology and the law. *Annual Review of Psychology, 27*, 359–404.

Tapp, J. L. (1977). Psychology and the law: A look at the interface. In B. D. Sales (Eds.), *Psychology in the legal process* (pp. 1–15). New York: Spectrum.

Taylor, S., Jr. (1986, July 1). High court, 5–4, says states have the right to outlaw private homosexual acts. *New York Times*, pp. A1, A19.

Terry v. Ohio, 391 U.S. 1 (1968).

Tetlock, P. E. (1983). Cognitive style and political ideology. *Journal of Personality and Social Psychology, 45*, 118–126.

Tetlock, P. E. (1984). Cognitive style and political belief systems in the British House of Commons. *Journal of Personality and Social Psychology, 46*, 365–375.

Tetlock, P. E., Bernzweig, J., & Gallant, J. L. (1985). Supreme Court decision making: Cognitive style as a predictor of ideological consistency of voting. *Journal of Personality and Social Psychology, 48*, 1227–1239.

Texas v. Johnson, 491 U.S. 397 (1989).

Texas v. White, 7 Wallace 700 (1869).

Thomas, C. (1996, April 8). *Judging*. Invited address, School of Law, University of Kansas, Lawrence, Kansas.

Thompson v. Oklahoma, 487 U.S. 816 (1988).

Thompson, W. C. (1989). Death qualifications after Wainwright v. Witt and Lockhart v. McCree. *Law and Human Behavior, 13*, 185–215.

Tinker v. Des Moines Independent Community School District, 393 U.S. 503 (1969).

Tomkins, A. J., & Oursland, K. (1991). Social and social science perspectives in judicial interpretations of the Constitution: A historical view and an overview. *Law and Human Behavior, 15*, 101–120.

Tomkins, A. J., & Penrod, S. D. (1996, August). *Use of social science evidence in the courts: Historical perspective*. Symposium paper presented at the meetings of the American Psychological Association, Toronto.

Toobin, J. (1996, July 8). Supreme sacrifice. *New Yorker*, pp. 43–47.

Tremper, C. R. (1987). Organized psychology's efforts to influence judicial policy–making. *American Psychologist, 42*, 496–501.

Tucker, W. H. (1994). *The science and politics of racial research*. Urbana, IL: University of Illinois Press.

Tushnet, M. (1992). Thurgood Marshall and the brethren. *Georgetown Law Journal, 80*, 2109–2130.

Twiss, B. (1942). *Lawyers and the Constitution: How laissez faire came to the Supreme Court*. Princeton, NJ: Princeton University Press.

Ulmer, S. S. (1970). The use of power in the Supreme Court: The opinion assignments of Earl Warren, 1953–1960. *Journal of Public Law, 19*, 49–67.

Ulmer, S. S. (1984). The Supreme Court's certiorari decisions: Conflict as a predictive variable. *American Political Science Review, 78*, 901–911

Ulmer, S. S., Hintze, W., & Kirklosky, L. (1972). The decision to grant or deny certiorari: Further considerations of cue theory. *Law and Society Review, 6*, 637–643.

Underwager, R., & Wakefield, H. (1992). Poor psychology produces poor law. *Law and Human Behavior, 16*, 233–243.

United States v. Bayless, 95 Cr. 533 (S.D.N.Y.) (1996).

United States v. F. W. Darby Lumber Co., 312 U.S. 100 (1941).

United States v. Hatter, No. 95–1733, United States Court of Appeals for the Federal Circuit (1995).

United States v. Nixon, 418 U.S. 683 (1974).

United States v. Virginia, 116 S.Ct 2264 (1996).

Urofsky, M. I. (1991). *Felix Frankfurter: Judicial restraint and individual liberties*. Boston: Twane.

Urofsky, M. I. (1997). *Affirmative action on trial: Sex discrimination in Johnson v. Santa Clara*. Lawrence, KS: University Press of Kansas.

Van den Haag, E. (1960). Social science testimony in the desegregation cases: A reply to Professor Kenneth Clark. *Villanova Law Review, 6*, 69–79.

Van Natta, D., Jr. (1996, April 2). Judge assailed over drug case issues reversal and an apology. *New York Times*, pp. A1, A10.

Vinson, F. M. (1961). Work of the federal courts. In W. F. Murphy & C. H. Pritchett (Eds.), *Courts, judges, and politics* (pp. 54–57). New York: Random House.

Volokh, E. (1992). Freedom of speech and workplace harassment. *UCLA Law Review, 39*, 1791–1872.

Wainwright v. Witt, 53 L.W. 4108 (1985).

Warren, E. (1977). *The memoirs of Earl Warren*. New York: Doubleday.

Wasby, S. L. (1981). Oral argument in the ninth circuit: The view from bench and bar. *Golden Gate University Law Review, 11*, 21–79.

Wasby, S. (1992). *Amicus* brief. In K. L. Hall (Ed.), *The Oxford companion to the Supreme Court of the United States* (pp. 31–32). New York: Oxford University Press.

Wasby, S. L., Peterson, S. A., Schubert, J. N., & Schubert, G. (1991). *The Supreme Court's use of per curiam dispositions: The connection to oral argument.* Paper presented at the meetings of the Midwest Political Science Association, Chicago.

Webster v. Reproductive Health Services, 109 S.Ct. 3040 (1989).

Wells, G. L., & Loftus, E. F. (1984). *Eyewitness research: Then and now.* In G. L. Wells & E. F. Loftus (Eds.), *Eyewitness testimony: Psychological perspectives* (pp. 1–11). New York: Cambridge University Press.

Wells, G. L., & Murray, D. M. (1984). *Eyewitness confidence.* In G. L. Wells & E. F. Loftus (Eds.), *Eyewitness testimony: Psychological perspectives* (pp. 155–170). New York: Cambridge University Press.

Werth, J. L. (1998, August). *Psychologist's and advocate'e perspective.* Symposium paper presented at the meetings of the American Psychological Association, San Francisco.

West Coast Hotel Co. v. Parrish, 300 U.S. 379 (1937).

West Virginia State Board of Education v. Barnette, 319 U.S. 624 (1943).

Whipple, G. M. (1909). The observer as reporter: A survey of the "Psychology of testimony." *Psychological Bulletin, 6,* 153–170.

Whipple, G. M. (1910). Recent literature on the psychology of testimony. *Psychological Bulletin, 7,* 365–368.

Whipple, G. M. (1911). The psychology of testimony. *Psychological Bulletin, 8,* 307–309.

Whipple, G. M. (1912). The psychology of testimony and report. *Psychological Bulletin, 9,* 264–269.

White, E. (1978). *The American judicial tradition: Profiles of leading American judges.* New York: Oxford University Press.

Wigmore, J. H. (1909). Professor Munsterberg and the psychology of testimony. *Illinois Law Review, 3,* 399–455.

Will, G. (1996, July 4). Expanding the boundaries of free speech. *Kansas City Star,* p. C–11.

Williams v. Florida, 399 U.S. 78 (1970).

Wilson, B. (1988). The making of a constitution. *Judicature, 71,* 334–338.

Wines, M. (1994, April 21). House votes to allow data on bias in death–row pleas. *New York Times,* p. A9.

Wiseman, R. L., & Schenck-Hamlin, W. J. (1981). A multi-dimensional scaling validation of an inductively-derived set of compliance–gaining strategies. *Communication Monographs, 48,* 251–270.

Witt v. Florida, 54 L.Ed. 2d 294 (1977).

Wood, S. L. (1996, August). *Bargaining and negotiation on the Burger Court.* Paper presented at the meetings of the American Political Science Association, San Francisco.

Woodward, B., & Armstrong, S. (1979). *The brethren: Inside the Supreme Court.* New York: Simon and Schuster.

Yarmey, A. D. (1984). *Age as a factor in eyewitness memory.* In G. L. Wells & E. F. Loftus (Eds.), *Eyewitness testimony: Psychological perspectives* (pp. 142–154). New York: Cambridge University Press.

Yarmey, A. D. (1986). Ethical responsibilities governing the statements experimental psychologists make in expert testimony. *Law and Human Behavior, 10,* 101–116.

Youngstown Sheet and Tube Co. et al. V. Sawyer, 343 U.S. 579 (1952).

Name Index

Adler, R., 39, 41
Allport, F., 139
Ambuel, B., 197, 199
Armstrong, S., 18, 35, 106–107
Asch, S., 118
Associated Press. 49, 102

Baldus, D. C., 144, 145
Bales, R. F., 90
Ball, H., 63, 64, 69
Barbash, F., 31
Barnum, D. G., 61
Barrett, G. V., 164
Baum, L., 22, 25, 30, 35, 46, 48, 59, 64, 65, 66, 86, 108, 109, 110, 111, 114, 115, 118, 119, 122, 150, 151
Baxter, L. A., 77
Berger, C. R., 78
Berkman, H., 16, 51, 52, 146
Bermant, G., 159

Bernzweig, J., 43, 44
Bersoff, D. N., 126, 158, 160, 161, 162, 163, 164, 166, 196, 203, 206, 208, 209, 214, 215, 216- 217, 218, 223, 224
Binet, A., 130
Bird, C., 88
Biskupic, J., 13
Bolick, C., 51
Borgida, E., 160, 161, 162, 163, 164
Boster, F. J., 78
Bradley, R. C., 121
Brenner, S. J., 109, 117, 118, 119, 120
Breyer. S., 42
Brittain, C. V., 217
Brown, B. B., 217
Bruner, J., 37, 38
Bugliosi, V., 69
Burgoon, M., 78
Burka, P., 30
Burtt, H. E., 90, 135

Caldeira, G. A., 28, 61, 62, 71, 150, 151
Cardozo, B., 46–47, 48
Carelli, R., 41
Carp, R. A., 22, 23, 24, 51, 52
Cartwright, D., 92
Casper, J., 150
Cattell, J. McK., 130
Chaiken, S., 37
Charen, M., 11, 46, 47
Chemers, M. M., 100
Chi, M. T. H., 42
Christie, R., 77
Clark, H. R., 110
Clark, K. B., 135, 137–138
Clark, M. P., 135, 137–138
Clasen, D. R., 217
Clay, R. A., 4
Collins, B. E., 38
Compston, C. L., 66
Congressional Research Service, 46
Cook, S. W., 139, 140
Cooper, P. J., 96, 97, 107, 111

243

Subject Index